MARRIAGE STUDIES

Reflections In
Canon Law and Theology

Volume Three

**Edited By
Thomas P. Doyle, O.P.**

**Canon Law Society of America
Washington, DC 20064**

©Copyright 1985 by Canon Law Society of America
ISSN: 0278-5242
ISBN: 0-943616-25-5

CONTENTS

INTRODUCTION

During the past twenty years western society has experienced the profoundly disturbing phenomenon of a divorce epidemic. Joined with this have been other problems: the restructuring of the family, change of societal values about marriage, new and different forms of the man/woman relationship, the erosion of socio-cultural supports for marital and family stability. This complex phenomenon could hardly be ignored by religious and secular leaders. The reality of millions of shattered marital relationships within so short a span of time prompted professionals in many fields to ask *why*. In the search for answers we have learned much about the marriage relationship as both a natural and sacred reality and, finally, as a sacrament.

Marriage, the fundamental human institution, serves secondary human institutions such as church and society. In turn it is shaped to a great degree by these institutions which it serves. This is especially true if we look at spousal and parental roles, expectations of marital behavior, the nature and durability of the interpersonal commitment. The divorce explosion has forced us to abandon many of our presumptions about marriage and to look deeply into the essential aspects of marriage. Religious and secular scholars have unceasingly sought to finalize the meaning of the marriage bond and the reasons why marriage, as a special kind of human relationship, relates as it does to the growth and health of human societies, both secular and religious.

The Canon Law Society of America has produced a volume of studies which is the result of research into the meaning of marriage at a time when it appears quite fragile. The editors are proud to present MARRIAGE STUDIES III, with a preface by the Most Reverend John R. Keating, Bishop of Arlington. It was Bishop Keating's monumental doctoral dissertation, *The Bearing of Mental Impairment on the Validity of Marriage*, that led canonists and theologians into new areas of insight about what is required of a consenting spouse. Now, twenty-one years later, Bishop Keating looks back on this intervening period and offers some thoughts on the future of marriage scholarship.

In any original essay, Theodore Mackin, S.J., carefully and critically examines Ephesians 5:21–33 and the Church's traditional defense of the consummated marriages of Christians as being absolutely indissoluble because of their reflection of the Christ/Church image.

Robert Smith examines the question of troublesome marriages in the Pauline community of Corinth. The stability of the marriage bond appears to relate to the ability of the couple to live up to certain uniquely Christian demands in the context of the Christian community. Here we see the beginnings of the realization that marriage as a natural reality was capable of having a profound effect on the growth of the Church.

Thomas Doyle, O.P., contributes an examination of the unique nature of human sexual communication and its specific impact on the formation of the man-woman interpersonal relationship. This study, based in great part on the talks and writings of Pope John Paul II, examines his notion of the "nuptial meaning of the body."

Paul Glick, a noted social scientist and demographer, examines the divorce explosion from another viewpoint. He analyzes statistical data relating to the instability of the marriage bond in the context of family composition. Doctor Glick looks at population trends, marriage and divorce levels, and the existence of a sizeable segment of the minor population living in single parent families. Lawrence Wrenn responds to Doctor Glick's article with observations on the impact of this data for canonists.

Sacramental marriage, which is not just an institution but a vocation, exists in a social and cultural environment that does not always fully support it. As a sacrament, marriage plays a role in God's plan for his earthly people. Raymond Finn, O.P., examines the question of the *faith* required for an effective and valid sacramental union. Closely related to the faith quotient is the inseparable relationship of contract and sacrament for the baptized. Father Finn's contribution is the concluding section of his doctoral dissertation, the content of which is summarized for the readers as a kind of preface to the article. It looks to the historical roots of this canonical fact of contract/sacrament inseparability and poses some profound questions for its application today.

Tomás Rincón examines in depth and detail the various implications of civil marriage for Catholics. This article, which first appeared in the Spanish journal *Ius Canonicum*, examines the historical development of the Church's legislation which led to canon 1012 of the 1917 code. Contemporary canonical and theological writing on the separability thesis is examined in the light of the theological basis or grounding for the sacramentality of marriage. Father Rincon moves to the conclusion that the legislated inseparability could be no other way, given the doctrinal basis of the question.

Since the promulgation of *Gaudium et spes* the notion of conjugal love has come under scrutiny by theologians and canonists alike. John Connery, S.J., presents a study of the unique kind of love that marks Christian marriage beginning with its historical roots in the Genesis account of creation and ending with some considerations of the vital importance of love in understanding the meaning of marriage as it is presented in the conciliar document and in the new canons.

We trust that these fine contributions will prove to be of great assistance in the fascinating search for the full meaning of the bond of marriage.

THE EDITORS,

THOMAS P. DOYLE, O.P.
EDWARD DILLON
ELLSWORTH KNEAL
MICHAEL PLACE

FOREWORD

In the past two decades, especially in North America, we have witnessed the phenomenon of a soaring divorce rate and the prevalence of remarriage. Who can doubt that the stability of the marriage bond has been seriously eroding? This is true of marriages among Catholics as well as non-Catholics. To defend the exclusivity and permanence of marriage today is a challenge to the faith of Christians, especially in our age of high tech communications that display the dichotomy so bluntly, so inescapably—the growing brittleness of male-female interpersonal relationships, often presented as culturally desirable . . . and the gospel mandate of indissolubility, often presented as a remnant of an irrelevant and boring past.

Should the Church's best efforts to shore up the stability of marriage depend more on research, or on aggressive pastoral practice? Is the avenue to renewed stability to come from the pulpit, from the marriage tribunal, from prayer, from family life programs . . . or must it come eventually from a shattering reawakening of society that it is losing hold of its foundations?

The Church has long depended on calm, clear and collected scholarship, the kind exemplified in this valuable volume. It is almost a truism in the Church that the study of marriage has always been, and shall always be, the pre-eminent and most practical area of both scholarly and popular endeavor and conversation.

There is a natural link of (1) solid scholarship, which leads to (2) sound pastoral practice, which in turn leads to (3) a steady and sure conscience in God's people regarding indissolubility. More than ever, there is now a palpable tension between human authority and divine authority in the governance of the marriage bond. One of the signs of genuine, well-grounded renewal within the people of God today is the presence of honest and objective scholarship searching both the biblical and secular data regarding marriage. No doubt of it—one of the surest signs of church renewal in the wake of Vatican II is the emergence and prominent place of solid scholarship regarding the marvel and mystery called marriage.

MOST REVEREND JOHN R. KEATING
BISHOP OF ARLINGTON

EPHESIANS 5:21–33 AND RADICAL INDISSOLUBILITY

Theodore Mackin, S.J.

The Issue

In his instruction on divorce in the Markan, the Lukan and the shorter Matthean versions of the Synoptic tradition, Christ is recorded as saying explicitly that a husband is forbidden to end his marriage by dismissing his wife. But beyond forbidding dissolution in this way did Christ also declare the impossibility of doing so—the impossibility of dissolution by this unilateral dismissal or by any other exercise of human authority?

From the Fathers of the Church to the present, Christian teachers have found the impossibility at least implied in this same instruction. How indeed would a man commit adultery in marrying a dismissed wife (Luke 16:18; Mt. 5:37), and how would a man commit adultery in attempting remarriage after dismissing his wife (Mk. 10:11; Luke, ibid.), unless in both cases the attempt at dissolution were null and one of the second set of partners were as a consequence still married?

Thus was sown the seed of the notion that in the matter of dissolving marriages human authority is not only constrained by the divine command but is known by divine revelation to be ineffective.

But at the same time and in the same tradition the seed of doubt was sown as well. In the longer, narrative version of Matthew's record Christ is reported as stating an exception. On marrying after dismissing his wife a husband does not commit adultery as long as he has dismissed her because of her *pornéia* (whatever this may have been). So his dismissal must have been effective in dissolving. What is more, in his instruction in I Corinthians 7 Paul forbade a Christian wife to abandon her husband; but he added that if she did in fact abandon him, one of her options must be to remain unmarried (vv. 10 and 11). The key terms in the Greek of the original here are telling. For "abandon" Paul used the verb, *chorízein,* commonly designating one kind of divorce under Roman law. For "unmarried" he used the same noun, *ágamos,* that he used in verse 8 to designate those of the Corinth community who had never married. So if we take Paul's words in verses 10 and 11 at their literal value, we find him

1

acknowledging that a Chrsitian wife can dissolve her marriage. But if we say (as most Catholic interpreters have said) that Paul meant the woman must not try to marry again because she was still the wife of the husband she had abandoned, we must admit that he chose words most apt to mislead his Corinthian readers.

Thus even short of reckoning with Paul's instruction in the same letter to Christian spouses abandoned by their non-Christian spouses (the New Testament source of the later Pauline privilege), we have from him and from the longer Matthean version at least the well-founded suspicion that the human will is not absolutely ineffective in dissolving marriages.

The ensuing struggle in the Church has been to answer two inextricably linked questions. First, what in fact do we know from the New Testament about the effectiveness of the human will in dissolving marriages? Is it incapable of dissolving as well as forbidden to dissolve? Secondly, since whatever the effectiveness, certainly it has limits, where are these limits? If some marriages are beyond its dissolving reach, what puts them there?

The Church's teachers have answered the second of these questions more confidently than they have the first. To be sure, for centuries they have both attenuated the impermissibility of dissolving and determined the human authority to dissolve. Paul himself and the Matthean editor began this. Fathers and bishops have allowed remarriage after dissolution because of adultery and equivalent crimes—from the beginning until now in the Catholic East, until the twelfth century in the West. Since at least the fourth century in both East and West dissolution of unconsummated marriages of Christian spouses (sacramental marriages therefore) has been permitted so that one or both spouses may take the vows of religious life. Since the twelfth century the Pauline privilege has been used to dissolve consummated marriages at first not sacraments, where one spouse subsequently accepts baptism and the other refuses to live in peace or abandons the marriage without fault on the convert's part.

Since the publishing of their apostolic constitutions in the sixteenth century by Paul III and Pius V, popes have used their "power of the keys" to dispense from the law of indissolubility erstwhile polygamous Catholic converts who were unable to recall which of their multiple wives was first and authentic, or who were unwilling to live with her if known—and thus freed them for a second and sacramental marriage with the wife of their choice. Gregory XIII extended the use of this power even to dissolving the marriages of slave spouses who had been separated violently, even where these marriages later became sacraments by the baptism of both the separated spouses. The possibility of such dissolution internal to these marriages was explained as their not having been consummated since becoming sacraments.

For the last four centuries, then, this has been the Catholic teachers' answer, in doctrine and in discipline, to the second of the questions posed above: The limit of any authority on earth to dissolve marriages is set at the consummated sacrament. If a marriage is known to be a sacrament (because both spouses are baptized Christians), and if it is verified as consummated since becoming a sacrament, no authority exercised on earth can dissolve it. But if it is proved to be not a sacrament—or if, though verified as a sacrament, it is proved to be not consummated as such—the one authority of the Bishop of Rome can dissolve it.

The Catholic teachers would be seriously remiss in their office of teaching if they did not show the divine warrant for their setting the pale of absolute indissolubility at the consummated sacramental marriage.[1] This warrant they find in chapter 5 of Paul's Letter to the Ephesians. This argument drawn from verses 21 through 33 of this chapter is, in brief, the following. Through the Apostle, God has revealed that the marriage of any two Christians is an earthly image of the love of Christ and his bride, the Church. The Christian spouses' baptismal character makes the marriage such an image. But the earthly image must correspond to its heavenly model. Since the latter, the love relationship of Christ and the Church, is indestructible, so too is the earthly image, the Christian spouses' marriage. But this is so only where the imaging is complete, where their sacramental marriage images fully the Christ-Church union. This it does not do until the spouses have consummated their marriage by complete sexual intercourse, until they have become "two in one flesh" analogously as Christ is (according to Ephesians 5:30) "two in one flesh" with his bride, the Church. In a word, the imaging earthly marriage is indissoluble because the imaged marriage of Christ and his Church is indestructible.

This theology of absolute indissolubility is what occasions the question I will seek to answer in this essay. At the risk of complicating it needlessly, let me formulate the question in this progressively unfolding sequence.

---

[1]The redundancy "absolute indissolubility" is almost excused by the need to distinguish two species of indissolubility legislated obliquely by Catholic marriage law. In the revised code of law, canon 1056 states that indissolubility is one of the essential properties of every marriage. But this natural indissolubility does not block the dissolution of non-sacramental marriages by use of the Pauline Privilege, nor of unconsummated sacramental marriages by papal authority. Canon 1056 says also that in a marriage that is a sacrament this indissolubility gains "a special firmness." It gains therefore finally indissoluble indissolubility, otherwise called, in the vocabulary of Catholic jurists, radical indissolubility.

Let us grant for now the arguable assumption that every marriage of two baptized spouses is a Christian sacrament. Let us grant also the accuracy of the explanation that every such marriage is a Christian sacrament in that it images the love relationship of Christ and the Church. Finally let us grant a third assumption, namely that despite having a metaphoric marriage as one of its key terms, the statement that the Christ-Church relationship is indestructible is both intelligible and accurate.

Granting these assumptions has an inescapable consequence. One must accept that the argument-by-analogy drawn from them to prove every sacramental marriage's indissolubility implies a cause-effect nexus between the two analogated marital relationships. Not only may one say that the imaging earthly marriage is indissoluble *as* the model Christ-Church marriage is indestructible. One must also say that the former is indissoluble *because* the latter is indestructible.

Since this is so, the cause-effect link should be verifiaable and intelligible. Does the indestructibility of the Christ-Church relationship *cause* every consummated sacramental marriage to be indissoluble? If it does, how does it do so? What kind of causation is this?

We can ask the same question about cause and effect in a different way. If one grants the deontological validity of the assertion that every marriage of two Christians *ought* to image the indestructible love of Christ and the Church in the spouses' intent and effort to make their marriage indissoluble, what cause moves this assertion on to accurate ontology in the claim that every consummated marriage of two Christians is in fact indissoluble? Here the usual perilous step in moral reasoning reverses direction. That is, how does one get from the "ought" to the "is" in this matter?

How have the Church's magisterial teachers explained this causation—if they have? How have the theologians explained it? When we examine (as we shall) a few typical explanations, will we find them to be conclusions drawn validly from what Paul says in Ephesians 5:21–33 about Christian marriages?

THE MAGISTERIUM'S USE OF EPHESIANS 5:21–33

One does not expect to find carefully detailed explanation in the Church's magisterial statements of doctrine. It is their nature to say which elements of the Christian religion are to be accepted in faith. Some of these elements are known through theological reasoning from divine revelation; they are the conclusions of this reasoning. In the magisterial statements one reads the conclusions.

In the Catholic teachers' use of Ephesians 5:21–33 one finds these two elements: a brief and informal exegesis, and from this exegesis a conclusion drawn about sacramental marriages and their indissolubility.

The Council of Florence

The Council of Florence turned to the consideration of marriage almost as an afterthought. The council met in 1439 in Florence as the continuation of the Council of Basel. Its intent was to reconcile the differences dividing the Greek and Roman Catholics and to reunite the two churches. Not a word was said about marriage in the *Decretum unionis Graecorum* of July 6, 1439,[2] despite the Greek church's centuries-long acceptance of divorce on the ground of adultery, and subsequent remarriage.

But after the departure of the Greeks and with the late arrival of the Armenian Catholics the council did take up the issue of marriage. On November 22 of the same year the representatives of the two churches signed the *Decretum pro Armenis*. The paragraph on marriage is the last in Part 5, which is a full statement of the Roman Catholic doctrine of the sacraments at that time.

> The seventh sacrament is the sacrament of marriage, which is a sign of the union of Christ and the Church, according to the words of the Apostle, "This is a great sacrament; in this I refer to Christ and the Church. . . ." A three-fold good of marriage is acknowledged. The first is offspring, to be procreated and nurtured for the worship of God. The second is fidelity, which each spouse owes to the other. The third is the indissolubility of this marriage deriving from the fact that it images the indissoluble union of Christ and the Church. . . .[3]

The statement takes from Augustine's *De bono coniugali* his enumeration of the three good things in marriage which excuse its use. But it converts his *sacramentum* to indissolubility, substituting the noun *indivisibilitas* for his *sacramentum*. It ascribes this indissolubility of sacramental marriages to the fact that they image the indissoluble union of Christ and the Church. The kind of cause-effect relationship is not made clear in the formulation, ". . . propter hoc quod [matrimonium] significat indivisibilem coniunctionem Christi et Ecclesiae." But the statement leaves no doubt that the earthly marriage's imaging of the divine indestructible relationship produces the former's indissolubility.

[2]Denzinger-Schönmetzer, nn. 1300–1308, pp. 331–332.
[3]Denzinger-Schönmetzer, n. 1327, p. 336.

The Council of Trent

One-hundred-twenty-four years later the bishops of the Council of Trent made a more careful use of Ephesians 5. They sought to provide evidence, against the Reformers' denial, that Christ himself made marriage a sacrament.[4]

> Christ himself, he who instituted and perfected the holy sacraments, has by his passion merited the grace which would complete the natural love [of husband and wife], which would seal the spouses' indissoluble unity, and would sanctify them. The Apostle intimated [*innuit*] this when he said "Husbands, love your wives as Christ loved the Church and gave himself up for her," and then added shortly afterward, "This is a great sacrament; I say this in reference to Christ and the Church."

The statement asserts the natural indissolubility of marriages, but qualifies this claim by adding that through his passion and death Christ merited grace which, when applied, would "seal" this indissolubility. The Latin verb is *confirmaret*.

Unlike Florence's *Decretum pro Armenis* this statement says not that Christian marriages' imaging the Christ-Church relationship makes them sacraments and indissoluble marriages. It says rather that Christ's grace is available to make marriages indissolubly indissoluble, and implies that those made such are sacraments. It concludes that Paul intimated this, and to support this interpretation quotes verses 25 and then 33 of Ephesians 5. Perhaps the implicit *argumentum* here is that Christ's sealing grace renders a marriage indissoluble when Christian husbands love their wives as Christ loves the Church; or perhaps that because Christ's sealing grace renders the marriage of two Christians indissoluble, husbands must love their wives as Christ loves the Church. The logical *consequentia* must be guessed at—if indeed a consequence is established at all.

Leo XIII's Arcanum divinae sapientiae

Pope Leo XIII published his encyclical letter, *Arcanum divinae sapientiae,* on February 1, 1880, in part as an attempt to counter the secularizing of marriage in the Catholic nations of Europe that had begun in the preceding century and was then nearing completion. Since taking marriages under secular authority made divorce available to Catholics, he

---

[4]They dealt with marriage in their twenty-fourth session, in the Fall of 1563. Their argument against the Reformers is in the theological statement that prefaces their dogmatic canons on marriage (Denzinger-Schönmetzer, nn. 1797–1800, pp. 415–416).

sought vigorously to vindicate marriage's indissolubility. For this effort he used Ephesians 5 by reasoning in the following way.[5]

He explained that what Genesis 2 reveals about marriage Paul set forth in Ephesians in a more detailed way. The Apostle confirmed that Christ raised marriage to the dignity of a sacrament. His grace in this sacrament can bring spouses to holiness; by conforming their relationship to Christ's mystical marriage with the Church they find their love brought to completion; and their union, which is by nature permanent (*individua*), is joined even more firmly by the bond of divine charity.

Here too one must guess at the intended cause-effect nexus. Leo names clearly three effects of Christ's grace in Christian marriages. He seems to say that they are caused by these sacramental marriage's conformation to, their imaging of, Christ's union with the Church. What is unclear is the cause of this conforming that itself causes the three effects.

Is the cause of the conforming the grace of Christ? If it is, does Leo imply this in order to sustain the doctrine that every marriage of two Christians is a sacrament; that even apart from the presence or absence of Christian faith in the spouses Christ's grace *makes* their marriages images of the Christ-Church union? Or does he allow that Christ's grace causes the conformation where and if the spouses accept this grace in faith and work with it? If he implies the latter, he risks undermining the doctrine recalled just above.

Or does he simply take for granted that Christ's grace works its conforming effect through the spouses' baptism; so that the cause-effect nexus is this, that Christ's grace through the spouses' baptism produces their marriages' conformation to the indestructible Christ-Church union, which conformation produces in turn the indissolubility of the spouses' marriage? To verify this interpretation one would have to find in the encyclical more exact analysis than it provides.

Pius XI's Casti connubii

The use that Pope Pius XI made of Ephesians 5 in his encyclical letter of December 31, 1930, is the use most commonly known among students of the Catholic theology of marriage.

Pius drew heavily on post-Tridentine ecclesiology to restate the boundaries of marriage's indissolubility. Although Christ himself, in the Synoptic instructions, reaffirmed the natural indissolubility of all marriages, his authority exercised on earth by the popes can dissolve these indissoluble marriages if they are not sacraments; or even if they are

[5]*Acta Sanctae Sedis* 12 (1880) 338.

sacraments, if they have not been consummated as such. But consummated sacramental marriages can be dissolved by no authority exercised on earth. This is God's will, and to explain how it is Pius turns immediately to Ephesians 5.

> If we seek reverently to find the intrinsic reason for this divine command . . . we shall find it readily in the mystical imaging of Christian marriage, found in its perfection in those Christian marriages that are consummated. The Apostle, in his Letter to the Ephesians . . . tells us that Christian marriage images that most perfect union which subsists between Christ and the Church: "This is a great sacrament; but I refer to Christ and the Church." And this is a union which, as long as Christ lives and the Church lives by him, can surely never cease or be dissolved.[6]

Pius acknowledges that one does not account for the indissolubility of consummated sacramental marriages by simply appealing to God's will. One must verify an intrinsic reason for it, a cause internal to the marriages themselves. This reason is that such marriages image perfectly the indestructible union of Christ and the Church. *Therefore* they themselves are indissoluble. He does not say that because they are indissoluble they image perfectly. Rather, because, being consummated sacraments, they image perfectly, they have as an effect of this imaging the indestructibility of the model they image. The power of the model enters through the imaging and reproduces in the imaging marriage the indestructibility of the model.

Gaudium et spes

The bishops of the Second Vatican Council stated their mind on marriage's indissolubility in article 48 of their chapter on marriage in *Gaudium et spes,* their pastoral Constitution on the Church in the Modern World.[7] They looked first not to the sacrament as the cause of indissolubility in Christian marriages, but to the covenantal commitment of spouses in any and all marriages.

> As a mutual gift of the two persons this intimate union, as well as the good of the children, imposes total fidelity on the spouses and argues for an unbreakable oneness between them.[8]

[6]*Acta Apostolicae Sedis* 20 (1930) 552.

[7]Constitutio Pastoralis de Ecclesia in Mundo Huius Temporis, Pars II, Caput 1, "*De Dignitate matrimonii et familiae fovenda,*" in Sacrosanctum Oecumenicum Concilium Vaticanum II, *Constitutiones, Decreta, Declarationes* (Romae, 1966), pp. 754–757.

[8]Ibid., p. 755.

The nature itself of marital love demands permanence; and the children produced by this love need the permanence of their parents' marriage.

But in the immediately succeeding paragraph the bishops turn to the analogy in Ephesians 5.

> Christ our Lord has blessed this love [*dilectionem*] abundantly, this love which has so many facets, which springs from the divine source of charity, and which is built on the model of Christ's union with the Church.

Thus far the Christ-Church union is the model of marital love of any two spouses, not only of Christians. But then the bishops confine their attention to Christian spouses alone: "Christ comes to them through the sacrament of marriage, just as in Old Testament times God came to Israel through a covenant of love and fidelity. . . ." They seem to say not that the Christian spouses' love images that of Christ and the Church, but that Christ's love for them is marital. He loves them in and by his love for the Church.

Christ abides with these spouses, lives in them, so that his love may produce in their marriages the effect that it produces in the Church—a fruitful and permanent love.

> Moreover he remains with them, so that just as he has loved the Church and given himself up for her, so too the spouses by their reciprocal self-giving may love one another with a fruitful and perpetual love. The love native to marriage is taken up into divine love; there it is ruled and enriched by Christ's redeeming strength and by the saving action of the Church—so that the spouses may be joined to God.

The movement of causation is significantly different here from what the earlier magisterial documents said it to be. Here there is no assumption that the baptism of any two Christian spouses makes their marriage an image of Christ's marital union with the Church, and therefore indissoluble. Rather Christ acts in the spouses' love, acts in it through the Church, and thereby empowers it to be fruitful and perpetual. The logic of causation here seems closest to that of Trent among the earlier documents: Christ empowers Christian spouses to love one another as he loves the Church; he graces their marriages with the gift of indestructibility.

If this is what the bishops of both Trent and Vatican II meant to say, they left in their theology of indissolubility a place for the wills of the spouses to ply their causation of the indissolubility. Love involves the will and its free decisions, or it is not love.

THE THEOLOGIANS

When one turns from the spare theology of indissolubility in the magisterial documents to the more detailed efforts of the theologians, one goes first and almost instinctively to Augustine. He was of course not the first of the Fathers to draw on Ephesians 5 for instruction concerning marriage. But those earlier than he saw in the passage primarily an elucidation of the Church's relationship to Christ, and only secondarily a reference to the nature of Christian marriage. They drew from it mainly moral and religious demands on Christian married life.[9]

How exactly Augustine reasoned to indissolubility from the *sacramentum* of Ephesians 5:32 remains to be seen. But if during his sojourn in Milan he read or heard Archbishop Ambrose commenting on the Gospel of Luke, he became acquainted with one interpretation of that verse that had taken root in Christian thought.

Ambrose reasoned that the marriage of two Christians must have been joined by God, for Christ said "No man can come to me unless the Father who has sent me draw him." Thus, since a man and woman can be Christians only if made so by God, it follows that their marriage too must have been made by God. For Proverbs says (19:14) ". . . a prudent wife is from the Lord." Thus, as St. Paul says, marriage is a great *sacramentum* of Christ and the Church. For Christ is the husband; the Church is the wife.[10]

Ambrose seemed convinced that Paul's *mystérion méga* is the marriage of the two Christians itself, and that their marriage is this because God it is who joined it. Closer questioning must then ask what among the several elements that make up a marriage is this *mystérion*, this *sacramentum*. This is what Augustine asked, and answered—indecisively.

Augustine and the Sacramentum of Marriage

Augustine completed his earliest treatise on marriage, *De bono coniugali,* in 401. There he sought for the reason in a man's marriage that forbids and even makes impossible his remarrying after dismissing his wife because of her sterility in face of his desire for children. He found this reason in the *sacramentum* of the man's marriage.

He explained the function of the *sacramentum* in making the second marriage impossible by setting it in analogy with the demands of monogamy in the marriage of a bishop. The latter must be a man of one wife (i.e.,

---

[9]See on this point Edward Schillebeeckx, *Marriage: Human Reality and Saving Mystery* (New York: Sheed and Ward, 1965), p. 281.

[10]In *Exposito Evangelii secundum Lucam*, Lib. 8, n. 9: *PL* 15, col. 1767–1768.

he may not remarry in widowhood) because his marriage must signify the union of many nations gathered in submission under the one heavenly spouse, who is Christ. He adds that this union will be completed only in eternity.

> Therefore just as the *sacramentum* of several marriages in Old Testament times signified the future multitude of all peoples on earth subject to God, so the *sacramentum* of the monogamous marriages of our time signifies the future union of all of us subject to God in the heavenly city.[11]

The *sacramentum* of a Christian marriage here lies in its signifying not the present union of Christ and the Church, as in Ambrose's Commentary on Luke, but the future union of all people with Christ in the one Church. From this, Christian marriages' indissolubility can be taken not as an ontological effect of their imaging the present Christ-Church union, but as a vocation they have been given in the eschatological work of Christ in the Church.

The demand on the bishop for monogamy in order to sustain his *sacramentum* has no causal relationship to the demand of all Christian marriages that they be indissoluble. Rather this demand on the bishop can no more than illustrate Augustine's meaning when he asserts that so too the *sacramentum* of the unordained married can put a demand on their marriages.

Where does Augustine get this notion of marriage's *sacramentum*? Because he does not say it is not clear that Augustine teaches, here in *De bono coniugali,* that the *sacramentum* in Christian marriage consists of their imaging Christ's here-and-now relationship with the Church. Therefore one cannot draw from *De bono coniugali* the theology of radical indissolubility that says the indestructibility of the *signatum* (the Christ-Church union) causes the indissolubility of the *signum* (the marriage of two Christians).

In his *Tractatus 9 in Ioannem* Augustine set forth an analogy that would be used by medieval theologians to argue that the marriages of Christians are sacraments of the New Law, and to explain the way in which they are.[12]

Asking and answering why Christ came to the wedding feast at Cana in Galilee Augustine offered two reasons: first, in order to honor marriage as

---

[11]*PL* 40, col. 788.
[12]*PL* 35, col. 1459.

good (a point the Manichees ought to notice); second, to reveal the *sacramentum* of marriage, its hidden meaning, and thus to make its chastity more firm. (Chastity here could be the virtue that excludes adultery in two senses: infidelity during a lasting marriage, and divorce followed by remarriage.) How was this revealed? In that the groom at Cana was an image of Christ; so that, by implication, the bride was wedded to an unfailing husband.

Thence Augustine's illustrative analogy: just as a virgin who has vowed chastity is involved in the Church's marriage to Christ, so this wife is involved in that marriage by her vow to her husband, who is the image of Christ.

The *sacramentum* in this case is the hidden meaning of marriage (of marriage, be it noted, not exclusively that of two Christians). This meaning seems to lie in the wife's being involved in the Church's marriage to Christ by virtue of her vow to her husband. As a consequence her relationship to him is assumed into that of the Church with Christ (as is the vowed virgin's relationship). And being thus assumed, it participates in the characteristics of the Christ-Church relationship—one of which is its indestructibility. Whether by coincidence or by design this will become the most commonly used interpretation of the *sacramentum* of Ephesians 5:32 among the many offered by theologians of later centuries.

Yet another sense of the *sacramentum* appears in Augustine's essay, *De nuptiis et concupiscentia,* which he wrote in two books in 418, and in which he made the most formal use of the analogy in Ephesians 5.[13]

Rehearsing the three goods of marriage by way of arguing for the indissolubility of Christian marriages, Augustine writes the following:

> For not only fertility, whose fruit is the child, is urged on the Christian married; and not only chastity, whose bond is fidelity; but also a certain *sacramentum* of their marriage is urged. Hence it is the Apostle says, "Husbands, love your wives just as Christ loved the Church."[14]

Then for the first time Augustine makes a distinction within the marital *sacramentum.* There is the *sacramentum* itself, and there is its *res,* its substantial effect. This he names as the Christian spouses' lifelong perseverance in marriage. Immediately he adds as an apparent explanation,

---

[13]Book I is in *PL* 44, cols. 413–437; Book II in ibid., cols. 438–474.
[14]Ibid., Book I, cap. 10 (col. 420).

"For this is what is maintained between the living Christ and the living Church, that they never for all eternity be separated by divorce."[15]

But in saying this Augustine does not reason that indissolubility is in the Christian marriage as an effect caused there by the Christ-Church union or by the marriage's imaging this union. Rather—and here emerges the new sense of *sacramentum*—it is an effect simply of their being Christians. Augustine uses another analogy to prove his point: just as an apostate does not lose the *sacramentum* of his baptism by his apostatizing, neither do the Christian spouses lose the *sacramentum* of their marriage by divorcing.

Reaching for even more thoroughness Augustine adds that the cause of the spouses' remaining married to one another despite their attempt at divorcing is that there survives ineradicably in their souls *quiddam coniugale,* "a certain marital something." Again this seems analogous to the baptismal *sacramentum* in the soul of every Christian. Augustine seems to intend this "certain marital something" as a synonym for the *res* of the marital *sacramentum*.

> . . . just as the soul of an apostate Christian, in a sense abandoning his marriage with Christ, even though he loses his faith does not lose the *sacramentum* of faith that he received in baptism. Or if he has lost it by apostasy, he would get it back in returning. But he who apostatizes has it to intensify his punishment. . . .
>
> Thus for as long as they live there remains a certain conjugal something which neither separation nor union with another can remove. But it remains to indict them for their crime, not as the bond of their covenant.[16]

With this a cause-effect alignment seems to emerge in Augustine's explanation of the *sacramentum*. It itself is the Christian marriage's quality as image of the Christ-Church union. This in turn causes an effect in the spouses' souls, which Augustine calls the *res* of the *sacramentum,* and apparently also the "certain marital something." Its permanence in these souls is analogous to the permanence of the baptismal *sacramentum* in the soul of every Christian. This seems finally to pinpoint it: the irreducible cause of indissolubility in Christian marriages is this "something." Or is it? From earlier in this passage Augustine said that the *res* is the permanence itself.

In trying to sort out and align the cause-effect relationship here one must reckon with a significant term at the end of the last quotation above. This is

[15]Ibid.
[16]Ibid.

"the bond of the covenant" (*vinculum foederis*) already another synonym for the *res* of the *sacramentum*, along with the "certain marital something."

So it seems now that it is the bond that is indestructible. Or does Augustine deny this in concluding that in the divorced couple the *quiddam coniugale* remains as the cause of their condemnation but *not* as the bond of their covenant?

Confusion mounts even more from something Augustine says in chapter 21 of this Book I, where the bond of the covenant seems to be the union of spouse with spouse. In this passage he accounts for the passing down of original sin's concupiscence from generation to generation. He denies that anything natural in marriage, anything caused in it by God, passes it down. He exonerates offspring (*proles*) and fidelity (*fides*). Then he personifies the *sacramentum* in order to exonerate it as well.

> The *sacramentum* of marriage would reply, "Before the sin it was about me that the words were said in Paradise, 'A man will leave his father and mother and shall cleave to his wife, and the two shall become one body (Genesis 2:24)'." "This is a great *sacramentum*," says the Apostle, "in Christ and in the Church (Ephesians 5:32)." Therefore that which is great in Christ and in the Church is quite small in each and every husband and wife, but is the *sacramentum* of inseparable union.[17]

Does a new shade of meaning of the *sacramentum* appear here, and a new cause-effect alignment with the *res*? Here Augustin calls the *sacramentum* the inseparable union itself, not this union's imaging of the Christ-Church union. This husband-wife union is the small *sacramentum*, as the Christ-Church union is, according to Paul, the great *sacramentum*. Here the cause of indissolubility is not, as it was above, the *res sacramenti*, the bond of the covenant, and neither is this cause the marriage's imaging the Christ-Church union.

If the modern student of his thought becomes progressively more unsure of Augustine's own understanding of the *sacramentum* of marriage, this must only reflect Augustine's own indecision. For he made one last effort, a year later than *De nuptiis et concupiscentia*, in his last essay on marriage, *De adulterinis coniugiis* (on Adulterous Marriages).[18]

Here he uses again the analogy with the baptismal *sacramentum*. Just as this is not deleted from the soul of an excommunicated Christian, so too the

---

[17]Ibid., col. 427.
[18]In *PL* 40, col. 473.

bond of her covenant (again the *vinculum foederis*) remains in the soul of a dismissed wife. It will vanish only when her husband dies, unlike her baptismal *sacramentum,* which remains in her soul forever because God never dies.

This is slightly more decisive. Since her baptismal *sacramentum* never dies, that which eventually does die in the wife at her husband's death, the covenantal bond, must by equivalency and contrast be her marital *sacramentum*. And this is the bond of her covenant. But a bond of whom with whom? Of wife with husband, so that the bond is their marital commitment? Or of her bond with God, her commitment to him to remain with her husband as long as he lives?

In any case here, in his last word on the subject, Augustine does not say that marriage's *sacramentum* consists of its imaging the Christ-Church relationship. He does not say it is the cause of marriage's indissolubility. Rather it is itself an indestructible effect of a cause he does not name.

Later Theologians' Use of the Sacramentum

Before examining how a few theologians of later centuries used the *sacramentum* of Ephesians 5:32 to explain sacramental marriages' indissolubility it will help to inventory the varied and even confused interpretations of it that they inherited from Augustine.

In his *De bono coniugali* Christian marriages' *sacramentum* consists of their imaging the final, eschatological union of all peoples in submission to Christ.

In his *Tractatus 9 in Ioannem* this *sacramentum* is Christian marriage's hidden meaning, namely the wives' involvement in the Church's marriage with Christ, the assumption of their marriages into that union of the Church with Christ.

In *De nuptiis et concupiscentia,* Book I, chapter 10, the *res sacramenti* appears. This is the spouses' lifelong perseverance in marriage. It is either the effect of "a certain marital something" or is this *quiddam coniugale* itself. Or the *res* is the effect of the *sacramentum* itself, which in turn consists of the marriages' imaging the Christ-Church union. A third name for the *res* is the "bond of the covenant."

In Chapter 21 of this Book I the bond of the covenant is the union of spouse with spouse.

Finally in *De adulterinis coniugiis* the *sacramentum* itself appears to be the bond of the covenant—the bond which unites wife to husband but which ceases at his death, unlike her baptismal *sacramentum* binding her to God, which never ceases because God never dies.

1. Thomas Aquinas

Thomas' treatise-in-miniature on the Christian sacraments in his *Summa Contra Gentes,* Liber IV, cap. 56–78, is more characteristically his own because when he wrote it he was, in contrast with his composition of *Commentaria in IV Libros Sententiarum* of Peter Lombard, no longer a young *Sententiarius* in the University of Paris where he had been locked into the schema of treatment established a century earlier by Lombard and was beholden to the opinions of his respected predecessors and contemporaries.[19]

In chapter 78 of the *Summa Contra Gentes,* Book IV, Thomas first asks and answers why marriage is a sacrament in the Church.[20] His answer is that this is because it is oriented to the good of the Church—because it is a union of a man and a woman for procreation and nurture oriented to the good of the Church.

He continues that marriage's sacramental nature consists of its imaging sensately a spiritual reality. He names this reality in the following way.

> And just as in the other sacraments a spiritual reality is imaged by a sensate action, so in this sacrament the union of Christ and the Church is imaged according to what the Apostle wrote to the Ephesians: "This is a great sacrament. I say this in reference to Christ and the Church."[21]

Thomas appears to take for granted that the clause, *Hoc sacramentum magnum est* in the Latin Vulgate version of Ephesians that he read, has Christian marriages as its referent. But he is explicit that these marriages are sacraments in that they image the Christ-Church relationship.

Then he accounts for Christian marriages' indissolubility on the principle that the sensate image must correspond to the spiritual reality which it images.

> Therefore because the union of husband and wife images the union of Christ and the Church, the image must correspond with that which it images. Now the union of Christ and the Church is a union of one person with one person, and a union that is per-

---

[19]The short treatise on the sacrament of marriage in the *Supplementum Summae Theologiae* bears Thomas' name but is no more than Reynaldo of Piperno's adaptation of the material in Thomas' Commentary of the Sentences arranged according to the method of the *Summa* after Thomas' death along with the rest of the *Supplementum.*

[20]*Summa Contra Gentiles,* Editio Leonina manualis (Romae, 1934).

[21]Ibid., p. 543.

petual. . . . It follows necessarily then that a marriage, in so far as it is a sacrament of the Church, must be of one man and one woman, and must be a union that is indissoluble.[22]

Does Thomas propose implicitly this causal nexus in producing the Christian marriage's indissolubility, that the *signatum* that is monogamous and indestructible (the Christ-Church relationship) causes its *signum* (the Christian marriage) to be both? Does the causation function in the imaging?

It is difficult to find the answer to this question in the passage's succinct argumentation. Earlier in this, his *Responsio,* Thomas hinted at a causal nexus by grace. He explained there how and why grace is conferred on the spouses by this sacrament. It is that all sacraments effect what they image. The union of Christ and the Church is itself a grace. So, since the Christian husband and wife image this union, they too must be graced.

This is the juncture in explaining the links of causation in sacramental marriage at which Thomas could have said (but did not) what some later Scholastics have said. Scheeben, for one, argued that the character and grace of baptism join the Christian spouses, specifically as spouses, to a Christ who has already espoused to himself his bride-Church, and has done so in an indestructible union of love. Consequently this union redounds causally in the Christian spouses' union to make it, too, indestructible. Hence it is that the spouses' baptism exercises a prior causality in producing their marriage's indissolubility.

Thomas at least does not say this here in the *Summa Contra Gentes.* He is clear that it is as spouses, through their marriage, that Christian husbands and wives are joined to Christ in his indestructible union with the Church: "And because the sacraments effect what they image, we must hold that grace is conferred on the married through this sacrament, *grace through which they belong to the union of Christ and the Church.*"[23]

Curiously Thomas does not round off his explanation by adding here that it is when the Christian spouses consummate their marriage by sexual intercourse that it becomes finally indissoluble. Years earlier he had made this qualification in his commentary on Lombard's *Liber Sententiarum* (Lib. IV, Dist. 31, Quest. 1, Art. 2).There he reasoned that marriage is indissoluble except by death. But there are two kinds of death, and the diverse kinds of marriage that can be dissolved are proportioned to each kind of death. A marriage that has been joined physically in sexual

[22]Ibid.
[23]Ibid., italics added.

intercourse is dissolved by physical death. A marriage that has been joined
[only] spiritually in marital consent can be dissolved by the spiritual death
that spouses undergo in pronouncing the vows of religious life. A conclusion implicit in this is that it is physical intercourse that makes a marriage
invulnerable to any dissolution other than physical death.[24]

When Thomas did his commentary on Ephesians he again, of course,
used the Latin of the Vulgate, "*Sacramentum hoc magum est.*"[25] The
context of this commentary is his explanation of the three ways in which a
husband and wife are joined. These are through affective love (not *caritas*
in this case, but *affectus dilectionis*); through agreement of minds and wills
(*per conversationem*); and through sexual intercourse (he finds this third
way of joining in the Biblical affirmation ". . . and they will be two in one
flesh").

Again Thomas simply takes for granted that Paul referred to this third
kind of joining when he wrote in Ephesians 5:32, "This is a great
sacrament"; he adds that in saying this Paul interpreted the spouses' sexual
intercourse according to its mystical meaning. That is, the intercourse is
sacrae rei signum, an image of a sacred reality. He names this sacred
reality as the union of Christ and the Church.

The conclusion Thomas draws from this is not that the marriages of
Christian spouses are indissoluble. This consideration does not surface in
his commentary. But he continues with an interesting reflection. He says
that from this point in Ephesians 5 Paul reasons according to the literal
meaning of words. Thus in the Old Testament some passages refer to
Christ alone (for example Psalm 21:18, "They have pierced my hands and
my feet; they have numbered all my bones."). Other passages can be
applied to both Christ and other persons—to Christ principally and to

---

[24]In the same Book IV, Dist. 27, Quest. 1, Art. 3, Sol. 2, ad 2m, Thomas offered another
reason for the final indissolubility of the consummated sacramental marriage. It is that before
consummation by the first sexual intercourse the marital union images the communion of
grace of the individual person with Christ, and this communion can be lost through sin. But
the marital union becomes formally the sacramental sign of the Christ-Church union in sexual
intercourse because it then becomes indissoluble, and the reality of the union of Christ and the
Church is indissoluble.

Note that Thomas here does not say that the consummated marriage is indissoluble because
it now images the indestructible Christ-Church union perfectly. Rather, because as consummated it is now indissoluble, it thus images perfectly. He drew this indissolubility
because of consummation from the assumption that the husband's power over his wife is not
perfect before the first sexual intercourse.

[25]This commentary is in *Sancti Thomae Aquinatis Opera Omnia* (Parmae, 1862), Tomus
XIII, *Exposito in Omnes S. Pauli Apostoli Epistolas: In Epistolam ad Ephesios, Lectio X*. His
commentary on Ephesians 5:32 is on pp. 497–498.

others as to images of Christ (*in figuram Christi*). Such is Paul's statement in Ephesians 5:33, "You too [husbands], each one of you must love his wife. . . ." It appears, Thomas explains, that Paul wrote this of Christ principally, referring to his love for the Church; but also of husbands as images of Christ (again, *in figura Christi*). In them the command is to be made manifest and fulfilled.

Thomas thus apparently lodges Paul's instruction concerning the love union of husbands and wives within exhortation, not within doctrinal declaration. That is, he sees Paul instructing the husbands and wives of Ephesus about how they can and ought to love one another, not about the ontology of their marriages.

2. Mathias Scheeben

In his *Mysterien des Christentums*, completed in 1865,[26] Mathias Scheeben set his treatise on marriage in a contemporary context. This was the effort of Catholic theologians to verify that in the marriages of Christians the contract and the sacrament are inseparable, and that as a consequence their marriages must be regulated exclusively by church authority. This was the ecclesiastical side of the struggle with certain Catholic governments in Europe which insisted that in such marriages contract and sacrament are separate, so that civil authority rules the contract, while ecclesiastical authority rules only the sacrament, which is no more than the religious ceremony.

Scheeben argued the ecclesiastical position by explaining how it is that every marriage of two Christians is a sacrament. This demonstration he drew from the theology of the mystical body of Christ. He reasoned that by their baptism any two Christian spouses are already members of Christ's body. Already, even before marrying, they live within the indestructible union of Christ and his Church. As members of his bride they are already wedded to Christ.

Consequently when they marry they do so within the Church as the body of Christ, within the indestructible union of Church-bride-body with Christ-husband-head. Scheeben did not interpret this as the spouses' being simply lodged within an indestructible relationship and assumed into its indestructibility. Rather he saw them taken into the dynamics of Christ's unfailing love for the Church and its unfailing response to him. Since they were taken into it before marriage by their baptism, their relationship in

---

[26]This rich compendium on Catholic theology was published in English, *The Mysteries of Christianity* (St. Louis, 1941). The treatise on marriage is in Part VI, chapter 21.

marriage is taken into it. They cannot unite in marriage as other than members of Christ's body, which is also his Church-bride. Since the Christ-Church union is the sacrament of God's saving action, so too is their marriage a sacrament by participation in this saving action.[27]

Scheeben did not at this point draw the conclusion that the Christian spouses' marriage therefore participates in the indestructibility of the Christian relationship. This was not his concern in the chapter. But the conclusion was there to be drawn easily.

3. Pierre Adnès

The French canonist, Pierre Adnès, published his book-length treatise, *Le Mariage,* at the outset of the Second Vatican Council.[28] His thought typifies that which in the decades before the council explained the competence of supreme Catholic authority to dissolve marriages that are Christian sacraments but unconsummated as such.

Three conjoined reasons, according to Adnès, account for this competence.[29] The first is that Christ has given to the apostle Peter and his successors the "power of the keys to bind and to loose." This is a power not their own by nature, but God's; they exercise it only as his instruments and ministers.

The second reason lies in the nature of the marriage vows. Since the spouses create their marriage by consenting freely in a contract, their obligation of permanence is of the kind that arises from contracts and vows generally. But supreme authority in the Church can dispense from such obligations for serious causes.

The third reason is that some marriages show precisely such serious causes. For example, where the marriage vows in a particular case create a serious obstacle to eternal salvation, it is expedient and even necessary to free the spouses from their obligation to them. To go back to reason two, the Church is convinced that its vocation to lead men and women to salvation includes the power to dispense from vows when they result in such danger.

---

[27]In his volume, *Der Brief an die Epheser* (Düsseldorf, 6th ed. 1966), Heinrich Schlier seems to reason as Scheeben does here. He insists that Paul not only compared the husband-wife relationship with that of Christ and the Church in order to exhort that the former imitate the latter as its model. Rather, Paul made the husband-wife relationship to be the working out in history of what Christ began in the Church: "The love of the husband for his wife, and therefore their relationship, is in fact to be understood as the execution and fulfillment (*der Nachvollzug*) of the love of Christ for the Church." (Ibid., p. 255.)

[28]Pierre Adnès, *Le Mariage* (Tournai, 1963).

[29]Precisely this explanation is in pp. 165–170.

But not even this reason of compassionate charity extends papal authority as far as competence to dissolve sacramental marriages once they have been consummated. Christian spouses who have consummated their marriage by a single act of sexual intercourse must perforce live on in danger of eternal damnation.

Why this limitation in the papal power of the keys to dissolve the disastrous marriage? In reply to this Adnès rejects the explanation that began with Hugh of St. Victor in the twelfth century, namely that a non-consummated marriage images only the union of Christ and the souls of the just through grace, a union which can be dissolved by sin; whereas a consummated marriage images the union of Christ with the Church, which is indestructible.

Adnès reasons that the union of Christ and the Church is not a purely moral union, but neither is it a physical union properly speaking. As the doctrine of the mystical body of Christ proposes, it is a union containing both these elements simultaneously while transcending them both.

He continues, explaining that by the spouses' consummating it in sexual intercourse their marriage reaches its fulness and thus its full ability to image the relationship of Christ and the Church. It can and does image fully its own mystical meaning. To be more precise, Adnès explains this fulness by pointing out that until sexual consummation the husband-wife union is only moral; but with intercourse their union is made physical as well, and thus a perfect, a complete image of the union of Christ and the Church, a union which is indestructible.

Finally the conclusion to this ratiocination: the image (the consummated Christian marriage) must conform to the essential laws of its divine archetype under the pain of forfeiting its quality as image. Implicit in this conclusion is that a consummated sacramental marriage cannot not thus conform, and therefore cannot forfeit its quality as image of the indestructible divine archetype.

Indissolubility as a Gift to Christian Marriage

Within the last fifteen years a few Catholic theologians have suggested a different kind of nexus of causation that makes Christian marriages indissoluble. They do not contend that what is given about such marriages—that they are images of the indestructible union of Christ and the Church—simply makes them to be indissoluble, as if the cause of their indissolubility were somehow in the imaging. They have also skirted Scheeben's accounting for this indissolubility by the spouses' assumption, through their baptism, into the mystical body of Christ, with the consequence that as married they are assumed also into the indestructible union of this body, the Church, with Christ the head and bride.

If I understand them, they are saying that through the marriages of Christian men and women who come together in faith and love, God works out his plan to save human beings. To do this he creates a love-union with them. This plan and its intent to form this union make up the mystery, the *sacramentum*, that Paul said in Ephesians 5:32 was both hidden and revealed in God's creating the first man and woman in one flesh. The mystery has been realized most perfectly in the union of Christ and the Church, in their becoming one flesh. But this mystery can also be realized, and is realized, in the faith-and-love motivated marriages of Christian men and women. The more clearly their marriages image the union of Christ and the Church, the more they are sacraments. The more they image it, the more they become indissoluble because they must image also its in-destructibility.

1. Joseph Ratzinger

Such seems Joseph Ratzinger's reasoning in his essay, "Zur Theologie der Ehe."[30] He concludes, "The more a person succeeds in living and forming his marriage out of faith, the more is his marriage a sacrament." The place of Ephesians 5 in this interpretation is that it draws out, extends the prophetic reach of the Old Testament, of those prophets who pictured Yahweh's covenant with Israel as a marriage. The creating of the husband-wife covenant, especially among Christians who live by faith, is the working out of this mystery. To work out the mystery to its completion they must live their marriages indissolubly.[31]

2. Walter Kasper

Walter Kasper sees a linear continuum from Christ's teaching in the synoptic passages to Paul's in Ephesians 5.[32] In the former, Christ made a prophetic declaration: it is God who joins men and women in marriage. His covenant with the human race is imaged in marriage; he works out his saving intent in their marriages.[33]

In Ephesians Paul teaches that in the marriage of two Christians Christ is present *in* his saving work, in his sanctifying of the Church. In this work

---

[30]In H. Greeven, J. Ratzinger, et al., *Theologie der Ehe* (Göttingen, 1969), pp. 81–115.
[31]Ibid., p. 92.
[32]Walter Kasper, *Theology on Christian Marriage* (New York, 1980), translated from *Zur Theologie der christlichen Ehe* (Mainz, 1977).
[33]Ibid., pp. 48–49.

Christ and the Church are in covenant, in an unconditionally faithful covenant. This strengthens the Christian spouses to be faithful in their own personal covenant.

> The indissolubility of marriage is therefore not based exclusively on the law of the Church, nor is it simply a moral norm or a metaphysical principle. It is rooted in the sacramentality of marriage itself. *Since the covenant of marriage makes God's covenant in Jesus Christ sacramentally present,* adultery is not primarily a sexual failing for a Christian, but an offense against a person's being in Christ.[34]

Kasper would be more helpful to his readers if he had explained analytically what he meant by this clause (in italics) which stands, intentionally or unintentionally, as the pivot of his brief argument that the marriages of Christian spouses are indissoluble because they are sacraments in the sense of Ephesians 5:32. But in any case he is a witness of the theological change of mind that now sees indissolubility in Christian marriages as a gift, a grace coming to them from Christ, rather than as an ontologically given quality in their character as images of the Christ-Church union.

3. Jean Beyer

Jean Beyer, a professor of canon law at the Pontifical Gregorian University, has added specificity to this interpretation of the sacrament in Christian marriages as Christ's gift to them, and hence of their indissolubility as his gift. He seems to make each an effect of the indwelling and active Holy Spirit.[35]

He reasons that the salvation of the Christian, which begins in his or her baptism, is a union of love with God. Ephesians 5 explains the Christ-Church union in the light of baptism, since it is in baptism, according to Paul, that Christ cleansed the Church and took her to himself. So baptism is the nuptial rite of Christ and the Church. The richest meaning of marriage, according to Paul, is that it images this marriage of Christ and the Church.[36]

Now the love of the Church for Christ, Beyer continues, is the Holy Spirit. But this is the same Spirit who dwells in all followers of Christ

---

[34]Ibid., italics added.

[35]Jean Beyer, "Il mistero dell'amore e l'indissolubilità," in Adnès, Bertrams, Beyer, et al., *Amore e Stabilità nel Matrimonio* (Roma, 1976), pp. 43–51.

[36]Ibid., pp. 44–45.

(Romans 8:11), who prays in them all (Romans 8:15), who lives in them in their every approach to God and Father (Romans 8:27). What the Spirit has accomplished in joining the Church to Christ he accomplishes in every Christian.

But the love that the Spirit generates in Christ and the Christians, and therefore in the Church as a whole, is unalterable (Romans 8:35–38). The love in the union of Christ and Church is indissoluble; the eternal Spirit makes it so. This same Spirit it is, again, who joins Christians and Church to Christ.

Here enters a given characteristic of marital love. This love, which is the kind of love uniting Christians as Church with Christ, is a reciprocal and equal self-giving. Therefore the love must be not only a reciprocal gift but also an unreserved gift.[37]

But because in Christians this human marital love is elevated and strengthened by the union of Christ and his spouse the Church (of which Christians are members), the love acquires the only depth that can bring on its indissolubility, its character as an image of Christ's eternal love. Because God is the origin and cause, through his Holy Spirit, of the marital love of Christian spouses, they can love one another without reserve.

Beyer seems to bring this argument to a climax in the following conclusion about the necessity that the marital love of Christians be indestructible.

> This love would not be the image of divine love if it were not definitive, permanent, indissoluble—if it were not to join and fix itself in the love of God at death and by death. The indissolubility of marriage reflects the permanence of divine love which the institution of marriage must manifest in order to retain the *sacramentum magnum* of divine love for man saved in Jesus Christ.[38]

To this even a student most critical of the traditional Catholic theology of indissolubility must say "Amen." But he or she could also suggest that what Beyer's reasoning has concluded to is not that the marriage of every pair of Christian spouses is an indissoluble sacrament, but that its imaging the love of Christ and the Church and thus being an indissoluble sacrament is contingent on the permanence and unfailingness of the spouses' love for one another. The critic could add that whether the spouses' love is such depends on their free cooperation with the gift of indissolubility, offered to them, as Beyer seems to say, by Christ through his Spirit.

[37]Ibid., p. 48.
[38]Ibid., p. 51.

CRITIQUE: PART I

Paul's Intent in Ephesians 5:21–33

18. And do not get drunk with wine (in which there is dissipation), but be filled with the Spirit, 19. singing to one another in psalms and hymns and spiritual canticles, singing and chanting to the Lord in your hearts, 20. giving thanks always and everywhere to our God and Father in the name of Our Lord Jesus Christ, 21. deferring to one another in the fear of Christ, 22. wives to their own husbands, as to the Lord, 23. because the husband is the head of the wife, just as Christ is the head of the Church, being himself the savior of her, his body. 24. Therefore just as the Church defers to Christ, so too must wives to their husbands in all things.

25. Husbands, love your wives just as Christ loved the Church and gave himself up for her, 26. so that he might make her holy by cleansing her in the bath of water that is joined to the word, 27. so that he might himself present the Church to himself in her splendor, having no stain or wrinkle or anything of this kind, but so that she might be holy and blameless. 28. [Earthly] husbands must love their wives in this way, as their own bodies. In loving his wife a man is loving himself, 29. for no man has ever hated his own flesh, but he nourishes it and cares for it, just as Christ does the Church, 30. for we are members of his body. 31. "For this reason a man will leave father and mother and will cling to his wife, and the two of them will become one flesh." 32. This mystery is a great one (I say this in reference to Christ and the Church). 33. So, let each of you love your own wife as you love yourself; and let the wife reverence her husband.[39]

Paul's intent in this marriage portion of Ephesians 5, what he means to say abut marriage and to the Christian married, is ruled by his overarching intent for the entire letter. This intent is to enlighten his readers about God's plan of reconciliation set from all eternity, his *mystérion*. The plan is that through Christ's death and resurrection he break down the ancient barriers of hostility, and unite Jews and Gentiles in one community, the Church. The executing of this plan has already begun in Christ's death and resurrection and the forming of the community. It is essential to understand that this community is quickened by Christ's love given through his Spirit.

---

[39]This is my translation done from the text of *The Greek New Testament*, ed. Kurt Alland, et al., (London, 1966), pp. 676–677.

The presentation of this thesis occupies Ephesians 1:3 through 3:21. Beginning in Chapter 4 Paul spells out gradually the consequences of this *mystérion* for the Christians' conduct of life. He gives instruction in how to live in such a way as to manifest the *mystérion*; in places the instruction elides into exhortation.

The first such instruction-exhortation is in 4:1–6. Here Paul urges his readers to acknowledge that different persons have received different gifts of the Spirit, some to be apostles, others to be prophets, others pastors, others teachers. But all gifts are from the one same Spirit. All are intended for the building up of Christ's body, the Church.

From 4:17 to 5:18 the substance of the instruction is that new Christians give up the conduct of the old life that his readers have already abandoned, and that they put on a new life, even a new self. Here the *Haustafeln* begin, the inventory of kinds of conduct to be avoided, such as lying, foul talk, drunkenness.

At 5:18 Paul turns to the kinds of conduct that *will* come from those who live by the Spirit and exhorts his readers to them. He singles out three personal relationships in the Ephesian community, and in every community of his time, for explicit instruction: that of husband and wife, that of father and children, and that of master and slave. At every point in his exhortation to love, deference, obedience, care in these relationships the motive is the love of Christ—his love at work in the Christians and their loving fear of him.

We do not get accurately at what Paul urges on husband and wives in verses 21–33 unless we read accurately the syntax and rhetoric of verses 18–21. The shift in the exhortation from conduct to be relinquished to conduct to be adopted is clear in verse 18. It contains a slightly veiled play on two contrasted notions of "getting drunk"; and the second quasi-strophe of the contrast sets the controlling principle for what follows until the end of this chapter 5 and on into the next:

> 18. And do not get drunk with wine (in which there is dissipation), but be filled with the Spirit. . . .

The clauses that follow in verses 19 through 21 have as their verbs in the Greek text a series of participles, with each clause urging a kind of conduct that comes of being "filled with the Spirit":

> 19. . . . singing to one another in psalms and hymns and spiritual canticles, singing and chanting to the Lord in your hearts,
> 20. giving thanks always and everywhere to our God and Father in the name of Our Lord Jesus Christ,
> 21. deferring to one another in the fear of Christ. . . .

Before bridging from verse 21 to verse 22 we must get exactly the meaning of the verb in verse 21 that for the five centuries since the New Testament was first translated into English has been read as "be obedient to" or "be subject to." It is *hypotassómenoi,* in participial form (along with the verbs in the clauses preceding it) in the middle voice. The verb was used commonly in *koiné* Greek; its most generic signification, translated in English, is "defer to." It does not necessarily signify "be subject to" because it is predicable of the attitude of persons who are in fact not subject to one another, and in doing what the verb signifies do not literally subject themselves. Thus scholars who seek the truth in debate rather than victory may defer to one another in the way that *hypotássesthai* signifies. Or commanders in the same army who want shared victory rather than ascendancy may do the same. Siblings, neither of whom has power or authority over the other, may defer to one another in this sense. What the verb signfies specifically in particular instances within this generic signification is to be ascertained from the context.

A far more grievous misreading of this passage, and possibly a deliberate one at that, is in the transition from verse 21 to verse 22. Again virtually all English translations still make of verse 22 an independent sentence, indeed the start of a new paragraph, with its verb in the imperative mode, thus: "Wives, be subject to your husbands as to the Lord."

This is not what the Greek of the passage says. To begin with, verse 22 in some of the most ancient manuscripts does not even have a verb of its own, not even a last participle in the series of participles that begins in verse 19 with "singing." What it does say would be more intelligible in translation if, after the phrase in verse 21, ". . . deferring to one another in the fear of Christ," there were inserted "for example. . . ." Then wives' deference to their husbands would be the first example of the multiple kinds of deference Paul will urge, and verse 22 would be a continuation without pause of the thought begun in verse 21: ". . . deferring to one another in the fear of Christ, [for example] wives to their husbands as to the Lord. . . ."

It is interesting to contrast this verb with which Paul instructs wives in conduct toward their husbands with the verb he later uses to instruct children in conduct toward their fathers. There it is *hypakóuein,* which signifies nothing other than to obey. Paul puts that verb in the imperative mode. The contrasting choice of *hypotássesthai* in its participial form to instruct wives says clearly enough that he urges (not commands) them to some other kind of deference than obedience.

In verses 23 and 24 Paul proposes for the wives a model of their deference to their husbands. This is the deference that the Church shows to Christ. He also gives them a reason for their so deferring: because their relationship to their husbands imitates, or ought to imitate, that of Christ to the Church. He is its head; it is his body. So too the husband is as head to his wife; she is as body to him the head. In proposing this model Paul says something that is an added cause for the Church's deferring: Christ is the savior of her, the body.

> 23. . . . because the husband is the head of the wife, just as Christ is the head of the Church, being himself the savior of her, his body.
> 24. Therefore just as the Church defers to Christ, so too [must] wives to their husbands in all things.

To clarify this exhortation, to give his reason for urging deference on the wives, Paul introduces two metaphors and makes an analogy from them. The Church is a body; Christ is the head of this body. The husband too is a head, and his body is his wife.

Paul joins the two metaphors in an analogy and uses this for two purposes. The first is illustrative, to make clear the kind of deference wives must practice. The other is deontological, to verify why wives ought to so defer. He does not draw an ontological conclusion from the analogy, such as that just as Christ's body is inseparable from him, the head, so too the wife as body is inseparable from her husband as head.

In verses 25 to 30 Paul turns to the husbands to instruct them about the kind of love in which they ought to hold their wives, and to exhort them to this love by explaining why they should love them thus. Here the verb which designates their way of deferring *is* in the imperative: *ándres agapáte*.

> 25. Husbands, love your wives just as Christ loved the Church and gave himself up for her,
> 26. so that he might make her holy by cleansing her in the bath of water that is joined to the word,
> 27. so that he himself might present the Church to himself in her splendor, having no stain or wrinkle or anything or this kind, but so that she might be holy and blameless.
> 28. [Earthly] husbands must love their wives in this way, as their own bodies. In loving his wife a man is loving himself,
> 29. for no man has ever hated his own flesh, but he nourishes it and cares for it, just as Christ does the Church,
> 30. for we are members of his body.

Here Paul uses the same two metaphors—Christ as head of a body that is the Church; the husband as head of a body that is his wife—and introduces a third one, that of Christ as husband, the Church as his bride. This he does in verses 26 and 27, which contain images of the ancient bridal preparation (her prenuptial bath) and of the ceremonial presentation of bride to bridegroom. In Paul's time this was usually done by the *prónubus,* the "friend of the bridegroom," but here Paul has Christ acting as *prónubus* to himself.

From the three metaphors Paul constructs his illustration-exhortation somewhat clumsily, all the moreso because in verses 26 and 27 he found it helpful to include what are probably verses from a *Christus* hymn, and thus introduced the third metaphor.

It is doubtful that Paul intended to draw from his analogy that husbands should do all for their wives that he pictures Christ having done for the Church in verses 26 and 27. Nevertheless these verses have hortatory and deontological valence for husbands. *Because* Christ's love for his bride drove him to such extraordinary care for her, so husbands should love their wives in an equivalent way and degree. At this point in verses 28 and 29, Paul enlists as a reason for the husbands' loving their wives with equivalent care the same reason he had earlier given for the wives deferring to their husbands. The two of them are related as intimately as head and body. Not only this, but the husband it is who is head—which Paul apparently meant to be the place of affectivity in this metaphoric anatomy, since he adds for persuasion, "No man has ever hated his own flesh, but he nourishes it and cares for it. . . ."

It is significant that verse 27 tells of an accomplishment eschatological in nature and intent, and future in realization. Christ gave himself up for the Church so that he himself might present her to himself as bride, holy without blemish, in her full beauty. But this does not tell of an effort fulfilled, a goal attained. It tells rather of what is under way, of what is being accomplished progressively, of what will be realized fully only in a future climax of attainment.[40]

---

[40]Markus Barth makes this point in the following way in his exegesis of the Greek of verse 27: *hína parastése autos heautô éndoxon tēn ekklēsían.* The position of the adjective "resplendent" (*éndoxon*) in the Greek text and the article before "Church" (*tēn ekklēsían*) indicate that resplendent has predicative force. That is, the Church as bride is not already a virtuous and beautiful girl. But she is one who will be made wise and beautiful.

"In addition the change, in the same verse 27, from the participial construction describing the Church—*mē échousan spílon ē hrutída*—to the finite subjunctive with *hína ē hagía kai ámomos* ("so that she might be holy and blameless"), indicates that the Church is not already a bride spotless and unwrinkled, but one who will be made such. The reference here is to the

Therefore if one wishes to reason from the perfections of the Christ-Church relationship to the perfections that are given in the husband-wife relationship, and wishes to include indestructibility among these perfections, the perfections in the former relationship are not pictured as finished and full. Or if one wishes to reason in reverse order, saying that the marriage of two Christian spouses does in fact image the Christ-Church relationship, it images a relationship which is incomplete, is in progress, and which will realize its perfection in an eschatological future. It would follow, then, that if the earthly marriage's imaging is to be faithful to its heavenly model, the former's perfections will be seen as incomplete, in process of realization, to be realized fully only in the future. The marriage's indissolubility would be among these perfections in progress toward realization.

Paul's Use of Analogy

Nowhere in this passage does Paul use the metaphor picturing Christ as husband and the Church as his bride to construct the analogy that has been drawn so commonly in the Catholic theology of marriage through the centuries, the analogy featuring Christian husband and wife as united in marriage the way Christ and Church are united. Consequently the theological commonplace that the earthly marriage is an image of the marriage of Christ and the Church cannot draw on Ephesians 5 as its source.

The analogy whose parts Paul does set out has the husband as head of the body which is his wife, just as Christ is head of the body which is the Church. Nowhere does Paul say, in virtue of this analogy, that the first of these unions is an image of the latter. He does not say it is such an image at all. If readers of the passage wish to say he does, they must get this by deduction from what Paul says, and justify the deduction.

Nowhere in developing this analogy does Paul say that the union of Christ as head with the Church as body is indestructible, although one may assume safely that he thought it so. Consequently the conclusion that in virtue of the head-body analogy the marriages of Christian spouses are indissoluble cannot be drawn from the analogy.

Down through verse 30 the issue of marriage's indissolubility enters only indirectly and implicitly. The issue is there only by implication in Paul's insistence that husbands love their wives as Christ loves the Church, with a love that is surely unfailing. Whether Paul saw the Church's love to

---

eschatalogical future of the Church." Markus Barth, *Ephesians 4–6, The Anchor Bible* (New York, 1974), p. 268.

be reciprocally unfailing in either of the Christ-Church metaphors—whether in'that of head-body or in that of husband-wife—is not clear. From his elaboration of the second of these metaphors one may best conclude that it is Christ's loving treatment of the Church that is intended to capacitate her to return to him an unfailing love. There is nothing in the metaphor suggesting that unfailingness is simply a given in the Church's reciprocated love. Consequently one cannot draw from this metaphor the conclusion that the indestructibility of love in Christian marriages is antecedantly given.

Paul's attention to marriage's indissolubility is more nearly explicit in verses 31 and 32.

> 31. "For this reason a man will leave father and mother and will cling to his wife, and the two of them will become one flesh."
> 32. This mystery is a great one (I say this in reference to Christ and the Church).

Certainly Paul intends to splice these two figurative assertions of the intimacy of marital union, his own assertion that wife and husband are as united as head and body, and the assertion borrowed from Genesis 2:24 that husband and wife are as one body. The symmetry of the two figures is not exact. Paul's metaphor makes the husband the head, the nobler and ruling member vis-à-vis the body. The Genesis metaphor evokes no such clear image. The verse in Genesis itself says that the man and woman become "as one flesh" (in Hebrew, *lebāsār' ehād*). Most probably taking the Greek translation of the same passage in the Septuagint for his use, Paul adopts its "one flesh" (*mía sárx*). But though the image is blurred and the noun disputable, the meaning is clear enough. For the ancient author, in verse 24, interrupted the parable narrative to make his own comment. He, not the fictional Adam, says that a man becomes one body with his woman. Having just had the man say, in verse 23a, that the woman is his intimate and constant companion, he himself now identifies another feature of their union: they become "one body."[41]

---

[41]Genesis 2:24, which Paul reproduces as Ephesians 5:31, continues, emphasizes and seeks to clarify the thought of 2:23a, where Adam said of the woman, "This one at last is bone of my bone and flesh of my flesh."

It is not incorrect but it gets at only minimal meaning to take this as saying that the man and woman are of the same physical stuff. The word-pair, "flesh and bone," appears more than once in the Old Testament. Taken togeher they can signify flesh weakness and bone strength. And together they signify more than physical strength and weakness. Flesh weakness and bone strength are antitheses in combination, and the antithesis includes not only the two

Despite centuries of patristic, theological, canonical and magisterial interpretation that claims it does, the expression does not designate sexual union in genital intercourse; or it does so only remotely. It designates primarily that the man and woman stand as one person before the people and the law. A legitimate inference here would be that in seeking legally to dismiss his wife, a man would try to get rid of his own person. Paul captured the thought in Ephesians 5:28b and 29a: "In loving his wife a man is loving himself, for no man ever hated his own flesh. . . ."

This moral and legal one-body status of the man and woman has for its immediate created cause the man's conduct reported in verse 24a, "This is why a man leaves his father and mother and cleaves to his woman [wife]. . . ." The two verbs in the statement belong to the language of covenant relations—"to abandon" (Hebrew *azav*) and "to cleave" (Hebrew *davao*).

> The latter verb is used especially in OT Deuteronomic contexts in clusters of covenant words to speak about loyalty to covenant partners. . . . Conversely, the term *azav* refers to abandoning one covenant commitment for the sake of another. The two terms in Gn 2:24 also speak of terminating one loyalty and the embrace of a new one. Thus it substantiates the covenant formula of 2:23a ["This one at last is bone of my bones, etc."].[42]

Obviously Paul found this passage in Genesis perfectly suited to clarify his interpretation of the two relationships he used in his analogical reasoning. It helped him to present his vision of Christ's relationship with his people, the Church, as a covenant. He says in verse 32 that the typological reference of the first covenant of the primeval man and woman to the second Christ-Church covenant is a great *mysterion,* a rich foreshadowing. Through this reference the foreshadowing illumines also the second relationship, that of husband and wife living within the Christ-Church covenant. Theirs too is by God's will to be a covenant. It is to have the characteristics of the primeval covenant: one-personhood before the law, companionship and sharing in all of life, unfailing fidelity. It is to have also the characteristics of the foreshadowed Christ-Church

---

extremes but all points between them. In effect the man says that the woman is his companion, his helpmate who shares his strength and his weakness and all points between them. This bespeaks constancy, permanence. *Gaudium et spes'* designation of marriage as a man's and a woman's intimate sharing echos this strikingly. Walter Brueggemann develops this interpretation of Genesis 2:23a in his essay, "Of the Same Flesh and Bone (Gn 2:23a)," *Catholic Biblical Quarterly* 32 (1970) 532–542.

[42]Brueggemann, p. 540.

covenant within which it is set, most notably the husband's self-giving love even unto death, and the wife's deferential submission to being loved in this way.

Paul's last words in the passage make a clear return to this point. Since they are his last words, one may rightly guess that this is the thought he wanted to make most emphatically. In these last words he comes from analogy, metaphor and Torah down to the earthly conclusion that he draws from them all: "So, let each of you love your own wife as you love yourself; and let the wife reverence her husband."[43] That this is an exhortation substantiates the interpretation that the context of the entire passage is exhortation, *paraklésis,* and that the theology of marriage is in the passage in service to the exhortation. It supplies the reasons for the kind of love and conduct to which Paul urges the Christian spouses.

CRITIQUE: PART II

Metaphor and Analogy in the Theology of Indissolubility

If one decides to use a metaphor to clarify a point of religious fact or event, one must take care (1) not to substitute the metaphor for the fact or event, and (2) not to change what is known already of the fact or event in order to fit the demands of the metaphor. How necessary is this exercise of care can be seen in the theology of the mystical body of Christ. This metaphor of Christ as head of a body may be useful to illustrate how, through the Holy Spirit, Christ works to guide and to energize Christians, analogically as the head (or more exactly the brain) guides and energizes the members of the body. But reify the metaphor, or go too far with its demands, and one could reduce Christian persons to psychological and moral passivity, as hands, feet, etc., are passive to the stimulus and guiding of the brain.

So too it is false to draw from the metaphor of the body of Christ, as one theology of the automatic sacramentality of all Christian marriages does, that Christians are in some way organically joined to Christ, with the consequence that apart from their choice in the matter they are in union with him—as the limbs of a body have no choice about being neurally in union with the brain. What is true from the metaphor is that apart from

---

[43]There is no dissimulating Paul's choice of a Greek verb designating the wife's attitude whose first meaning is "to fear" (*phobêin*). But in view of all he has just said about the husband-wife relationship he obviously intends not servile fear but reverential fear—a fear analogous to the kind a human being ought to have for even an infinitely loving God. For this reason I have chosen to translate the verb as "to reverence."

persons' choice God acts in them through Christ and the Spirit. But this is ineffectual in forming union with them unless they react positively, through free decision letting God's action work its effect in them.

The same is true about automatic indissolubility. Set aside the fact that Ephesians 5:21-33 nowhere proposes the analogy whose poles are the relationships respectively of husband-Christ to the bride-Church and of earthly husband to earthly bride, but proposes rather the analogy of Christ-head of his body-Church and of husband-head of his body-wife. From the fact that in the first metaphor of this second analogy the head and body are functionally inseparable (no body and head would separate themselves from one another), one cannot use this as a mediating metaphor for the Christ-Church relationship so as to produce the conclusion that real-life husbands and wives are inseparable.

An added reason for this impossibility is that there is an unassimilated variable in the second metaphor of this analogy, the metaphor of husband-head and wife-body. This variable is the power of free decision in the partners to the union.

Presumably Paul intends that the mode of predictability of "husband" and "wife" in the metaphor is that of a concrete universal. These sub-stantives refer to all husbands and wives, or at least to all Christian husbands and wives. But the real-life referents of this predication have the power of decision. The endurance of their union comes under this freely useable power. If the analogy using the husband-wife metaphor does not accept and include this fact, at least this pole of the analogy has no referent in reality. Consequently the analogy as a whole can say nothing conclusive about real-life marriage.

I have said that the use of an analogy and its metaphors must not alter nor force the nature of the reality it is intended to clarify. In this case the metaphors Paul uses in Ephesians—Christ as head of the body that is the Church; husband as head of the body that is his wife—must not force the nature of the sacrament.

Each of the Church's sacraments has its created matrix, that human experience out of which the sacrament is formed. In baptism the matrix is the immersing in water or at least the washing with it. It is not merely water itself, idle in a reflecting pool. In the Eucharist the matrix is the blessing, breaking, sharing and eating of bread, and the blessing, pouring out, sharing and drinking of wine. The matrix here is not merely bread and wine in themselves, perhaps reposing at a food fair.

In a sacrament the human, pre-sacramental matrix's meaning—its ex-pressed signification for the people—is used intentionally by the Spirit to effect a meaning analogically similar to its merely human meaning. The Spirit makes of the bathing a cleansing in the rebirth into the person's union with Christ as savior. The Spirit makes of the blessing, sharing and consuming of bread and wine a nourishing and intensifying of the union with Christ (and of course of the union too of all persons already in union with him).

Marriage too has its human matrix. It differs somewhat in different societies and their cultures. But in *Gaudium et spes* the bishops at the Second Vatican Council identified this matrix when describing a marriage as a man's and a woman's intimate sharing, or companionship, in life and love, a sharing that begins and continues as a covenantal gifting of their persons to one another.[44] The self-giving and sharing, the bishops added, is most typical and complete in the spouses' sexual intercourse.[45]

When the spouses' specifically marital conduct is sacramental because evoked and impelled by their Christian faith and love, it loses none of its human characteristics. Since the self-giving and the sharing must be freely decided, this freedom continues where their conduct is sacramental. But freedom is by nature the ability to choose among alternatives and to choose among opposites. A man and woman can love one another with sharing and self-giving marital love only if they retain the capacity to end the sharing and self-giving.

(It is not widely known that in 1976 Pope Paul VI answered a question that follows necessarily from this freedom. If after their exchange of marital consent a man and a woman end their sharing and self-giving, does not their marriage come to an end? Catholic diocesan marriage courts in Utrecht and Haarlem, Holland, had answered this question about a marriage affirmatively in 1971. Pope Paul's authoritative judgment in the matter, in his annual address to the Roman Rota on February 9, 1976, was that spouses' cessation of love and sharing does not end their marriage and cannot end it. It cannot because it does not affect the essence of their marriage. This is not their self-giving and sharing. This essence is rather the juridical entity that their consent creates, the legal bond. Once created it is invulnerable to any subsequent act of will by the spouses. It is obvious that Paul's judgment constituted an interpretation of the minds of the bishops of Vatican II, namely that in *Gaudium et spes* they had not touched the essence of marriage. He also neglected to explain how this juridical bond, which exists independently of the wills of the spouses, can be the

---

[44]*Gaudium et spes*, no. 48.
[45]Ibid., no. 49.

matrix of the sacrament; how, as a consequence, it can image the union of Christ and the Church.)[46]

It seems, then, that when accurately understood the sacramental character of a marriage does the contradictory of investing this marriage with an indissolubility that is spontaneous, automatic, invulnerable to the wills of the spouses. This sacramentality helps to keep them loving one another, and helps to keep them loving freely. Christ's acting in their free love through his Spirit may indeed help strengthen this love to the point where they *could* never withdraw it. But to say this is wholly different from saying that the Spirit acts within their marital consent to make their marriage a legal bond that is invulnerable to their wills.

It is also wholly different from claiming the other alternative, namely, that the Spirit acts in their marital consent to make of their marriage an image of the indestructible union of Christ and the Church, and by its imaging to take from them the very possibility of ending their love for one another, their sharing and self-giving. Such a theology built on such a claim is out of touch with the reality of marriage.

The Demands and Limitations of Analogy

To understand what Paul says in Ephesians 5:21–33 about the permanence of the husband-wife union, the student must begin by drawing from his analogy what he himself put into it and presumably intended should be drawn from it.

To do this one must reckon with the structure of the kind of analogy each of whose two poles consists of a relationship. Such an analogy asserts that there is a same element of reality found in the two relationships, but that this element is in the two relationships in different ways. (If the analogy is designed aptly, the nature of the relationship in one pole is familiar to the readers or hearers. On being told that this nature is found also in a second relationship, they may come to understand this relationship as well.)

This essay has dealt continually with such an analogy that is found in Paul's letters, that which portrays Christ's relationship to the Church as a relationship of a person's head to his body. The element common to both poles of this analogy is the function of guiding and ruling. Paul assumes that his readers know that the head (i.e., the brain) does this for the body. He also expects that from this knowledge they will, thanks to his analogy, come to understand how Christ guides and rules the Church.

---

[46]See my volume, *Marriage in the Catholic Church: What is Marriage?* (New York: Paulist Press, 1982), for a more detailed examination of Pope Paul's discourse.

As I pointed out earlier, the analogy in Ephesians 5:24–29 by which Paul seeks to clarify his instruction to husbands and wives does not have the marital union as its element common to both poles. Paul does not say in the analogy that Christ and the Church are joined in a marital union that is indestructible. Hence he does not expect that from understanding this his readers will come to understand that their marriages, too, are indestructible. As I said just above, the common element he proposes is the head-body relationship, the guiding and ruling done naturally by the head. Because of his readers' familiarity with this, Paul surely expects that they will come to understand the guiding and ruling he means for husbands to exercise in regard to their wives—not the kind appropriate to a slave-master relationship, nor to a parent-child relationship, but proportioned to the relationship between the greater and lesser members of one body.

If one were to skirt Paul's intent in using the analogy and work only with the semantic content of its polar metaphors one could not draw from it the conclusion that the consummated marriage of any two Christians is indissoluble. To put it brutally, a head and body are not inseparable.

But one does not understand what a writer's analogy means to convey if one skirts his intent in using it. Certainly Paul's was not to argue for indissolubility. But even if one works with his intent, one cannot infer from the analogy that the marriage of any two Christians is indissoluble. One can infer from it only that their love ought to be as intimate and sustaining as the union of a head and body, which intimacy and sustenance find their arch-model in the union of Christ and the Church.

Metaphor in the Theology of Real-Life Marriage

A further difficulty in the way of finding spontaneous indissolubility in Paul's analogy appears when one considers that one of the poles of the analogy has a metaphor as one of its ingredients. The "body of Christ" that Paul pictures is not a concretely universal representation of a physical reality, as is "the wives" in the analogy's other pole. In the analogy Christ's body is a metaphor, a reification of the society we call the Church.

Provided that in dealing, in this analogy, with the pole across from the real-life husband and wife, one remains abstractly within this metaphor, one can say easily that the union of Christ and the Church is indestructible. One would thus have in the dominant pole of the analogy a source whence to draw a conclusion about earthly marriages—at least the conclusion that the spouses ought to strive to image this indestructibility.

But the real-life Church—not the reified, metaphoric Church—is not so amenable to abstract, a priori determination. In real life it is a society of human beings, some of them resolute in their fidelity to Christ, some of them not. Christ's effort, through his Spirit, of bringing men and women to fidelity is in its effects a continuing struggle. It is a struggle in which some work with the Spirit and remain faithful while others do not and fall away.

Therefore if one insists that as a prior and given fact determined by baptism any and every marriage of two Christians images Christ's real relationship with the real, non-metaphoric Church, he must find a place in his explanation for much struggle, in this struggle much cooperation with the Spirit and therefore much fidelity, as also much rejection of the Spirit and therefore much infidelity. He could then set about explaining how to draw from such contingency in the real relationship of the real Church with Christ the priorly determined fact of every Christian marriage's indissolubility.

The Consummated Sacrament and Indissolubility

We know from the history of the Catholic Church's doctrine concerning marriage's indissolubility that two major questions concerning this doctrine remained unanswered for centuries. The first asked if, according to God's will, marriages are vulnerable or invulnerable to dissolution. Once the Catholic authorities agreed on a qualified answer to the question, namely that some marriages are invulnerable while some are not, the second question demanded an answer: which are the marriages that are invulnerable and what makes then so?

By the time of Gregory XIII's apostolic constitution of 1585, *Populis ac nationibus,* the authoritative answer was fixed. A marriage that is a Christian sacrament and is consummated as such is invulnerable to the attempt of any authority on earth to dissolve it; but only a consummated sacramental marriage is thus invulnerable.

Two fragile assumptions made this answer possible. The first of these is an assumption about the nature of consummation that is rooted, in turn, in an assumption about the nature of marriage itself. The latter is that a marriage is in essence a contract in which a man and a woman exchange the good that is each party's right to his and her sexual acts that are apt for procreation. Once this definition is assumed it is easy to conclude that a marriage is consummated, which is to say completed, when the parties to the contract exchange their marriage's contractual good. They do this in their first complete sexual intercourse after their wedding vows, after making the contractual consent. Join to all this the kindred assumption that the contractual marital consent of any two Christians creates a marriage that is a sacrament, and one easily concludes that the first complete intercourse produces also the consummated sacrament, invulnerable to any human power of dissolution.

The second fragile assumption interprets the meaning of the term "one flesh" in Christ's instruction in Mark 10:8 and Matthew 19:6 (where the Greek *mía sárx* repeats the Septuagint's change from the "one body" of Genesis 2:24). This interpretation says that the reason Christ gave for the impermissibility and even the impossibility of a man's dismissing his wife is that in their marriage they become "one flesh," and that they do this not in their marital consent but by their sexual intercourse. For the consent creates only a spiritual and moral union, which images no more than the union of the Christian soul with Christ, a union vulnerable to destruction by sin. But the completing of the union by sexual intercourse makes it a physical union, which images the union of either Christ with the Church or of the two natures in Christ. Both unions are indestructible. Therefore as soon after their consent as the spouses have completed intercourse, their marriage gains the indissolubility Christ revealed it to have. This interpretation was reinforced by Pope Alexander III's exegetical determination, circa 1178, that in forbidding husbands to dismiss their wives and remarry Christ referred only to spouses who had consummated their marriage by sexual intercourse.[47]

The entire interpretation is vulnerable, and most vulnerable in precisely the assumptions I have just outlined. But before getting at these it is pertinent to glance at a seldom-noticed discordance of this theory from Paul's reasoning in Ephesians 5. To locate marriage's indissolubility in the Christian spouses' consummation by intercourse is to go beyond what Paul intended. Even if one presumes that in his exhortation to the spouses he urged them to image the union of Christ and the Church, he did not say that the perfect imaging of this union is accomplished in intercourse. He implied rather that it is accomplished in the husband's self-giving love and in the wife's deference, or submission, to him. One must invent and add to Paul's explanation in order to place the perfection of this love and of this submission in intercourse.[48]

---

[47]"Certainly what the Lord says in the Gospel, that a wife is not to be dismissed except for her adultery, is to be understood, by the interpretation of sacred Scripture [*sacri eloquii*] to refer to those whose marriage has not been consummated by sexual intercourse—intercourse without which a marriage cannot be consummated. Hence if the wife has not had intercourse with her husband, she is permitted to enter religious life." *Liber Decretalium*, Lib. 3, Titul. 32, Cap. 32, in *Corpus Iuris Canonici*, Editio Lipsiensis Secunda, ed. E. Friedberg (1881), Pars Secunda, Col. 579.

[48]Aquinas' explanation from his *In IV Sententiarum*, Dist. 27, that we have already seen—namely, that the spouses' imaging the Christ-Church union is perfect only in in-

But the teaching that it is the consummation of it as a sacrament that makes a marriage finally indissoluble is called into doubt more fundamentally because it is now doubtful that the concept of consummation retains any meaning.

As long as marriage was understood as a contract in the way explained above it was consistent to say that by their consent in the wedding vows the spouses exchanged the right to their sexual acts and thereby created the marriage, but still only an inchoate and incomplete marriage. It was also consistent to go on and say that the marriage is completed—consummated—as soon as the exchange is first realized in sexual intercourse.

But what becomes of this notion of consummation now that the Church's teachers no longer understand marriage as a contract, and therefore no longer interpret the act that creates a marriage as a contractual exchange of rights? In *Gaudium et spes* the bishops described marriage as a man's and woman's intimate sharing of marital life and love, and added that they create their marriage, according to the biblical model, by a covenantal gifting of themselves to one another.[49] Presuming that to consummate a marriage is to bring it from a state of incompletion to completion, and drawing from the understanding of marriage in *Gaudium et spes* as an intimate sharing of life and love begun by the spouses' giving over of their persons to one another, what would it mean to bring such a sharing, such a self-giving to completion?[50]

If in the attempt to understand consummation of marriage, the sacramental covenant, the Church's teachers were to use the notion as old as Aquinas, namely "the *perfect* imaging of Christ's love for the Church," the consequences of this would be severe. Christ's love for his bride, the Church, came to completion in his dying and rising from death. What would have to be found in the conduct of a Christian marriage if it were to

---

tercourse because only then is the husband's power over his wife fulfilled—draws on a psychology of sexual marital love that is hardly assimilable into the Christian sacrament.

[49]This understanding has been taken into the revised Code of Canon Law and formulated in canon 1057, §2: "Marital consent is an act of the will by which a man and a woman, in forming an irrevocable covenant, give themselves over to one another, and accept one another, with the intent of creating a marriage."

[50]How grievous is the inconsistency in the revised code where this defines the act creating a marriage as it does in canon 1057, §2, but then in canon 1061, §1 defines consummation in a way fitted only to the contractual exchange that the law itself has banished? Canon 1061, §1 is this: "A valid marriage . . . is ratified and consummated if the spouses have placed in a human way the marital act which is of itself apt for the procreation to which marriage is by nature oriented, the act by which the spouses become one flesh."

image this dying and rising perfectly? If not the husband's or both spouses' physical death, what analogical equivalent?

There is a logically prior difficulty hidden, but just barely hidden, in new canon 1061, §1 of the revised marriage law. The canon says that a marriage is consummated ". . . if the spouses have placed in a human way the marital act. . . ." The Latin of the adverbial modifier here is *humano modo*.

Since 1958 a few canonists and theologians have objected vigorously to a decision handed down on August 2 of that year by the Sacred Congregation of the Sacraments. The decision ruled that a marriage referred to the congregation's adjudication had been consummated even though the wife had had to drug herself into senselessness in order to survive intercourse emotionally. The consultors of the congregation ruled that she and her husband had consummated their marriage because he had deposited his semen in her vagina and had thus realized marriage's essential contractual exchange.[51]

At the same time a more fundamental and generic question was put to the same congregation. It asked whether in order to consummate their marriage spouses need have the capacity, both before and during the presumably consummating intercourse, to place a truly human act. This was to ask if both must be aware of their conduct and carry it on by free consent. In replying the congregation distinguished two intentions in the spouses, and the effect of these intentions. In order that their intercourse be an exercise of the virtue of justice whereby each party discharges a debt owed in justice, both must be able to place a human act—in this case intercourse had knowingly and by choice. But in order to consummate the marital contract, to place that act which of its nature is apt for realizing marriage's primary end, neither awareness nor consent is needed. (Where both spouses are Christian this semiconscious and unintended penetration and semination were presumably thought also to consummate the sacrament.)

Some bishops' and theologians' reaction to this mechanistic interpretation had its effect in *Gaudium et spes'* own interpretation of consummation. Writing of the goodness of marital love, the bishops said that it is expressed uniquely in sexual lovemaking, in those good and worthy acts which manifest and intensify the spouses' self-donation to one another—provided these acts are accomplished in a human way (*humano modo*).[52]

[51] In Bouscaren-O'Connor, *Canon Law Digest* 5: 529–533.
[52] *Gaudium et spes*, no. 49.

This significant modifier, *humano modo,* was not left to rest half-noticed in the text of *Gaudium et spes.* The sub-commission which, beginning in 1966, worked at the first draft of the revised canons on marriage judged its inclusion to be necessary in their new canon defining a consummated marriage. Old canon 1015 of the 1917 code said that a marriage is consummated if that act takes place between the spouses to which the marital contract is oriented by nature. New canon 1061, §1, as I have indicated above (in note 50), simply repeats this formulation, but with the addition of *humano modo*: "A valid marriage is consummated if the spouses have placed in a human way the marital act. . . ."

But the consultors of the subcommission sensed a difficulty in including this modifier. In 1973, while their work was still in progress, they reported the difficulty in the following way.

> The question was raised whether a marriage is consummated even by copula that is physically complete but is had unconsciously or is extorted by force. It was pointed out that the reply according to the more common teaching thus far has been affirmative. . . . But according to some this teaching seems hardly consonant with that of the Second Vatican Council on marriage, and specifically with its teaching concerning the marital act. . . .
>
> Consequently it is proposed that the law as well state that consummation of marriage must be done in a human way [*humano modo*] if it is to be called true consummation.
>
> But it is objected that an essential trait of a fact in the law ought to be readily available to verification, whereas it is hardly possible to prove that a consummating act has not been done in a human way. Even though one could say that the act of a human being [*actus hominis*, e.g. the unconscious or extorted intercourse mentioned above] can be distinguished clearly from a human act [*actus humanus*, an act produced by reflection and decision], one ought not ignore the fact that in many such cases a human act is at least virtually present from marital consent already given and accepted.
>
> Even though the majority of the consultors judged that the words *humano modo* ought to be included in the determination of the act consummating marriage, they were unanimous in recommending that these be put within parentheses so that their doubts in the matter may be on record.[53]

---

[53]*Communicationes* 5 (1973) 79.

Although the parentheses were removed when the modifier was written into canon 1061, §1, no one among the Church's official teachers has to date resolved the doubt concerning the verifiability of the sexual intercourse that consummates a marriage—not the Pontifical Commission for the Revision of the Code of Canon Law, not Pope Paul VI while he still lived, nor to date Pope John Paul II.

In short, the officially teaching Church, admittedly lacking a criterion for judging the humanness of sexual intercourse, lacks a criterion for verifying that a marriage is consummated. Therefore as long as the marriages of Christian spouses are held to be indissoluble only if the spouses become two-in-one-flesh by intercourse that consummates this union, the Church has no criterion by which to distinguish indissoluble marriages from dissoluble. Reductively then it is to date of dubious value to reason theologically from Ephesians 5:21–33 and say that Christian marriages are indissoluble because in the physical union of intercourse the spouses image perfectly the union of Christ and the Church. Certainly this act's imaging such a union demands that it be accomplished in a human way. But this theology is in abeyance, and is in abeyance as the warrant for the doctrine of indissolubility, until the Church works out a humane psychology of sexuality that can understand what it means to communicate sexually in marital love in a human way.

CONCLUSIONS

The intent of this essay has been negative and in a sense destructive. It has sought to show that the radical indissolubility of consummated sacramental marriages cannot be proved from Ephesians 5:21–33. In an extended conclusion let me itemize the limits of what I think can be drawn from the passage about the permanence of Christian marriages.

Paul has no ontological intent in the passage. He does not in it assert the characteristic of marriage taken abstractly that is indissolubility. He does not even assert the indissolubility of the real-life marriages of Christian spouses. He certainly does not try to establish and explain their given and fixed radical indissolubility.

His primary intent is to exhort—to exhort Christian spouses indwelt by the Holy Spirit and moved by him to live their marriages in a way befitting their situation. Instruction is his obvious second intent. But it is instruction in the service of exhortation in order to explain which kinds of conduct befit their situation.

Therefore anyone who seeks to prove radical indissolubility from this passage engages in a task that is apart from its author's intent. He must find evidence that is accidental to what Paul intended to exhort and teach. He also deals with a concept about which it is difficult to show that it ever entered Paul's mind.

The passage offers no evidence that justifies the fixing of radical indissolubility at the point of consummated sacramental marriage. To argue in support of such marriage from Paul's use in the passage of the epigram, "They shall become two in one flesh," is to misinterpret Paul's own intent in using it. To begin with, in its document of origin, the Book of Genesis, it does not refer primarily to sexual intercourse. Its primary referent is the intimate union of husband and wife that makes them legally and morally the equivalent of one person.

Paul quotes this epigram to support his complex thesis, first that the two-in-one-flesh union of the first man and woman foreshadowed the union of Christ and the Church. Thus in their union Christ and the Church stand as on person before God and the world. Secondly, the firmness and intimacy of Christian marriages look backward to the one-personhood of Christ and the Church as to a model; and the spouses must imitate the union, the firmness, the intimacy in their own marriages. Paul does not give sexual intercourse a function in this thesis.

In setting forth his thesis Paul uses a pivotal analogy that is constituted partly of a metaphor predicated of Christ and the Church. This metaphor does not picture Christ as husband of his bride Church, the metaphor that is the middle term of the traditional theological argument that tries to prove radical indissolubility from this passage. Paul's analogy uses rather the metaphor picturing Christ as the head of his body, the Church. To devise for the traditional argument the metaphor whose structure is "As Christ is to his bride the Church so is the Christian husband to his wife," is to extemporize an analogy that is not Paul's, but one whose discrete elements lie unrelated in the passage.

The contingency of marital love and union, not their supposed character as given and fixed states, runs through Paul's thesis from beginning to end. Since Christ's work, as Paul saw it, is to gather the entire human race into union with himself in the Church, the *mystérion* of this union that is the union of the first man and woman refers to this universal union. The *mystérion* is not limited in its reference to only the marriages of Christian spouses. But Christ's union with all the human race is replete with contingency, with failures as well as successes. It is an enterprise in process. In substance it is as much a striving as it is a completed state. Therefore what can be inferred from Paul's thesis about the permanence of marriages generally as a concrete universal, and about the permanence of individual marriages, is that in them too the realization of permanence is contingent, that it too is in substance a striving.

The idea that the marriage of two Christians images the Christ-Church union is not in the passage. That the idea has been assumed so widely and persistently by Catholic teachers to be Paul's comes from the historically early and exegetically mistaken interpretation that the epigram, "This *mystérion* is a great one," refers to the husband-wife relationship. Join to this the Latin Fathers' translation of *mystérion* into *sacramentum,* and Augustine's suggestion in *De bono coniugali* that this *sacramentum* consists of a Christian marriage's imaging the eschatological union of Christ and the Church, and the eisegesis is complete. The imaging function of Christian marriage has been read into the passage.

What can be inferred about imaging from the passage is the following. Paul urges on Christian spouses a model for the reciprocally (and asymmetrically) deferential love they should have for one another. The model is Christ's love for the Church and its love for him. Thus, *if* the spouses imitate this model in their love, they will image it.

It is not sophistic to point out that the fact that Paul urges the Christian spouses to embody this model in their marriages implies that he thought they might not be doing so. Otherwise why urge them? Plainly he was reckoning with the contingency of the Christian spouses' imaging the divine model. He cannot have been taking for granted that all their marriages in fact image it.

That the marriage of two Christian spouses image the Christ-Church model in its fidelity and permanence is an effect, according to the logic of Paul's exhortation, of the spouses' being filled with the Holy Spirit and impelled by him in their conduct. This does not argue for the given and fixed indissolubility of their marriages. Men and women can refuse the Spirit. This is taken for granted everywhere in the New Testament, and nowhere more than in Paul. That is, Christian spouses can as freely refuse the operation in themselves of the necessary cause of their marriage's faithful permanence as they can welcome and cooperate with it.

My conclusion of conclusions: Whoever would support theologically the doctrine that the marriage of two baptized Christians cannot end short of death once it is consummated must find the premises for his argument elsewhere than in Ephesians 5.

THE STATUS OF MIXED MARRIAGES
IN THE CORINTHIAN COMMUNITY

ROBERT J. SMITH

A. The Situation

The exact status of marriages between believers and non-believers was a troublesome issue within the Christian community at Corinth which occasioned severe criticism and controversy and demanded a certain adaptation in the apostle's gospel proclamation. Various opinions have been offered as to the precise nature of the difficulty.

Some authors who have critically studied and evaluated First Corinthians have indicated that the precise nature of the problem concerned the recent conversion and baptism of the Christian spouse. Concluding that conversion and baptism into the Christian community was considered a radical commitment demanding absolute adherence to Christian faith, some authors have speculated that the Corinthian community regarded any formal contact with one's former state of infidelity as being "quasi-magically contaminated,"[1] even if made indirectly through an infidel spouse.

Some authors have suggested that the issue confronting Paul concerning the questionable orthodoxy of such marriages was prompted by the spiritual implications of regeneration and re-creation as attributed to baptism. In essence, some Christians at Corinth had been advocating repudiation of the infidel spouse and abandonment of the existing marriage; in doing so, they attributed to baptism, "the rabbinical principle that entrance into Israel (chosen community) freed the proselyte from all former bonds."[2] The matrimonial union of two unbaptized persons was regarded as henceforth non-existent after the Christian baptism of one spouse.[3]

---

[1]Aloysius Ambrozic, "Indissolubility of Marriage in the New Testament: Law or Ideal?" *Studia Canonica* 6 (1972) 279; cf. Paul Hoffman, "Jesus Sayings About Divorce and its Interpretation in the New Testament," *Concilium* 55 (1970) 62; Thomas Considine, "Pauline Privilege," *Australasian Catholic Record* 40 (1963) 115–116.

[2]Kugelman, "The First Letter to the Corinthians," *Jerome Biblical Commentary*, p. 264.

[3]John O'Rourke, "Scriptural Background of Canon 1120," *The Jurist* 15 (1955) 133.

Other authors attempt to explain the questioning of the legitimacy of such marriages on the basis of Paul's vision of the imminent parousia.[4] In advocating perfect continence as the radical call of Christianity, certain members of the Corinthian community instructed recent converts to deny themselves the privileges of marriage in order to allow complete and total dedication to the life of the Spirit.[5]

Some have suggested that certain members within the community found it impossible to reconcile the apparent incongruity between the absolute demands of Christian life and the compromise of this demand in the marriage of a Christian brother or sister with an unbeliever. Consequently, certain members of the community recommended separation so that the spiritual life of the Christian spouse would be neither compromised nor impaired.[6]

B. Condition and Purpose of the Apostolic Privilege

In his response to the controversial situation in the Corinthian community, Paul invokes that authority given him in his capacity as servant and apostle of Jesus Christ. Verses twelve to sixteen of I Corinthians 7 respond to the two pressing questions facing certain Christians at Corinth: are Christians allowed to remain in marriages with infidel spouses? What happens to these marriages when the infidel departs?[7]

In examining the Apostle's response it is apparent that Saint Paul attributed a certain stability to these marriages because of that blessing which faith afforded such unions through the Christian spouse. The Apostle envisioned the believer as one confronted with a definite Christian apostolate: "to consecrate in holiness the infidel spouse and their children through the presence and power of faith."[8]

In the hope of achieving the desirable goal of consecration and holiness within marriage, Paul exhorted the Christian to remain with the infidel spouse should the latter be willing to live in peace. Ambrozic suggests Paul's conception of these unions as being "slavific arrangements willed by the Lord within which the husband and wife sanctify each other and their

---

[4]Pierre Dulau, "Pauline Privilege: Is It Promulgated in the First Epistle to the Corinthians?" *Catholic Biblical Quarterly* 13 (1951) 149; Kugelman, p. 264.

[5]Dulau, p. 149.

[6]John Hurd, *The Origin of I Corinthians* (New York: Seabury Press, 1965), p. 168.

[7]Ambrozic, p. 279.

[8]Edward Schillebeeckx, *Marriage: Human Reality and Saving Mystery* (New York: Sheed and Ward, 1965), p. 161.

children."[9] In essence, the Christian spouse was not to initiate separation nor was separation to be justified simply by conversion and baptism.

Pagan culture and religion rejected as essential to marriage the Christian concepts of permanence and fidelity; in effect, the infidel could depart from a marital union without fear of contravening a divine law or command of Christian faith. In responding to this problem, Paul firmly stated that separation was not to be initiated by the Christian. Termination of the union was to be effected by the unbeliever: "if the unbeliever separates, let it be so; in such cases, the brother or sister is not bound."[10]

The purpose in Paul's instructing the Christians that they were "not bound" was to restore them to that peace which they received in conversion.[11] Departure was not to be so burdensome as to deny the convert that peace which was the essence of Christian faith.[12]

The blessing of Christian faith which Paul indicated as influential in affecting the quality of holiness within a marital union was also relied upon as ground for declaring released the brother or sister if the infidel departed or refused to live in peace. Paul exhibited a genuine concern for the well-being of the Christian partner and the stability of the correlative virtues of faith and peace. Concern for the person was concern for the faith and "if one is faithful to God's call, one should not be forced to suffer the loss of the very peace that God's call promises."[13] Paul was caught in a certain dichotomy: "the words of Christ forbid divorce but the call of Christ begets peace."[14] In the resolution of alternatives, the Apostle opted for the value of Christian peace, "the choice of concrete situation over commandment."[15]

C. Separation or Remarriage

Whether Paul permitted merely separation or divorce and remarriage has been a point of controversy for centuries. The text does not explicitly state that remarriage is a viable option for the Christian whose infidel spouse has

[9]Ambrozic, p. 279.

[10]I Cor. 7:15.

[11]Thomas Thompson, "A Catholic View of Divorce," *The Journal of Ecumenical Studies* 6 (1969) 64.

[12]Dominic Crossan, "Divorce and Remarriage in the New Testament," in *The Bond of Marriage,* ed. William Bassett (Notre Dame, Indiana: Notre Dame Press, 1968), p. 29.

[13]Thompson, p. 64.

[14]Hoffman, p. 62.

[15]Ibid.

departed. What Paul does state, however, is that the "brother and sister is not bound."[16]

The meaning of this phrase is subject to various interpretations. It could imply that the Christian is "not obligated to oppose the separation and involve himself in a life of marital discord, antagonism and continued wrangling."[17] One author interprets this phrase as suggesting that the "Christian man or woman should not feel so bound by Christ's prohibition of divorce as to be afraid to depart when the unbelieving partner insists on separation."[18] It has even been interpreted as qualifying one's zeal in pursuing the possible conversion of the infidel spouse: "don't feel responsible for the loss of the soul."[19]

Other reasons are offered which support an even broader interpretation of the phrase. In comparing Paul's use of the phrase in I Corinthians 7 with passages in other Pauline epistles using the same expression, it is argued that the phrase implies more than one's freedom from cohabitation, but "freedom from the bond itself."[20]

One author analyzes the Greek word *chorizestho* (let him depart) as used in this text and compares it with its use in Matthew 19:6 where Christ says: "What therefore God has joined together, let no man put asunder (*chorizestho*)." The suggestion is that the unbeliever renders or puts asunder the marital bond through his act of departure.[21]

Two other opinions exist in favor of Paul's implicit consent to divorce and remarriage. One argues that the favor accorded the Christian is more than separation because separation, without real divorce, was foreign to Greek and Roman law.[22] The other opinion holds that I Corinthians 7 is

---

[16]I Cor. 7:12–16: "If a brother has a wife who is an unbeliever, and she is content to live with him, he must not send her away; and if a woman has an unbeliever for her husband, and he is content to live with her, she must not leave him. This is because the unbelieving wife is made one with the saints through her husband. If this were not so, your children would be unclean, whereas in fact they are holy. However, if the unbelieving partner does not consent, they may separate; in these circumstances, the brother or sister is not bound."

[17]Kugelman, p. 264.

[18]Archibald Robertson and Alfred Plummer, *A Critical and Exegetical Commentary on the First Epistle of St.Paul to the Corinthians* (New York: Charles Scribner and Sons, 1914), p. 96.

[19]Dulau, p. 152.

[20]Ambrozic, p. 279. See also James Hackett, "The Pauline Privilege and the Right to Remarry," *Resonance* 4 (Spring, 1967) 48–59.

[21]Brian Byron, "I Corinthians 7:10–15: A Bias for Future Catholic Discipline on Marriage and Divorce?" *Theological Studies* 34 (1973) 430.

[22]Crossan, pp. 28–29.

one of two instances where remarriage is permitted following divorce,[23] both of which appear to be in service to the same religious value, namely, that peace to which God calls the Christian.[24]

Those who do not find permission for divorce and remarriage in I Corinthians 7 argue from the verses themselves. Paul does not explicitly mention the possibility of another marriage. It would appear unlikely that what Paul so clearly prohibits in verse 10 would be regarded by him as permissible in the next few verses.[25] If, in fact, Christ forbids divorce and remarriage, would not all Christians be bound by this divine precept, without exception?[26] These authors would affirm the reality of separation but deny the possibility of remarriage.

D. Scriptural Implications

What is unique to I Corinthians 7: 10–16 was Paul's enunciation of a divine principle and consequent affirmation of an apostolic exception.[27] Paul accepted Christ's precept prohibiting divorce as normative for Christian marriage. Christians were expected to fulfill the divine command of the Lord. Christians who remarried "were in conflict with the Lord's teaching: they were to return or remain unmarried with the view of ultimate reconciliation."[28]

One author suggests that the issue confronting Paul was broader in scope than that addressed by Christ in His divine command against divorce.[29] What confronted Paul was desertion as initiated by the infidel spouse; what Christ prohibited was divorce as understood in the active sense of the term.[30] As Byron notes:

> I would propose . . . that Saint Paul realized that Christ had not included the *deserted* party in his doctrine on divorce and that in a particular circumstance, viz., when the deserter is an unbeliever,

---

[23]The second instance can be found in the Gospel of Saint Matthew, which some authors suggest addresses itself to marriages within the forbidden degree of consanguinity and affinity.

[24]Ambrozic, p. 280.

[25]David Dungan, *The Sayings of Jesus in the Churches of Paul* (Philadelphia: Fortress Press, 1971), p. 97.

[26]Ibid.

[27]Petrus Huizing, "The Indissolubility of Marriage and Church Order," *Concilium* 38 (1968) 45–47; Bruce Vawter, "The Biblical Theology of Divorce," *CTSA Proceedings* 22 (New York: St. Joseph Seminary, 1968) 239–250.

[28]Brian Byron, "General Theology of Marriage in the New Testament and I Cor. 7:15," *Australasian Catholic Record* 49 (1971) 7.

[29]Brian Byron, "The Brother and Sister is not Bound," *Blackfriars* 52 (1971) 518.

one who does not accept the Christian doctrine of marriage, and hence when there is no likelihood of reconciliation the deserted Christian is free. I do not think it is stretching a point to say that Paul realized that Christ had not included this case (of desertion) in his teaching because the term divorce had a strong, active transitive sense among the Jews. It meant, *to put (someone) away, to send (someone) away.* The Christian teaching forbade anyone to *send away* a wife or husband. It forbade anyone *sent away* to remarry, presumably because there was an obligation of reconciliation. . . . Christ's teaching, therefore, amounted to this: it is sinful *to break up* a marriage (a) by sending away a spouse; (b) by marrying a dismissed spouse and by the dismissed spouse entering such a marriage, and (c) by deserting.[31]

It is Byron's belief that desertion by the infidel caused the commitment of the Christian to be without meaning or purpose. It was not that the Christian withdrew his commitment; the commitment was present but "having no recipient, ceased to exist."[32]

When Paul makes his decision in I Corinthians 7:15, he is making a particular application of a more general principle. An unbeliever who separates from a Christian can realistically be regarded as making an unconditional and final break. The union may be regarded as in fact finished. The more general principle behind this is that, while neither party may make such a definitive break, if one does and abandons the other in a way that prudently and practically can be considered final, the deserted party is unbound and free to marry again.[33]

Certain authors disregard consideration of apostolic authority as the influential force in Paul's resolution of the Corinthian problem. According to their view, the essential force was the Christian spouse whose predicament demanded a moral concession in favor of the virtues of Christian faith and peace. As Thomas Thompson states:

The implication of the context of Paul's letter is that divorce is allowable not on the basis of any special extraordinary authority, but on the basis of the demands of the situation itself which could

[30]Ibid.
[31]Ibid.
[32]Byron, "I Corinthians 7:10–15: A Basis for Future Catholic Discipline," p. 440.
[33]Ibid.

make it necessary for those involved to obtain a divorce. The "authority" in question is not that of a judge—in fact, we must speak of a principle rather than a power. Paul is establishing . . . a scale of values, not a legal authority; nor is he basing his authority on any legal principle.[34]

Byron concurs with Thompson when he states that Paul's directive was a "statement concerning the party those marital status was not discussed by Jesus."[35]

Paul presented the reality of Christian faith as a power and principle of Christian existence. It was a power which could effect consecration and holiness within marriage; it was a principle to be protected and preserved should faith and peace be impaired by the departure of the unbeliever.

The preservation of faith and peace was the primary motive in Paul's instruction to the Christian that he was "not bound" to the commitment. Later developments in canonical discipline regarding extrinsic and intrinsic indissolubility and sacramental and non-sacramental marriage were unknown to Paul and did not serve as the basis of his declaration. Neither can one determine the scope of the apostolic exception by equating "unbeliever" with unbaptized.[36] To infer that later canonical developments served as cause and motive for Paul's resolution of the problem was described by one author as a "misrepresentation of the grossest sort."[37]

Paul's resolution was based on a hierarchy of Christian values. For Paul, marriage was more than a social institution; it was a sacred reality which demanded a full and total commitment on the part of the Christian. Preservation of marital life and concurrent growth in holiness were specific objectives of the Christian apostolate. The bilateral qualities of commitment and preservation advanced the cause of salvation by offering the Christian a certain peace in which to realize the values of Christian faith.

The fulfillment of one's life of faith and the preservation of peace presupposed the presence of a spouse equally dedicated to the preservation of the union. The departure of an infidel spouse denied this essential

[34]Thompson, p. 57.

[35]Byron, "I Corinthians 7:10–15: A Basis for Future Catholic Discipline," p. 440.

[36]Byron, "General Theology of Marriage," p. 9; traditional ecclesiastical *praxis* has understood the Pauline Privilege as applying to the marriage of two unbaptized people. The matter was officially clarified in a response from the Holy Office on June 10, 1937: *Acta Apostolicae Sedis* 29 (1937) 305.

[37]Thompson, p. 63; for an example of this methodology, see William O'Connor, "The Indissolubility of the Ratified, Consummated Marriage," *Ephemerides Theologicae Lovanienses* 13 (1936) 642–722.

quality of mutuality and seriously endangered the Christian's commitment of faith and call to peace. In such cases Paul declared the Christian released from the obligation of his commitment.

In essence, Paul conceived the presence of faith and peace as important, and in certain circumstances, more important than the mere stability of an impossible or intolerable marriage. In contemporary terminology, Paul conceived indissolubility "in service to Christian peace and conditioned by it."[38] One could possibly suggest then that the "solution found in I Corinthians 7 was not based on the principle of a lesser but possible good, but rather on a higher value, in comparison with which the permanent value of marriage was less significant."[39]

[38]Crossan, p. 37.
[39]Thompson, p. 63.

THE MORAL INSEPARABILITY OF THE UNITIVE AND PROCREATIVE ASPECTS OF HUMAN SEXUAL INTERCOURSE

Thomas P. Doyle, O.P.

The Basic Question and its Urgency

Sexuality is an essential dimension of every creature yet for the human person sexuality differs radically from that of any other form of life. There is probably no aspect of humanity that is more influential, powerful and mysterious than sexuality. Just as sexuality itself is mysterious, so is its ultimate form of expression, intercourse. Unlike the sexual joining of the lower animals which is ordered to reproduction, that of the humans has a two-fold finality: it is ordered to the continuation of the species and to communication between persons. Consequently it is really more precise to refer to the sexual joining of the lower animals as "copulation" and to that of humans as "intercourse."

The meaning of "unitive" and "procreative"

The reproductive aspect of human sexual intercourse is called "procreative" because it enables persons to participate in God's act of creation. The communicative aspect is called "unitive" because it is a language whereby a man and a woman are able to communicate a commitment to one another and at the same time experience "being one." This commitment is grounded in conjugal *love*, a unique or special kind of love which is rooted in the will and is manifested by the giving of oneself to the other.[1]

In fact people can have sexual intercourse which is neither unitive nor procreative. In spite of this, can these two aspects be *morally separated*

---

[1]Sacred Congregation for Catholic Education, *Educational Guidance For Human Love* (Rome: 1983), n. 32, p. 12: "In synthesis, sexuality is called to express different values to which specific moral exegencies correspond. Oriented towards interpersonal dialogue, it contributes to the integral maturation of people, opening them to the gift of self in love; furthermore tied to the order of creation, to fecundity and to the transmission of life, it is called to be faithful to this inner purpose also. Love and fecundity are meanings and values of sexuality which include and summon each other in turn, and cannot therefore be considered as either alternatives or opposites."

without at the same time (a) dishonoring God, the Author of life; (b) redefining the meaning of sexual intercourse and its place in marriage; and, (c) having negative side-effects within culture and society?[2]

It is one thing for couples to choose to have sexual intercourse for non-procreative and/or non-unitive purposes, e.g., for recreational purposes; yet it is quite another matter for a re-direction of the purpose of intercourse to be socially or culturally accepted. Such a re-direction would influence the meaning and stability of marriage, the nurture of children, and the role of the family in society. Essentially the moral separation of the unitive and procreative aspects of intercourse can amount to a dehumanization of intercourse. Thus it would become a "thing," subject to exploitation and abuse. Such exploitation not only degrades the very meaning of sexuality but holds a potential for psychic, spiritual or even physical harm to persons.

Searching for the meaning of sexual intercourse

The unitive and procreative aspects of sexual intercourse are ontological realities: they take their meaning from the nature of the human person. Sexual intercourse also serves other ends; intercourse can be sought or experienced for other reasons because of its effects on the person. Among these functions are actual reproduction, the actual communication of love and/or affection, the release of tension, and the attainment of physical and psychological pleasure.

Pleasure is a powerful function of intercourse and because of this it has much to do with the confusion related to the search for the meaning of intercourse. One way or the other sexual intercourse produces pleasure and this, combined with the fact that intercourse is sub-rational, needing to be under the command of reason, is related to much of the popular definition of what sex is all about.[3]

Sexual intercourse has an intrinsic meaning based on its nature. Never-

---

[2]Alternatives to the traditional monogamous marriage arrangement all involve not simply human relationships but sexual relations. See James and Lynn Smith, *Beyond Monogamy* (Baltimore: Johns Hopkins, 1974); Jesse Bernard, *The Future of Marriage* (New York: World Publishing, 1972); Nena and George O'Neill, *Open Marriage* (New York: Avon Books, 1973).

[3]William May, "Sexuality and Fidelity in Marriage," *Communio* 5 (1978) 284: "As a desire, a drive, it is unconscious and instinctual in origin and character, an aspect of our being that helps us to recognize that our life, our being, is not exhausted by consciousness. But it is a serious error to infer from this that the sex drive is something subhuman, subpersonal, merely brute irrationality."

theless the meaning of intercourse is influenced by myths, taboos, etc., and by predominant social behavior.

Because of its relationship to human generation, which has an element of mystery about it, as well as the powerful and unique kind of pleasure attached to intercourse, society and culture have repeatedly developed myths, taboos and superstitions which in turn have led to the growth of restrictions and norms surrounding sexual behavior. The sexual urge needs to be under the control of reason yet this urge cannot be completely grasped by human reason. Hence the development of the myths, etc., which filled the gap of ignorance. These myths, taboos and superstitions with their contingent rules and norms cannot totally define the meaning of sexual intercourse since there is often an arbitrary and therefore distorted dimension in the relationship between the intrinsic nature of human sexuality and the myths.

The other powerful factor in shaping the meaning of intercourse is societal behavior. Sectors of the population tend to define the meaning and purpose of intercourse by what the majority are doing in this regard. Human beings knew about sexual intercourse before they banded together as a society. Therefore it is difficult to see how the meaning of intercourse can be determined from sociological findings. In most if not all societies the mores governing behavior are based on what is acceptable and what is unacceptable. This in turn is based to an extent on the myths and taboos. As societies become more materialistic and secularistic, or sophisticated in a worldly sense, the myths disappear and behavior patterns cease to be influenced by values no longer considered valid. There must be an authentic value system concerned with sexual behavior which is based on the intrinsic meaning of intercourse.[4] This intrinsic meaning of intercourse rests on the correct understanding of the unitive and procreative aspects and their inseparability. Historically the development of the myths which led to culturally or even legally enunciated standards of behavior was often grounded in a need to protect one or both of these aspects from abuse.

Sexual intercourse can take place in a variety of contexts, each of which is related in a different way to the unitive and procreative aspects. Intercourse can take place within marriage, outside of marriage, prior to

---

[4]This point is well illustrated in any history of marriage. See the classic, E. A. Westermarck, *The History of Human Marriage* 3 vols., 5th edition (New York: 1922). A more recent though not as thorough work is B. I. Murstein, *Love, Sex and Marriage Through the Ages* (New York: Springer Publishing Co., 1974). More specialized studies include V. Bullough and J. Brundage, *Sexual Practices and the Medieval Church* (Buffalo: Prometheus Books, 1982), and G. Duby, *Medieval Marriage* (Baltimore: Johns Hopkins, 1978).

marriage, within forbidden degrees of blood relationship. The circumstances or context will bear directly upon whether or not the two aspects are fulfilled or separated. Marriage has always been accepted as a context for intercourse. There has always been controversy and conflict as to the social and ethical acceptability of intercourse in extra or pre-marital contexts. Incestuous intercourse (siblings, parents) is a nearly universal taboo, while consanguineous intercourse (cousins, etc.) has been accepted in some cultures. The degree of acceptability of the various non-marital contexts for intercourse has a bearing on the role and development of the concepts of marriage and family within a society.[5]

The Church has long sought a theology of human sexuality that accurately reflects the true nature of man. The moral inseparability of the unitive and procreative aspects of intercourse becomes more than a command when it is grounded in the authentic nature of sexuality. The Church's understanding of sexuality is grounded in the essential goodness of the person. The contemporary teaching, typified in recent papal and magisterial pronouncements, is well grounded in historical and scriptural sources.[6]

There is an urgency to this question of the moral inseparability of the unitive and procreative aspects of intercourse. The Church must proclaim this inseparability because the acceptance of the possibility of separating the two aspects can have a profound effect on marriage and family life, and respect for human life in general.

THE INSEPARABILITY OF THE UNITIVE AND PROCREATIVE ASPECTS

The Church teaches, and rightly so, that the unitive and procreative aspects of sexual intercourse are morally inseparable. The nature of this intimate and profound language rules out intercourse *solely* for pleasure or recreation. Many, however, see the Church's teaching as a dogmatic statement cut off from the reality of contemporary life. If the reasons for the Church's teaching are presented the entire matter can be seen in a positive light.

The *first* and fundamental reason for the moral inseparability is

---

[5]See Abel Jeanniere, *The Anthropology of Sex* (New York: Harper and Row, 1967).
[6]The standard texts: Pius XI, *Casti Connubii* (1930); Vatican II, *Gaudium et spes* (1965); Paul VI, *Humanae Vitae* (1968); S. Congregation for the Doctrine of the Faith [S.C.D.F.], *Declaration on Certain Questions Concerning Sexual Ethics* (1975); John Paul II, *Familiaris Consortio* (1981); and S. Congregation for Catholic Education, *Educational Guidance in Human Love* (1983). See also John Paul II, *Original Unity of Man and Woman* (Boston: St. Paul Editions, 1981) and *Blessed Are the Pure of Heart* (Boston: St. Paul Editions, 1983).

grounded in the complex nature of human sexuality. *Secondly*, marriage as a natural institution and as a sacrament demands this moral inseparability. *Thirdly*, since human sexuality and sexual activity have a social dimension, the moral separability of the two with the consequent depersonalization of sexual intercourse leads to negative consequences in society.

THE NATURE OF HUMAN SEXUALITY

The human being is unique in that it is the only being created by God for its own sake. The person is good or worthwhile because he is a person. A human being is not a highly developed form of animal life with intelligence and rationality. There is a radical difference between the human person and every other form of animal life and this difference lies in the fact that the person is created in the image of God. This unique imaging is expressed in the person's ability to love. This capacity transcends all levels of intelligence, all degrees and kinds of physical appearance and health, and every kind of social stratification.

> God created man in his own image and likeness: calling him to existence through love, he called him at the same time for love. God is love and in himself he lives a mystery of personal, loving communion. Creating the human race in his own image and continually keeping it in being, God inscribed in the humanity of man and woman the vocation, and thus the capacity and responsibility, of love and communion. Love is therefore the fundamental and innate vocation of every human being.[7]

Love (self-gift) is meaningless unless it is shared with another person. The person cannot give of himself to a lower animal since the animals cannot, by their very nature, receive this gift. A person may share a kind of affection with an animal such as a pet, but this is not love.

The Genesis account of creation explains the extent and nature of human love. The human person is able to love and thus to achieve true self-actualization only with a creature equal to him:

> When God Yahweh says that "it is not good for man to be alone" (Gen. 2:18), He affirms that "alone" man does not completely realize this essence. He realizes it only by existing with someone and even more deeply and completely, by existing for someone.[8]

[7]John Paul II, *Familiaris Consortio*, November 22, 1981 (Vatican City: Polyglot Press, 1981), n. 11, p. 19 (hereinafter referred to as *FC*).
[8]John Paul II, audience of January 9, 1980, in *Original Unity*, p. 107

In his "original solitude" man, the human person, was isolated among all of the other creatures yet he was essentially complete, possessing the ability to love.[9] The Genesis account says that it "is not good for man to be alone." A change was needed and this change was directly related to man's uniqueness as a person able to love.

Pope John Paul II, in his commentary on this passage of Genesis, posits that the reference to man's falling into a deep sleep could indicate a return to the moment preceding man's creation ". . . in order that, through God's creative initiative, solitary 'man' may emerge from it again in his double unity as male and female."[10] Upon waking from sleep, the man, now male, discovers the woman, the helper fit for him. Man's reaction to the woman points to his realization that she shared a similar nature with him:

> In this way the man (male) manifests for the first time joy and even exaltation, for which he had no reason before, owing to the lack of a being like himself. Joy in the other human being, in the second "self," dominates the words spoken by the man (male) on seeing the woman (female).[11]

The fact that man's original solitude was substantially prior to his companionship with the woman indicates that she is not merely a duplication of the man (male) with incidental anatomical differences. Following upon the original solitude there is the "original unity of man and woman." The two share a similar nature yet they are quite separate and different. The human, man, is created in two modes: as male and female. It is vital to understand that man and woman share the same essence yet there is a difference and a complementarity about them that enables man and woman to be something that would be impossible had man not been created in two modes. It is significant that man's potential for love becomes real with the creation of the woman.

The concept of "original unity" is expressed in "giving life to that *communio personarum* that man and woman form. . . ." The potential for loving and thus for imaging God is realized in this communion of man and woman:

---

[9]Original solitude was necessary for man to realize his radical difference from every other creature. From this came the need to create another "self" in order that man, as male and female, might be complete and capable of fulfilling his being. See John Paul II, audience of October 10, 1979, in *Original Unity,* pp. 43–49.

[10]John Paul II, audience of November 7,1979, in *Original Unity,* p. 64.

[11]Ibid., p. 66.

. . . we can deduce that man became the image and likeness of God not only through his own humanity, but also through the communion of persons which man and woman form right from the beginning. . . . Man becomes the image of God not so much in the moment of solitude as in the moment of communion.[12]

From Adam's sleep emerges "man," yet two different ways of being "man." In these two ways, male and female, we have a key to understanding the human body and its role for accomplishing God's plan for man. The two modes of being human are expressed by means of the body. Male and female bodies are each composed of similar bone and flesh tissues, similar blood types, digestive organs etc., yet there is an all-pervasive difference that transcends human corporeality and that difference is sexuality.[13] It is no accident that there is an intimate relationship between the *communio personarum* of man and woman that enables man to image God, the fact that the distinguishing factor of the two modes of being human is sexuality, and the fact that through sexuality man both expresses love, the gift, and shares in the power to generate life.

Since human sexual interaction is not only ordered to generation but to communication, it is called by a special name, "intercourse." The sexual joining of the lower animals is properly referred to as "copulation" which differs from intercourse. Intercourse is not sub-rational but a response of the will. It is not simply the joining of sexual organs but the joining of two persons.

The relationship of the body to the person

Personhood is expressed through the body, but the body is not merely a shell or a kind of vehicle which is directed and used by the person. In truth the body is also the person because it is through the body that the person exists and expresses his or her fundamental purpose of imaging the creator. The divider between the two modes of being a person is sexuality, the sexual differences being much more than biological. The reason why man's potential for love as a gift can ever be realized is grounded in sexuality:

Sexuality is a fundamental component of personality, one of its

---

[12]John Paul II, audience of November 14, 1979, *Original Unity*, p. 73.

[13]S.C.D.F., *Declaration on Certain Questions Concerning Sexual Ethics*, December 29, 1975, p. 3: ". . . it is from sex that the human person receives the characteristics which, on the biological, psychological and spiritual levels, make that person a man or a woman and thereby largely condition his or her progress towards maturity and insertion into society."

modes of being, of manifestation, of communication with others, of feeling, of expressing and of living human love.[14]

Through life in the body the person expresses and experiences love in a variety of ways from verbal expression to complete sexual intercourse. Because the human body is distinct from any other kind of body, the expression and reception of love is uniquely human. Sexual behavior and the different ways of sexual expression are evaluated from the context of the meaning of the person: some are acceptable and others are not.[15] Since intercourse is ordered to a twofold aspect of communication and procreation, acceptable modes of sexual expression will conform to these aspects.

The nuptial meaning of the body

The fact that the body expresses the person provides the basis for the theological insight of the nuptial meaning of the body. The capacity to give and receive and to form the *communio personarum* which brings forth the image of God is built upon the sexuality of the male and female. They communicate this self-gift through the language of the body. The body is "nuptial" then because it is designed for communicating love. This nuptial meaning is not confined to the capacity for sexual intercourse. The nuptial meaning permeates the entire person, enabling the person, through the various modes of communication, to express love. Human sexual communication is unique because it takes its significance from the nuptial meaning of the person which is expressed through the body.

Only the human person relates to other persons out of choice and not instinct. He chooses whether and how to relate to another person. Communication is always through the body and it may be prompted by intense and total love, lust, emotional neutrality, apathy or deep-seated hatred. Nevertheless the human body is intended by God to be nuptial or giving in spite of man's capacity for other kinds of bodily communication. The person does not determine when the body will be nuptial since person and body are not separate realities. The person cannot simply use his or her body in a mechanistic way as if person and body did not constitute a natural whole.[16] The intellectual understanding of the nuptial meaning of the

[14]Sacred Congregation for Catholic Education, *Educational Guidance for Human Love* pp. 3–4.
[15]See William May, *Sex, Marriage and Chastity* (Chicago: Franciscan Herald Press, 1981), p. 10. Dr. May makes the helpful distinction that the human body and human sexuality are goods *of* the person and not goods *for* the person.
[16]One's definition of person determines many practical conclusions in the area of sexual ethics. See May, *Sex, Marriage and Chastity,* pp. 3–9, especially p. 8: "For the separatist

person should direct the will in choosing how the body is used in sexual communication.

It is possible to communicate sexually in ways that are clearly not nuptial. Sexual relations can be self-serving, can be ordered only to pleasure, or can be loving yet closed to procreation; but *should* they be? The misuse of the body in sexual communication can be a distortion of its nuptial meaning by a disruption of the inner person:

> Concupiscence, in itself, is not capable of promoting union as the communion of persons. By itself, it does not unite, but appropriates. The relationship of the gift is changed into the relationship of appropriation.[17]

Concupiscence has been wrongly interpreted as the sexual urge itself yet this can hardly be true if the twofold aspect of sexual intercourse is good in itself. The Holy Father calls concupiscence a wedge between the body and the person which threatens to rob the body of its donative or nuptial meaning, replacing this meaning with selfish pleasure and possessiveness.[18]

Human sexual intercourse can never be considered merely biological *in se* as is the case with that of the lower animals. Human intercourse is always unique and only analogous to the copulation of the lower animals. Intercourse is a language whereby a man and a woman communicate a

---

then, a person is a conscious subject of experiences that possesses a body, that is, a human being who happens to be either a male or a female." This definition of the "separatist" seems to describe the meaning of personhood found in A. Kosnik, et al., *Human Sexuality: New Directions in Catholic Thought* (New York: Paulist Press, 1977); see pp. 83–84: "Within this embodied view of human existence, sexuality is seen as that aspect of our fleshly being-in-the-world whereby we are present and open to that which is not ourselves, to that which is other . . . for us humans, the teleolgy of the pleasure bond is the intercoursing of subjectivities. . . . Subjectivity is embodied in neither a male nor a female body. . . . Our understanding of bodily existence requires that the specific structure of one's body colors the manner in which oneself and the world are experienced. . . . Sexuality further serves the development of genuine personhood by calling people to a clearer recognition of their relational nature, of their absolute need to reach out and embrace others to achieve personal fulfillment."

[17]John Paul II, audience of July 23, 1980, in *Blessed Are the Pure of Heart*, p. 77.

[18]Ibid., p. 76: "Lust in general and the lust of the body in particular attacks precisely this sincere giving. It deprives man, it could be said, of the dignity of giving, which is expressed by his body through masculinity and feminity and in a way 'de-personalizes' man making him an 'object for the other.' Instead . . . man becomes an object for man: the female for the male and vice versa. . . . The subjectivity of the person gives way in a certain sense, to the objectivity of the body; man becomes an object for man, the female for the male and vice versa."

special love. Pope Paul VI described the characteristics of this love in *Humanae vitae*:

> This love is first of all fully human, that is to say, of the senses and the spirit at the same time. . . . This love is total . . . it is a very special form of personal friendship. . . . Whoever truly loves his marriage partner loves not only for what he receives but for the partner's self, rejoicing that he can enrich his partner with the gift of himself. . . . Again this love is faithful and exclusive until death. And finally, this love is fecund for it is not exhausted by the communion between husband and wife but is destined to continue, raising up new lives.[19]

This unique nature of human sexual interaction (intercourse) flows from human nature and is related to the ultimate form of human gift, the cooperation with the Creator in the gift of life to a new person. Intercourse serves more than physical release or pleasure. It is ordered to generation but serves more than fertility.

Reproduction and procreation

Human fertility and the interaction that leads to conception and birth are inaccurately described as "reproduction." Man and woman are not merely reproducing. They are cooperating with the Creator since God creates the new person in the midst of the sexual intercourse and entrusts the child's nurture to the parents. The proper term for this process is "procreation."

After physical birth the new person is totally helpless, needing complete care. The parents provide physical and psychological nurture for the child, guiding it through the various stages of growth and human development. They also provide emotional and spiritual nurture, the latter being particularly important in view of the child's destiny to share eternity with the Creator.

The child is conceived through the physical act which is the ultimate word in the language of love. After birth, the parents draw the child into their own love relationship thus nurturing the child's incipient capacity for love. By living out their love for each other the parents bring out the image of God in their child. Procreation, then, involves more than the physical or biological dimension of the sexual relationship. Procreation is a process which is completed by nurture and is dependent on the total union of the man and woman in an on-going love relationship. Human fertility is more than physical cooperation; it is a vocation:

[19]Paul VI, *Humanae vitae*, July 25, 1968 (Washington, D.C.: USCC), n. 9, pp. 5–6.

The total physical self-giving would be a lie if it were not the sign
and fruit of total personal self-giving, in which the whole person,
including the temporal dimension, is present. . . . This totality
which is required by conjugal love also corresponds to the demands
of responsible fertility. This fertility is directed to the generation of
a human being, and so by its nature it surpasses the purely
biological order and involves a whole series of personal values.[20]

The male and female are not merely reproductive persons. They are
procreative persons for two reasons: they have the capacity for bringing
other human beings into existence through bodily cooperation, and they are
necessary for the proper nurturing of the gift of the ability to love. The man
and woman accomplish both of these aspects through their own conjugal
love:

Conjugal love reaches that fulness to which it is interiorly ordained,
conjugal charity, which is the proper and specific way in which the
spouses participate in and are called to live the very charity of
Christ who gave Himself on the cross.[21]

These two aspects of the procreational process, physical birth and
spiritual nurture, are dependant upon the unitive and procreative aspects of
intercourse. As procreative beings man and woman express the gift of love
in sexual communion, possible because of their complementarity. It is only
in this union that fertility can be exercised indicating that God's love is a
life-giving love. The love of the parents continues to be expressed and
strengthened through the language of intercourse. Thus intercourse as a
unitive act promotes the *communio personarum* of the parents in the midst
of which the child is raised. Even though individual acts of intercourse do
not result in conception they are still procreational acts if they foster the
love relationship of the parents.

The finality of intercourse transcends accompanying pleasure. This
finality is best explained by the word "procreation" since the *complete*
transmission of human life requires an ever-deepening love on the part of
the parents.

This unique nature of sexual intercourse becomes even more evident if it
is looked at in a three-dimensional context. Intercourse is a language that
expresses an already existing love with a view to continuing this love into

[20]*FC*, n. 11, p. 20.
[21]*FC*, n. 13, p. 23.

the future. Intercourse which takes place for pleasure alone, outside of the context of love, is isolated to the present.

If sexual intercourse is to be all that God has intended it to be then there must be a total, mutual acceptance of the man and the woman. As a unitive act intercourse implies a giving and not a taking. The man accepts the woman for who and what she is, not for what he would like her to be or for the pleasure she momentarily provides, and vice versa. A man and a woman cannot claim to accept one another unconditionally and at the same time reject the procreative aspect of themselves. This procreative aspect is not merely biological but is grounded in the nuptial meaning of the person. In their original unity man and woman respond to their complementarity in order to realize God's image through love. Man and woman can become "one flesh" precisely because they are procreative beings. This procreative aspect does not depend on the consciousness or will of the person: it is there whether or not the person knows or wants it. Because the person is capable of conjugal love, the gift of self, he is procreative in his very essence. Even sexual intercourse between infertile persons which expresses authentic love and is open to God's will is procreative.

The pleasure that accompanies intercourse as well as the natural tendency to complete a romantic relationship or even a romantic encounter with intercourse lead to the *de facto* separation of the unitive and procreative aspects. People want to have intercourse without the possibility of procreation and often without the added responsibility of an interpersonal relationship. If the parties do not accept each other as procreative beings then the gift of self is limited. Hence even the unitive aspect of intercourse is altered and is a conditioned communication.

Only the person bears a responsibility for sexual acts and sexual intercourse since the person acts from choice and not instinct. The decision to engage in sexual intercourse must be informed by what sexual intercourse *is* and not simply by the physical or emotional effects that accompany it. Ultimately the choice to engage in intercourse must be shaped by the fact that intercourse is an expression of a special kind of love between two procreative persons.

Some hold that the sexual faculties are essentially biological and become procreative and unitive when this is consciously willed and chosen.[22]

---

[22]May, *Sex, Marriage and Chastity,* p. 3: "The understanding of human sexuality dominant in our culture can, I believe, be properly described as separatist. By this I mean that the separatist understanding has severed the existential and psychological bond between life-giving or procreative meaning of human sexuality and its person-uniting, love-giving, unitive meaning. It regards the former as a biological function of sexuality. This biological

Those who follow this understanding also hold that there must be a sense of responsibility in having intercourse: responsibility to the relationship or at least to the experience. This approach focuses on the benefit of sexual relations to the persons. As such it is a pragmatic approach that does not direct the responsibility to the fact that sexual relations are intrinsically personal and procreational.[23] In other words, the responsible choice to have intercourse must be made with the full meaning of intercourse uppermost in mind.

Admittedly it is difficult to argue for an intrinsic meaning to human sexual intercourse while living in a secularist-materialist society. The morality of actions can easily be judged against a pragmatic set of standards since spiritual values are not that acceptable unless they can be rationally demonstrated. "What's wrong with doing it as long as nobody gets hurt?" is a commonplace justification for non-marital intercourse.

Summary

Only human beings are created by God with the capacity to relate in a manner beyond the physical and instinctual. The gift of self is made on a spiritual level and communicated through the body. Human sexuality is unique because it is the means by which this gift is communicated. At the center of this gift is the power to generate human life and the contingent responsibility to nurture such life. Sexual intercourse is a language which communicates the person. As such it is by nature both unitive and procreative. If one aspect is separated from the other then sexual intercourse can become neither unitive nor procreative.

HUMAN SEXUAL INTERCOURSE AND MARRIAGE

The procreative process demands stability in the man-woman relationship since the *communio personarum* cannot be a series of fleeting encounters with no real commitment. The welfare of society depends on the success of this process. Consequently every society from the most primitive to the most sophisticated has acknowledged God's design for man and woman in the institution of marriage.

The most common definition of marriage is that it is a stable relationship

---

function can become humanly and personally valuable when it is consciously willed and chosen, but in and of itself it is simply a physiological given."

[23]Ibid., p. 6: "When the human significance of sex is seen in this way the principle criterion for evaluating genital sexual activity focuses on the quality of the relationship established and/or expressed by such activity, on the affection, tenderness and fellowship that it both engenders and expresses."

between a man and a woman from which children are born and in which they are given their rudimentary preparation to enter the social group.

When marriage and family life become disrupted from within and when this disruption becomes widespread among families, the society in general is affected. These disruptions are almost always centered around the sexual dimension of the marital relationship. Consequently sexual relations outside of marriage have been proscribed to a greater or lesser degree in most secular and religious societies down through history.[24] Why is sexual intercourse so important that such attention is paid to it? The answer lies in the fact that the male-female relationship, procreative by nature, is the fundamental growth principle for society. Sexual intercourse as a unique human act is grounded in the essence of procreative man and thus reserved to marriage.[25]

The marriage community and the "one flesh"

Marriage is defined in contemporary theological language as the "community of the whole of life," a phrase taken from *Gaudium et spes* and repeated in the Code of Canon Law.[26] Neither of the commonly used Latin phrases (*communitas*—community, or *consortium*—partnership) fully capture the true meaning of the marriage relationship. Marriage is more than a "side-by-side" relationship of two loving people. It is this, a friendship, and more. Marriage is a oneness of two distinct persons which becomes possible because of their sexual complementarity, expressed through the body. This union has a completeness about it which goes beyond itself as it brings new life into existence.

In Genesis 2:23–24 we read that the man leaves his mother and father

---

[24]Historically it seems that marriage was treated under custom or family law. The public (civil) law only became involved when abuses or problems pressed intervention for the good of the community. Ancient law codes regularly mention penalties for adultery. In the Roman world marriage was under the domestic or family authority until widespread problems related to adultery, exposure of children and childless unions prompted Caesar Augustus to issue the *Lex Iulia de Adulteriis* (18 B.C.) and the *Lex Iulia de Maritandis* (11 B.C.) as civil law attempts to counteract family-related problems.

[25]See May, *Sex, Marriage and Chastity*, pp. 97–107. This section on marital chastity discusses the basis for the Church's traditional teaching. May also points out what he sees as the error of those who teach that the proscriptions against adultery are essentially cultural.

[26]*Gaudium et spes*, no. 48 defines the essence of marriage as the "intima communitas vitae." Canon 1055 of the Code of Canon Law uses the phrase "totius vitae consortium." Neither term adequately translates into English the meaning of the marital joining although *consortium* comes closest from an historical perspective.

because he is destined by nature to become "one flesh" with a woman. The preceding phrase in which the man exclaims that the woman is "bone of my bones and flesh of my flesh" describes the kind of union possible because of the male-female complementarity. The term "one flesh" does not refer exclusively to joining in sexual intercourse but to the complete union. Sexual intercourse, as a complete bodily joining, symbolizes and effects the joining of the persons. The spouses become completely "one" not because they are joined in sexual embrace but because of their conjugal covenant.

Exegetes hold that the word-pair "bone" and "flesh" is a common Old Testament covenantal formula which refers to strength (bone) and weakness (flesh). It implies the joining together of two distinct persons which together have the capacity to withstand every possible contingency in the relationship:

> The statement "this . . . is bone of my bones and flesh of my flesh" occurs again and again in the Bible as an expression of blood relationship, and implies a fully human unity and an attitude of peace which is characteristic of the pattern of life of the clan.[27]

The "one flesh" union of the marriage covenant is not only total but has the same degree of stability as a blood relationship, which can be severed only with death. Thus to be "one flesh" requires nothing short of the total gift of self to one's spouse and the unconditioned acceptance of the other as gift. The sign of this gift is the procreative sexual act whereby the spouses' mutual giving and receiving of each other is open to new life. Perhaps one of the best English-language explanations of the meaning of one flesh union is found in the traditional marriage vow formula: ". . . for better or for worse, for richer or for poorer, in sickness and in health until death do us part."

Marriage is more than an interpersonal relationship. It is a publicly pronounced, publicly acknowledged and publicly protected commitment. The spouses promise to become "one flesh" and to remain "one flesh" with one another. The man and woman may feel committed to one another and indeed may have expressed this commitment privately, yet it is not a marriage covenant until it is made according to the recognized formula. This public promise is necessary because of the potential for turning away from the relationship.

---

[27]Eduard Schillebeeckx, *Marriage: Human Reality and Saving Mystery* (New York: Sheed and Ward, 1965), p. 18. See also the excellent article by W. Brueggeman, "Of the Same Flesh and Bone," *Catholic Biblical Quarterly* 32 (1970) 532–542.

In spite of the sad reality of divorce, man and woman are basically capable of a permanent relationship. It is for this reason that Christian tradition uses the word "covenant" for the marriage agreement since it denotes a mutual commitment from which there is no turning back. After the covenant is entered into the spouses join in sexual intercourse which both symbolizes the totality of the marital union and continues to renew the covenant.[28]

Sexual intercourse is a profound and powerful language by which to express conjugal love. To be authentic, intercourse must be open to sharing the "one flesh" relationship with God's gift of a child. As a unitive act intercourse communicates the self-gift which the spouses continue to be to each other. As a procreative act intercourse is at once ordered to sharing this gift of love with a child while at the same time it enriches the marital community, the "one flesh" union, in which the child will be nurtured.

Marital consent and sexual intercourse

The 1917 Code of Canon Law referred to marital consent as an act of the will whereby the spouses exchanged the *right* to the body for procreative sexual acts (1917 code, c. 1081, §2). The 1983 code has changed this definition and expanded it. It no longer refers to the exchange of a right but to the giving and receiving of persons:

> Matrimonial consent is an act of the will by which a man and a woman by an irrevocable covenant mutually give and accept each other in order to establish marriage.[29]

After the spouses have made the marital covenant with one another they are truly married. If both are baptized the union is called a "ratified" marriage. When this covenant is consummated by sexual intercourse its stability is strengthened. For ratified marriages, the property of absolute indissolubility is added with consummation. What is it about sexual intercourse that it can have this effect on a marriage covenant? The answer is in the unitive-procreative nature of intercourse.

The above understanding of when marriage came about was more or less fixed with the "consensus-copula" debate between the theologians of the

---

[28]*Gaudium et spes*, no. 49: "Hence the acts in marriage by which the intimate and chaste union of the spouses takes place are noble and honorable; the truly human performance of these acts fosters the self-giving they signify and enriches the spouses with joy and gratitude." This same idea is repeated in *Humanae vitae*, no. 9, pp. 5–6.

[29]Canon 1057, §2. English translation from *The Code of Canon Law* (London: Collins Liturgical Press, 1983).

Paris and Bologna schools in the 12–13th centuries. The controversy was over what made a true marriage: the consent of the parties alone or their consent plus sexual consummation. The compromise resolution of the debate held that true marriage exists after consent but that it becomes absolutely indissoluble after consummation.

Gratian, the champion of the Bologna school, argued that sexual consummation transformed the spouses' marital consent into a true marriage. Consent was given to the marital *societas* which included sexual intercourse as an essential element. Gratian's understanding of the essence of marriage is remarkably similar to that of Vatican II. It was, for him, a joining of the man and woman to follow a singular way of life.[30] Gratian also employed an ancient Roman law term but with a new meaning. For the Romans *affectio maritalis* meant simply the will to be married.[31] For Gratian the same words meant much more: the attitude of the will to treat a spouse as a spouse ought to be treated. This was an attitude that was to accompany marital consent. It is important for our consideration because of its relationship to the unitive aspect of intercourse. For Gratian the marital society was a "one flesh" union in the complete biblical sense and for this reason he used this metaphor to describe not only the act of sexual consummation but the abiding reality of the marital community which comes about after consummation.[32]

Gratian's overall argument seems to say that the man and the woman are not involved in a true marriage until they are joined in sexual intercourse. They cannot be truly one without experiencing sexual intercourse nor can the purpose of their oneness, procreation, happen without sexual intercourse. Although sexual intercourse in itself does not constitute a

[30]C. 27, q. 2 in Freidberg, *Corpus Iuris Canonici,* vol. 1, col. 1062. "Sunt enim nuptiae sive matrimonium viri mulierisque coniunctio individuae vitae consuetudinem retinens." This is a standard Roman law definition of marriage. The Romans considered marriage to be radically different from the Christians, yet Gratian gave new meaning to the older definition by developing other concepts.

[31]Adolf Berger, *Encyclopedic Dictionary of Roman Law* (Philadelphia: The American Philosophical Society, 1953), p. 356: "*Affectio maritalis.* Conjugal affection conceived as a continuous (not momentary) state of mind. . . . It presumes the intention of living as husband and wife for life and procreating legitimate children." *Affectio* in the Roman law sense did not mean conjugal love or an attitude of charity between the spouses. For Grataian *affectio* distinguished marriage from concubinage although his interest was more moral than juridical. Basically the Christian understanding of *affectio* was the will to treat a spouse as a spouse ought to be treated. See also John Noonan, "Marital Affection in the Canonists," *Studia Gratiana* 12 (1967) 482–509.

[32]See John Alesandro, *Gratian's Notion of Marital Consummation* (Rome: Officium Libri Catholici, 1971), p. 578.

marriage, it is the ultimate sign of the fact that a marriage covenant has begun. Perhaps Gratian was saying what John Paul II so recently said:

> And the coming into being of marriage is distinguished from its consummation to the extent that without this consummation the marriage is not yet constituted to its full reality. The fact that a marriage is juridically constituted but not consummated corresponds to the fact that it has not been fully constituted a marriage.[33]

There is a difference between marriage as a juridical reality, the fulfillment of certain objective legal prescriptions, and the full, human entity of marriage which the legal entity presumes to exist. By their verbal expression of consent, the man-made language of the vows, the spouses create marriage as a juridical reality in the here and now. By this verbal consent they promise to become one; they enter into the covenant which exists because of their mutual gift. Somehow sexual intercourse is necessary as a complete expression of the meaning of the marriage covenant:

> The sacramental sign is determined, in a certain sense, by "the language of the body," inasmuch as the man and the woman, who through marriage should become one flesh, express in this sign the reciprocal gift of masculinity and femininity as the basis for the conjugal union of persons.[34]

The language of sexual intercourse is an exclamation of the meaning and purpose of marriage. In order to conform to the full import of the "one flesh" it cannot be anything other than unitive and procreative.

The Code of Canon Law refers to sexual consummation "humano modo," i.e., in a human fashion. The sexual language of the spouses must be free of violence and coercion or it is not an expression of the conjugal community. To carry the concept of "humano modo" one step further, one could argue that the sexual act must also be open to procreation in principle if it is to be fully human. No language quite captures the meaning of marriage or the full reality of the marital commitment like the language of sexual intercourse. To further illustrate this point, there are instances when intercourse alone is considered to be the sole expression of marital consent, sufficient to constitute the juridicial reality of marriage.[35]

---

[33]John Paul II, audience of January 5, 1983 in *L'Osservatore Romano* [English edition] 1–2 (766) (January 3–10, 1983) 7.

[34]Ibid.

[35]Certain canonists hold that in those instances when it is necessary to renew marital consent privately, sexual intercourse, performed lovingly between the spouses, suffices as an

The very nature of marriage as a union of two giving persons argues that sexual intercourse, as the unique marital communication of two nuptial persons, be unitive and procreative. In fact, these two aspects are almost synonymous with one another so that if one aspect is denied or willed away, the other is also absent. If the procreative aspect of the *person* is rejected can it be said that there has been a mutual giving and receiving of persons? The procreative aspect is intimately bound up with God's image in the person, unconditional gift. The key is in the openness to participating in the procreative process and not the actual phenomenon of procreation since many persons may find themselves, through no fault of their own, unable to have children.[36]

Because of what sexual intercourse *is* as a unitive and procreative act, we can draw certain basic moral conclusions. In the first place, sexual intercourse outside of marriage, though it may take place under circumstances of true caring, tenderness or even love and with a conviction that an interpersonal commitment exists, is not truly *unitive* because there has been no covenant. There has been no real self-gift to communicate through intercourse. The parties, no matter how emotionally and psychologically involved they may be, are still replaceable. They have not taken the risk of making a public commitment of an unconditional and permanent gift of self to each other.

Secondly, sexual intercourse which is habitually contraceptive is a "falsification of the inner truth of conjugal love, which is called upon to give itself in personal totality."[37] Sexual intercourse for personal pleasure alone is unnatural because it does not correspond to the uniquely human meaning of intercourse; it does not communicate the nuptial meaning of the body. When lust replaces love as the motivating factor for intercourse, the partners become turned in on themselves and intercourse has as its sole

---

expression and sign of consent. This situation would occur in cases of marriages invalid due to an undispensed impediment which ceases or is dispensed. It is not always necessary to renew consent according to canonical form. Rather, it may be renewed (canon 1158, §2) even privately and in secret. See James Brennan, *The Simple Convalidation of Marriage* (Washington, D.C.: Catholic University of America Press, 1937).

[36]*FC* n. 14, p. 27: "It must not be forgotten however that, even when procreation is not possible, conjugal life does not for this reason lose its value. Physical sterility in fact can be for spouses the occasion for other important services to the life of the human person, for example adoption, various forms of educational work, and assistance to other families and to poor or handicapped children." In other words, the conjugal love of the spouses prompts them to share this love with others in some way even if they cannot do it with their own child.

[37]*FC*, n. 32, p. 61.

purpose the attaining of orgasm. Thus the partners are taking and not giving and sexual intercourse becomes de-personalized.

Third, there is no room for sexual intercourse with a person other than one's spouse. It is dishonest to become "one flesh" through the language of intercourse with a person with whom one is not committed in the marriage convenant. Sexual intercourse as a language exclusive of the marriage covenant excludes the possibility of any exceptions to the obligations of total fidelity and the consequent prohibition against adultery.

Summary

The permanent man-woman relationship in marriage is possible but depends for its success on the continued giving of the parties to one another. As the natural way for children to be born and nurtured, the marriage relationship needs stability. The stability safeguards the pro-creative aspect of the relationship and is at once fostered by authentic sexual relations, i.e., those that are both unitive and procreative. If these two aspects are morally separated then the physical union of the man and woman is not a sign of the biblical "one flesh" union which they became by their covenant.

MORAL INSEPARABILITY AND THE SOCIAL DIMENSION OF INTERCOURSE

Although sexual intercourse is a personal and private act, it has a social dimension. To some extent society and culture have something to say about what sexual intercourse is all about. Conversely the commonly held sexual mores have an impact on society. Referring to the so-called sexual revolution of the past two decades, a recent Roman document said:

> The Church cannot remain indifferent to this confusion of minds
> and relaxation of morals. It is a question, in fact, of a matter which
> is of the utmost importance both for the personal lives of Christians
> and for the social life of our time.[38]

Many, of course, would not argree that morals have become bad. They would argue that values have changed and so have standards of sexual behavior. When the parameters of sexual behavior change it involves a widespread acceptance of sexual intercourse for other than unitive and procreative purposes. When the unitive-procreative aspects are separated from sexual intercourse does it follow that there will be certain negative effects in society at large? This is a vitally important question. It is not based on individual acts of sexual intercourse for non-procreative-unitive

---

[38]S.C.D.F., *Declaration on Certain Questions Concerning Sexual Ethics*, p. 4.

purposes, but the widespread acceptance of a trivialized and de-personalized theory and practice of sexual intercourse. Recent Roman documents, including *Gaudium et spes,* do not hesitate to make such a connection referring to widespread disorders of our time.[39]

Those who advocate a non-restrictive morality often base their value system on the belief that sexual intercourse and sexual pleasure is a personal right of the individual. Thus it is in fact divorced from the unitive-procreative aspects which require that sexual intercourse take place within the context of marriage. Sexual intercourse has become a form of recreation and a standardized dating habit for many. Casual sexual encounters, extra-marital sexual intercourse, homosexual genital expression are increasingly acceptable and even glamorized to an extent. *Open Marriage,* a book found on many Catholic and secular college campuses in the seventies, attempted to create a philosophy of creative infidelity which redirected marital commitment from the gift of self for the sake of the other to a commitment of one's growth. At the conclusion the authors write:

> Sexual fidelity is the false god of closed marriage. . . . Fidelity is then redefined in the open marriage, as commitment to your own growth, equal commitment to your partner's growth, and a sharing of the self-discovery accomplished through such growth.[40]

The authors advocate relationships with members of the opposite sex other than one's spouse. These relationships are supposed to enhance and augment the marital relationship of the open couple. They can include sexual relations:

> These outside relationships may, of course, include sex. That is completely up to the partners involved. If partners . . . do have outside sexual relationships it is on the basis of their own internal relationships, that is, because they have experienced mature love, have real trust, and are able to expand themselves, to love and enjoy others and to bring that love and pleasure back into their own marriage, without jealousy.[41]

There is no evidence that mutually acceptable adultery has contributed to overall marital stability; in fact the O'Neills, authors of *Open Marriage,* are themselves now divorced.

---

[39]*Gandium et spes,* no. 47; *FC*, n. 6, p. 12.

[40]Nena and George O'Neill, *Open Marriage*, p. 253.

[41]Idem. Although the O'Neills' book is 12 years old the morality it expresses is still in vogue. For a scientific study of the phenomenon of extra-marital sex, see Gerhard Neubeck, ed., *Extra-Marital Relations* (Englewood Cliffs, N.J.: Prentice-Hall, 1969).

Likewise there is no correlation between living together prior to marriage and marital stability. Sexual intercourse is looked upon as a right to be used if the parties feel comfortable with the relationship and no one is hurt. This same ethic can carry over to married life and becomes the rationale for extra-marital behavior. A more liberalized sexual ethic depends on the premise that extra-marital relations are not necessarily destructive of the person and not restricted to marriage by nature. We find this approach even among Catholic moralists.[42] Some refer to the so-called "pre-ceremonial" Christian couple, a man and a woman who "feel" committed to one another and are thus justified in having sexual relations.[43]

It is a fact that most of the barriers restricting sexual intercourse to marriage have fallen. Yet in spite of the technology of artificial contraception there is still a high rate of extra-marital pregnancy, but a disproportionately lower rate of birth due to abortion. Also, the wonders of the "open marriage" have not prevented the divorce rate from reaching new highs every year, leaving behind a trail of scarred former partners and a whole new minority in the general population, the child of the single-parent family.[44]

There are other social phenomena that have accompanied the gradual change in sexual morality: the high proportion of sexually transmitted

---

[42]For example, A. Kosnik, et al., *Human Sexuality: New Directions in Catholic Thought.* After discussing what they call "variant patterns" such as common law marriage (p. 145), swinging (pp. 147–148), adultery (pp. 148–149), all of which refer to marriage, the book then gives three approaches to moralitay. First, the traditional, of which they say "The strength . . . lies in its fidelity to a carefully developed legal understanding of marriage. Its weakness lies in the assumption that such activity is always destructive of human personhood without due regard for any empirical evidence that might support or repudiate such an assumption. This position does not appear convincing to many people of good will today" (p. 149). The *third* approach holds that such variations are largely private matters, depending on the consent of the participants and acceptable as long as nobody gets hurt (p. 150). The *second* approach, which the authors say is "most compatible with our own" (p. 150) says in part: "Variant marriage patterns depart to one degree or another from the Christian ideal of what marriage ought to be. Therefore they are not tolerated in at least most cases" (p. 150).

[43]See "Pre-ceremonial Christian Couples," *Église et Théology* 8 (1977), entire issue. The collection of essays attempts to create a spirituality and theological justification for pre-marital sex by positing that some couples have made a commitment that can justifiably be consummated before it is ratified.

[44]According to the National Center for Health Statistics there were the following statistics for 1981: 686,605 illegitimate births (up 20,858 from 1980); 29.6 percent of every 1,000 births were illegitimate and 49.2 percent of births to girls between the ages of 15–19 were out of wedlock. Also, there were 1,297,606 known abortions in 1980; 76.9 percent were

diseases including the new strains of herpes and AIDS and the higher instance of individuals seeking therapy for sexual dysfunction. The basic question is whether there is a cause-effect relationship between a sexual ethic that depends on the separation of the unitive-procreative aspects of intercourse and the aforesaid negative effects which abound in our society. The sexual permissiveness of the "new morality" is a by-product of the trivialization of sexual intercourse into another source of fun.

In positing that the separation of the unitive-procreative aspects of intercourse are at the root of this age's sexually related troubles we naturally add one more dimension to the overall argument in favor of moral inseparability of the two aspects or, more accurately, their inseparability from intercourse itself. In this context *Humanae vitae* was more prophetic than anything else:

> In defending conjugal morals and their integral wholeness, the Church knows that she contributes towards the establishment of a truly human civilization: she engages man not to abdicate from his own responsibility in order to rely on technical means; by that very fact she defends the dignity of man and wife.[45]

Ashley and O'Rourke refer to a "sexual future" which begins with the understanding of sexuality from the viewpoint of the person and extends to its impact on society. Their basic assessment is correct:

> The sexual revolution projects a future in which the Christian vision of human sexuality will appear ridiculous and unrealizable. Yet for Christians human sexuality is governed by norms of hope, a hope on which a truly human future must be built.[46]

The unitive-procreative aspect of intercourse is part of human nature. If man tries to change this meaning to suit a secularist-materialist outlook, then society itself will be changed.[47] The moral inseparability is a statement of what human sexuality is all about, telling us of the uniqueness of the human person and of his proximity to God.

---

performed for unwed mothers (763,476 abortions in 1974; 72.6 percent on unwed mothers). There were 2,495,000 marriages and 1,180,000 estimated divorces in the U.S. in 1982.

[45]*Humanae vitae*, no. 18, p. 12.

[46]Benedict Ashley and Kevin O'Rourke, *Health Care Ethics: A Theological Analysis* (St. Louis: Catholic Hospital Association, 1978), p. 305.

[47]See George Gilder, *Sexual Suicide* (New York: Quadrangle, 1973).

MARRIAGE, DIVORCE, AND LIVING ARRANGEMENTS: PROSPECTIVE CHANGES*

PAUL C. GLICK

In this time of rapid changes in the patterns of family life, considerable interest is expressed in demographic aspects of the current marital situation and in the likely developments during the next several years. Recent annual reports on vital statistics, marital status, and household composition shed light on relevant demographic changes in the American scene. By making reasonable assumptions about the implications of these changes for probable future developments, some important conclusions can be drawn about how marital patterns may develop during the next several years.

This study presents some pertinent features of the current marital and family situation, some projections of lifetime levels of marriage and divorce by selected social characteristics of today's young adults, and some of the likely consequences of these changes in terms of the living arrangements of adults and children projected for the year 1990.

OVERVIEW

Prospective trends of marriage and divorce during the 1980s will be determined in large part by the trend of the birth rate soon after the end of World War II. Persons born in the United States during the peak years of the baby boom have reached the main ages for first marriage. In fact, the number of young adults 18 to 26 years of age crested in 1982 and has started a gradual decline. However, the number of adults 25 to 39 years of age, who are in the period of life when most divorces occur, will not reach

*The U.S. Bureau of the Census received substantial support from the National Institute for Child Health and Human Development for the collection and processing of the unpublished data for June 1980 on marital history that are used extensively in this article. I wish to express my appreciation to Arthur J. Norton and James A. Weed for contributions they made toward the development of this study, and to Karen Smith for her assistance in preparation of some of the data cited in this article. An earlier draft of this article was presented at the Second Annual Social Science Colloquium at the University of Texas at Tyler, April 19, 1983; this version appeared in *Journal of Family Issues* 5 (1984) 7–26, © Sage Publications, Inc. Reprinted with permission.

a crest until about 1990, after which the number in that age range will decline. Thus, the present population includes the larger cohort with the highest probability of first marriage, and the population during the late 1980s will include the largest cohort with the greatest risk of divorce.

The actual number of marital events that occur in a given year depends, of course, not only on the pool of eligibles but also on the rate at which the events occur. The most recent data available on detailed vital statistics show that both first marriage and remarriage rates at critical ages had declined for most of a decade through 1979, while the divorce rate at critical ages had doubled (U.S. National Center for Health Statistics, 1981a, 1981b). Although preliminary data for more recent years indicate a slight rise in marriage and a slight decline in divorce, the underlying statistics suggest that the number of first marriages should decline before the end of the 1980s, while divorces and remarriages should rise moderately.

Some of the main factors that gave rise to the upsurge in divorce after the mid-1960s are not likely to cause correspondingly rapid changes during the 1980s (U.S. Bureau of the Census, 1979). The declining birth rate made it easier for unhappily married couples to maintain two households after divorce, but the birth rate is unlikely to decline further. The advancing educational levels meant that more young adults, especially women, were developing skills that made them more employable, but the increase in educational levels has about run its course. Also, the increase in the employment of women, a development identified by Cherlin (1981) and others as a prime factor underlying the rising divorce rate, seems destined to taper off (U.S. Bureau of the Census, 1979). Such anticipated moderations in relevant social changes are expected to slow down the rates of change in marriage and divorce during the 1980s. As a caveat, one must always acknowledge that unforeseen developments could occur, but by definition such potential developments are unpredictable.

CURRENT MARRIAGE AND DIVORCE LEVELS

Nearly all Americans eventually marry. About 95% of the population above 45 years of age in the United States in 1980 had married (Table 1). But the situation has been changing markedly among younger Americans. In 1970, 45% of the men and 64% of the women in their early twenties had already married, but by 1980, the corresponding figures had decreased to 31% and 50%. Whether this change means that more of the young adults were merely postponing their marriages, or whether a growing proportion of them were heading for lifelong singlehood, is a topic under much discussion today and one to which attention is devoted in a later section.

While marriage has been declining, divorce has been rapidly increasing. Evidence of the rising divorce level is apparent from the information in the second column of Table 1. Thus, the proportion of men in their early thirties in 1980 who had ended a marriage in divorce was already as large as that for men 45 to 54, even though the latter had been exposed to the risk of divorce for many more years. Among women, even more of the younger than of the older age group had experienced divorce. One consequence is that the current divorce level is well above the trend line that extends back for an entire century. Approximately how high the level may reach within the lifetime of today's young adults, even if the rate of increase should diminish, will be discussed below.

A large majority of divorced persons eventually remarry. According to Table 1, about five of every six men and three of every four women have become remarried after divorce before they reached the age of 75 years. But most of the divorce experience among those in the oldest age group occurred 35 to 40 years before the time of the survey in 1980. Meanwhile, the remarriage rates for divorced persons have been falling. It should not be surprising, therefore, if a similar survey made by the end of the 1980s were to reveal remarriage levels some five to ten percentage points lower than those observed in 1980. In a later section, information will be presented on variations among social groups in the tendency to remarry after divorce.

PROJECTIONS OF MARRIAGE AND DIVORCE

Various methods have been employed to arrive at reasonable estimates of the likely level of marriage and divorce during the lifetimes of persons who are currently young adults (U.S. Bureau of the Census, 1977; Cherlin, 1981; Weed, 1982). The approach used here is the one introduced by the U.S. Bureau of the Census (1977) in the analysis of data from the June 1975 Current Population Survey. Most of the source material used in the present study came from previously unpublished tabulations based on the June 1980 Current Population Survey, which covered information from 55,000 households scientifically selected to represent the noninstitutional population of the United States. Some new types of projections were prepared on the likelihood that young adults will ever marry and on variations in future marital experience for persons classified by selected social characteristics.

The method of projection applied here produces results that would be expected if the same increments in marriage and divorce observed between 1975 and 1979 for each five-year age group were to be experienced by younger adults during succeeding five-year periods before they reach the

TABLE 1
Marital History, Sex, and Selected Ages of Adults:
United States, 1980

Age at survey date and sex	Percent of adults ever married	Percent of married adults ever divorced	Percent of divorced adults ever married
Men			
20–24 years	31	8	39
30–34 years	86	23	68
45–54 years	95	23	77
65–74 years	95	16	85
Women			
20–24 years	50	14	61
30–34 years	90	26	55
45–54 years	96	23	71
65–74 years	94	15	78

SOURCE: U.S. Bureau of the Census, derived from unpublished Current Population Survey data for June 1980.

age of 75 years. For example, the projections imply that persons 25 to 29 years of age in 1980 would add as much marriage and divorce experience between 1980 and 1984 as persons 30 to 34 years old in 1980 had added between 1975 and 1979. This procedure implies, furthermore, that the direction of recent change will continue but that the amount of change will be smaller than that during the upsurge in divorce during the early 1970s. The resulting projections, together with estimates of the corresponding current levels for comparison, appear in Tables 2, 3, and 5. The information in Table 4 on remarriage after divorce is shown only for the current situation, because the technique used in this study proved to be inappropriate for projecting remarriage, as will be explained below.

PROSPECTIVE CHANGES IN FIRST MARRIAGE

Although nearly all adults who reach middle age have married, the timing is different for men and women, and the extent of marriage varies by race and educational level (Table 2). Because women usually enter marriage at a younger age than men, it is not surprising that the 1980 data show a much larger proportion married for women than men in their late twenties, regardless of race or education. But some of the difference may be attributed to a likely practice among some young mothers who have never married to misreport themselves as having been married, in order to mask their premarital childbearing. The relatively small proportions of college students who had married by the age of 25 to 29 years is probably a result of increasing numbers of persons in this age group who are attending postgraduate school or who are getting settled into their careers before marriage. Eventually, men who have been educated above the college graduation level are expected to have the highest proportion who marry within their lifetimes, whereas women college graduates are expected to have the lowest proportion among women.

These and other projections of the proportion of adults who may eventually marry are shown in the right half of Table 2. The results indicate that an expected 96% or 97% of those who were at the usual age for first marriage during the height of the baby boom of the 1950s (and who were about 50 to 54 years old in 1980) may become married before they reach the age of 75 years. Looked at another way, all but 3% of the men and 4% of the women in this age group have already married or may eventually marry. By contrast, the projections imply that substantially larger pro-

TABLE 2
Selected Marriage Statistics: United States, 1980

Age at survey date, race, and educational level	Percent who had married by 1980		Percent who may eventually marry	
	Men	Women	Men	Women
25-29 years old:				
All races	69	79	90	88
0–11 years of school	75	82	92	90
12 years	75	83	90	90
13–15 years	65	76	74	86
16 years	61	70	84	83
17+ years	57	62	93	83
White	71	81	89	90
Black	58	62	89	75
50–54 years old:				
All races	95	95	97	96
70–74 years old:				
All races	95	94	95	94

SOURCE: U.S. Bureau of the Census, derived from unpublished Current Population Survey data for June 1980.

portions of those who have been participants in the recent slump in first marriage (those currently 25 to 29 years old) may never marry; these proportions are 10% for the men and 12% for the women. Thus, if the projections prove to foretell the future marital experience of these young adults with reasonable accuracy, three times as large a proportion of them as compared with members of their parents' generation may be counted upon to spend a lifetime in singlehood.

If 10% to 12% of the young Americans of today never marry, it would mean, among other things, that this country would be changing from one of the developed countries with the smallest proportions never marrying to a country with one of the largest proportions never marrying. But among the less developed countries are many with much larger proportions of adults who remain unmarried (United Nations 1977; Table 25). The more that young adults postpone marriage, the more likely that the projected rates of lifelong singleness will become realized. Such a developmnent could mean that more young adults for a variety of reasons are joining a current trend or that more of those who are ill adapted to married life for their maximum happiness are choosing to remain unmarried.

A tripling during the last two decades in the proportion of children born out of wedlock is one of the most extreme happenings associated with the sharp decline in marriage. The proportion of children born to unmarried mothers rose from 5% in 1960 to 11% in 1970 to 18% in 1980 (U.S. National Center for Health Statistics, 1982). The proportion of women 20 to 24 years of age who had never married rose from 28% in 1960 to 36% in 1970 and to 53% in 1982 (U.S Bureau of the Census, 1982b). According to the most recent information, the figures by race showed that in 1980 "only" 11% of white births but 55% of black births occurred to unmarried mothers. Moreover, only one-half as large a proportion of white women as black women 25 to 29 years of age in 1980 had never married (19% versus 38%). In the absence of any distinct turning point in the upward trends in illegitimacy and postponement of marriage, one may reasonably assume that the trends will continue during the 1980s but at a more moderate rate.

As more young adults have delayed marriage, more of them have contributed to the recent upsurge in marriage-like behavior before they marry. Nearly one-half (43%) of these unmarried couples living together in 1975 involved a man and an unrelated woman who had never married (Glick and Spanier, 1980). The number of unmarried copules has been increasing at the extremely rapid rate of about 15% per year during the last decade, rising from 523,000 in 1970 to 1,863,000 in 1982 (U.S. Bureau of the Census, 1982b). Even if the rate of increase should moderate considerably, on the assumption that the slack in the growth of this practice is being gradually taken up, a reasonable prognosis is that the number of cohabiting unmarried couples may come close to doubling during the 1980s. Whether those who engaged in premarital cohabitation increase or decrease the chances that they will become divorced if they do marry is a subject on which available Current Population Survey data can shed no light. A definitive answer to this question may have to await private surveys a decade from now.

Prospective Changes in First Divorce

The occurrence of divorce was rather rare two generations ago, as may be seen by the fact that only 15% of persons 65 to 74 years old in 1980 reported that they had ended their first marriage in divorce (Table 3). By contrast, a much larger proportion of persons 40 years younger had already become divorced, despite their far shorter period of exposure to the risk of disrupting their marriage. Partly because women tend to marry two or three years sooner than men, the proportion of women, regardless of race or educational level, whose first marriage had ended in divorce by the time they were 25 to 34 years of age was somewhat higher than that for men. The quite small amount of divorce reported for black men by this age may reflect in part the relatively large undercount of young black men, probably including many divorced men with no fixed address. Among both men and women there tended to be negative correlation between divorce and educational level, with the smallest proportions divorced being for those with four years of college.

The projections imply that about one-half (49%) of the men and women 25 to 34 years of age had either ended their first marriage in divorce by the survey date or may be expected to do so before they reach the age of 75 years. This is three times the level of 15% for their parents or grandparents, that is, for those 65 to 74. The liklihood of the first marriage ending in divorce is closer to 60% for young adults with some college education but not a bachelor's degree. A relatively small proportion (about 40%) of young adults who graduated from college but took no postgraduate school training may be expected to become divorced after their first marriage. It appears that persons with the kind of personality and family background characteristics that result in their reaching the traditional goal of college graduation may also be most likely to achieve the goal of a permanent marriage. However, women who had gone on to postgraduate school evidently have a considerably greater likelihood of divorce after first marriage (over 50%); these women usually have the greatest probability of being career oriented.

If a two-year college degree becomes more of a norm than a high school diploma for those who do not aspire to gain a full college education, one might expect a corresponding diminution during coming years in the large proportion of women with one to three years of college whose first marriage ends in divorce. Likewise, if an increasing proportion of women with graduate school education successfully combine a professional or business career and marriage, that level of education would become more of a norm; therefore, one might expect the probability of divorce after first marriage among these women to decline to a level closer to that for women with terminal college graduation. In fact, there are data that suggest that a trend in this direction has already begun (U.S. Bureau of the Census, 1977).

PROSPECTIVE CHANGES IN REMARRIAGE

Although most divorced persons remarry some time before they reach the age of 75 years, the extent and timing of remarriage differs consider-

TABLE 3
Selected Divorce Statistics: United States, 1980

Age at survey date, race, and educational level	Ever married			
	Percent who had ended their first marriage in divorce by 1980		Percent who may eventually end their first marriage in divorce	
	Men	Women	Men	Women
25–34 years old:				
All races	20	24	49	49
0–11 years of school	25	29	51	53
12 years	22	25	51	48
13–15 years	22	24	58	55
16 years	12	13	40	39
17+ years	13	17	41	52
White	20	23	49	48
Black	9	26	52	58
45–54 years old:				
All races	22	22	33	27
65–74 years old:				
All races	15	15	15	15

SOURCE: U.S. Bureau of the Census, derived from unpublished Current Population Survey data for June 1980.

ably by sex, race, and educational level (Table 4). Men are consistently more likely than women to remarry. This tendency reflects such factors as the greater tendency for divorced men than divorced women to marry someone not previously married. Moreover, divorced men with custody of children evidently tend to become remarried relatively soon, partly because they may feel a need for a spouse to help with the rearing of their children and partly because they tend to be relatively affluent and hence rather attractive potential marital partners.

Among women in their thirties who have been divorced, the likelihood that they have remarried is negatively correlated with their educational level. Other things being equal, divorced women with no college education appear to remarry rather quickly, whereas those with more education either enter remarriage more deliberately or decide to remain unmarried. Another factor may be the younger ages at marriage and divorce of those with no college education. But despite the much greater concentration of blacks than others in the lower educational levels, black divorced persons have a distinctly low proportion remarried before the age of 40 years. Factors other than educational level must be involved in explaining this racial difference.

Women 65 to 74 years old in 1980 included a quite small proportion remarried after divorce among those with four years of college education.

TABLE 4
Selected Statistics on Second Marriages: United States, 1980

Educational level and race	Divorced after first marriage			
	Percent who had remarried by age 30–39		Percent who had remarried by age 65–74	
	Men	Women	Men	Women
All races	72	63	84	77
0–11 years of school	76	70	81	78
12 years	76	65	88	77
13–15 years	68	58	84	82
16 years	62	54	91	62
17+ years	64	46	88	69
White	72	65	84	76
Black	64	37	84	81

SOURCE: U.S. Bureau of the Census, derived from unpublished Current Population Survey data for June 1980.

Most of these women had become divorced many years ago, when the amount of career orientation was probably about as strong among women with a terminal college education as that among women with postgraduate school training today.

No projections of probable lifetime experience with remarriage are presented in Table 4. The method used in preparing the other projections for this study yielded results implying that more than 100% of young divorced persons may eventually remarry. Probably young divorced persons who had remarried were more likely to report fully and accurately on their marital history than those who had not remarried.

Vital statistics for the 1970s provide documentation of a sharp recent decline in remarriage rates. For example, the remarriage rate per 1000 divorced men dropped from 229 in 1972 to only 166 in 1979, the latest year for which rates have been published (U.S. National Center for Health Statistics, 1981b). Therefore, as observed above, it seems reasonable to expect the proportion of divorced persons now below 40 years of age who eventually remarry to fall well below the approximately 80% level (for those in old age today) to close to 70% or 75%.

Prospective Changes in Redivorce

Very few people below the age of 40 years have experienced two divorces. Specifically, among those in their thirties in 1980, about 90% had married; a little over one-fourth of this 90%, or 24% of all persons in their early thirties, had ended their first marriage in divorce; about two-thirds of this 24%, or 16% of all persons in their thirties, had remarried after divorce; and Table 5 shows that one-fifth of this 16%, or only 3%, of all persons currently in their thirties have already experienced redivorce. Later in this section, it will be demonstrated that a much larger proportion of those now under 40 will have become redivorced by the time they reach old age.

The level of education appears to be negatively correlated with the level of second divorce as well as first divorce. Especially noteworthy are the small amount of redivorce for men with postgraduate school training and the large amount for women with an incomplete college education. Whites are evidently more likely than blacks to become redivorced. As an indication of an upward trend in redivorce, the proportion of persons who had become redivorced was already higher in 1980 for persons in their fifties than for those in their seventies, even though they had been exposed to the risk of experiencing redivorce for many fewer years.

Projections of the extent of eventual redivorce yielded estimates of 61%

TABLE 5
Selected Statistics on Redivorce: United States, 1980

Age at survey date, race, and educational level	Remarried after first marriage ended in divorce			
	Percent whose second marriage ended in redivorce by 1980		Percent who may eventually end their second marriage in redivorce	
	Men	Women	Men	Women
30–39 years old:				
All races	19	22	61	54
0–11 years of school	21	26	58	59
12 years	21	22	59	51
13–15 years	17	35	81	57
16 years	17	21	62	41
17+ years	11	a	44	a
White	19	22	61	53
Black	16	18	48	51
50–59 years old:				
All races	26	26	36	31
70–74 years old:				
All races	19	18	19	18

SOURCE: U.S. Bureau of the Census, derived from unpublished Current Population Survey data for June 1980.

a. Very small base.

for the men and 54% for the women in their thirties in 1980. These levels are higher, but not extremely higher, than the projected 49% who may eventually have a first divorce. But those who become divorced once may tend to have personality configurations and family backgrounds that make them relatively prone to divorce after succeeding marriages. Moreover, remarried persons who had been divorced are familiar with the procedure and consequences involved in divorce.

The pattern of variation in redivorce by educational level over a lifetime is similar to that for redivorce among those currently in their thirties. Also, young whites appear to be more likely than young blacks to become redivorced before they reach old age. If the projections prove to be relatively accurate, remarried persons now in their thirties will be three times as likely as those now in their seventies eventually to become redivorced.

Because not all persons marry, and not all persons who do marry become divorced, and not all those who become divorced later remarry, and not all who remarry eventually become redivorced, the chances that the average young adult in the general population today will become redivorced before reaching old age are about one in five, as the following computation will show. If 90% of all persons in the United States in their thirties today finally marry, and 50% of the 90% (45%) become divorced, and 75% of the 45% (33%) remarry, and 60% of the 33% (20%) become redivorced, one may conclude that about one-fifth of all persons in their thirties today may expect eventually to experience a second divorce. Still fewer are likely to have a third divorce, perhaps about 5%. Thus, only a relatively small but not insignificant minority of young adults may eventually experience multiple divorces.

PROSPECTIVE CHANGES IN LIVING ARRANGEMENTS

The prospective changes in marriage and divorce discussed above may be expected to result in substantial changes in the living arrangements of adults and children during the years ahead. For instance, the rate of growth in the number of households between 1981 and 1990 as shown in Table 6 is expected to be only about one-half as rapid as it was between 1970 and 1981 (U.S. Bureau of the Census, 1982b). The growth that does occur is likely to be unevenly distributed by composition of household. These expected changes are based on the assumption made in preparing the projections shown in Tables 6 and 7, namely, that the direction of change in the number of households during the period 1970 to 1981 will continue for each type of household but that the amount of change during the nine years from 1981 to 1990 will be only two-thirds as great as that during the eleven years from 1970 to 1981. These projections are consistent with the anticipated general slowdown in various types of family change discussed in an earlier section.

Primarily because of declining marriage rates and rising divorce rates during the 1970s and the prospect that these trends will continue, married couple households may be expected to decline from 60% to 55% of all households between 1981 and 1990, while other households increase from 40% to 45%. But underlying these apparently moderate changes are greatly contrasting anticipated rates of increase among the several types of household. Thus, married couple households, according to the projections, will increase only 6% between 1981 and 1990, while households main-

TABLE 6
Type of Household by Race:
United States, 1981, and Projection for 1990

Type of household and race	1981	Projection, 1990	Percent change, 1981–1990
All races			
All households (thousands)	82,368	95,076	15.4
Percent	100.0	100.0	—
Married couple households	59.8	55.1	6.2
With children under 18	30.2	25.8	−1.9
No children under 18	29.6	29.3	14.2
Other, woman as householder	26.5	29.0	26.0
With children under 18	6.8	7.9	33.0
No children under 18	19.7	21.1	23.6
Woman living alone	14.2	15.4	25.0
Woman in unmarried couple	0.8	1.0	40.6
Other	4.7	4.7	16.3
Other, man as householder	13.6	15.9	35.4
With children under 18	0.8	0.9	32.7
No children under 18	12.8	15.0	35.5
Man living alone	8.8	10.3	34.4
Man in unmarried couple	1.4	1.8	51.6
Other	3.6	2.9	30.9
Black			
All households (thousands)	8,847	10,719	21.2
Percent	100.0	100.0	—
Married couple households	38.3	32.6	2.9
Other, woman as householder	44.3	48.0	31.3
Other, man as householder	17.4	19.4	35.7

SOURCES: Derived from U.S. Bureau of the Census (1982a, 1982b).

tained by a woman with no husband present will increase by 26%, and those maintained by a man with no wife present will increase by fully 35%. As more young adults postpone marriage and more young parents become divorced, the number of married couple households with children in the home is expected actually to decrease, while the number of one-parent households increases by one-third between 1981 and 1990. As time goes on, the experience of being a lone parent who maintains a household is becoming steadily much less unusual.

A large majority of childless households consist of adults living alone.

The rate of increase for these households during the 1980s is expected to be above twice that for all households. Although four-tenths of the one-person households are maintained by persons over 65 years of age, by far the fastest rate of recent growth has occurred among persons under 35 years of age who have never married or who have become divorced. This pattern of change seems likely to continue.

Unmarried couple households onstitute the smallest category shown in Table 6. As pointed out above, they have increased at an extremely high rate during the last dozen years and are expected to keep increasing at a faster rate than any other type of household. Even so, they are likely to account for only 3% of all households and 5% of all couple households by 1990. These levels are only about one-third as high as those for Sweden during the 1970s as reported by Trost (1979).

The high rate of increase for black households not maintained by a married couple seems likely to continue. The projections imply that nearly one-half (48%) of black households in 1990 may be maintained by a woman with no husband in her home.

Along with the changes in living arrangements of adults have gone corresponding changes in the living arrangements of children. Life in a home with two parents used to be close to unanimous among children under 18 years of age, but the proportion living in that manner has declined from 85% in 1970 to 76% in 1981 and may be expected to go down to 69% by 1990 (Table 7). Although a quite high level (82%) of white children were living with two parents in 1981, only about one-half as large a proportion of black children (43%) were doing so. By contrast, the growth in the number of children living with only one parent has been quite large and may be expected to keep increasing rapidly during the present decade. As one consequence, the contemplated proportion of children under 18 living with a lone parent in 1990 is about twice as large for black children as for all children (57% versus 27%). Most of the remaining children will be living with relatives other than their parents. However, about three times as large a proportion of black children as white children under 18 may be expected to be living apart from all relatives (12% versus 4%).

Only about 2% or 3% of the children under 18 in 1990 may be living with their father only, but at least another one in every ten may be living with their natural mother and a stepfather (Glick, 1979). According to unpublished research by Arthur J. Norton, about 59% of all children born in the early 1980s may expect to live with only one parent for at least a year before reaching the age of 18 years. Moreover, about two-thirds of these

TABLE 7
Living Arrangements of Children Under 18 by Race:
United States, 1981, and Projections for 1990

Living arrangements and race	1981	Projection, 1990	Percent change, 1981–1990
All races			
All children under 18 (thousands)	62,918	58,735	–6.6
Percent	100.0	100.0	—
Living with:			
2 parents	76.4	69.4	–17.9
1 parent	20.0	26.5	23.5
Mother	18.1	24.0	23.3
Divorced	7.8	11.3	35.7
Married	5.6	6.3	5.8
Separated	4.9	6.1	16.8
Widowed	1.8	1.7	–13.7
Never married	2.9	4.5	47.5
Father	1.9	2.5	25.4
Divorced	1.0	1.5	47.7
Married	0.5	0.5	2.0
Separated	0.4	0.5	28.0
Widowed	0.3	0.2	–27.1
Never married	0.2	0.3	49.1
All other	3.6	4.1	7.0
Black			
All children under 18 (thousands)	9,400	9,016	–4.1
Percent	100.0	100.0	—
Living with:			
2 parents	42.7	31.3	–29.8
1 parent	45.9	56.5	18.2
Mother	43.4	53.8	19.0
Father	2.5	2.7	4.2
All other	11.4	12.2	2.8

SOURCES: Derived from U.S. Bureau of the Census (1982a, 1982b).

children (close to 35% of all children) may expect to live with a stepparent during a part of their childhood.

The demographic sources throw considerable light on the differing living arrangements of young children, but they do not reveal the wide differences in the adjustment problems that the children face according to how they relate to the adults in whose homes they live.

DISCUSSION

In this article, recent information for the United States on marriage, divorce, and living arrangements has been used to arrive at reasonable projections of these variables. Underlying the projections is the implicit assumption that the direction of recent changes will continue but that the rate of change will be moderated during future years. As additional relevant information is gathered through demographic methods, the projections presented here can be appropriately revised.

This study documents the current and projected levels of marriage and divorce classified by selected social characteristics and demonstrates some of the consequences of these findings in terms of the differing distributions of living arrangements of adults and children. The recent and prospective changes in these aspects of family life reflect an increasing tendency for new family norms to develop. In the words of Thornton and Freedman (1982: 303),

> Although most young Americans continue to value marriage and plan to marry, these attitudinal changes are likely to motivate young people to marry later and postpone marriage to obtain an education and establish a career. . . . The growing acceptance of single life and of divorce may result in greater willingness on the part of married people to dissolve an unsatisfactory marriage, but the observed attitudinal changes may also increase marital fulfillment.

Despite anticipated further increases in divorce, lone living, and lifelong singlehood, the prospective future population seems very likely to continue to include a vast majority who live in one form of family group or another. An estimated 80% of the American population in 1990 will be living in homes maintained by a married couple (65%) or by a lone parent (15%). The remainder may be divided between persons living alone (8%) and all others (12%). Thus, the composition of households will probably continue to change but to consist predominantly of closely related family members.

REFERENCES

Cherlin, A. J.
  1981 *Marriage, Divorce, Remarriage.* Cambridge, MA: Harvard Univ. Press.
Glick, P. C.
  1979 "Children of divorced parents in demographic perspective." *Journal of Social Issues* 35(Fall): 170–182.

Glick, P. C. and G. B. Spanier
1980 "Married and unmarried cohabitation in the United States." *Journal of Marriage and the Family* 42(February): 19–30.
Thornton, A. and D. Freedman
1982 "Changing attitudes toward marriage and single life." *Family Planning Perspectives* 14(November/December): 297–303.
Trost, J.
1979 *Unmarried Cohabitation.* Västeros, Sweden: International Library.
United Nations
1977 *Demographic Yearbook, 1976.* New York: United Nations.
U.S. Bureau of the Census
1977 "Marriage, divorce, widowhood, and remarriage by family characteristics: June 1975," in *Current Population Reports,* Series P-20, no. 312. Washington, DC: Government Printing Office.
1979 "The future of the American family," in *Current Population Reports,* Series P-23, no. 78. Washington, DC: Government Printing Office.
1982a "Household and family characteristics: March 1981," in *Current Population Reports,* Series P-20, no. 371. Washington, DC: Government Printing Office.
1982b "Marital status and living arrangements: March 1981," in *Current Population Reports,* Series P-20, no. 372. Washington, DC: Government Printing Office.
U.S. National Center for Health Statistics
1981a "Advance report of final divorce statistics, 1979," in *Monthly Vital Statistics Report,* vol. 30, no. 2, supplement. Washington, DC: Government Printing Office.
1981b "Advance report of final marriage statistics, 1979," in *Monthly Vital Statistics Report,* vol. 30, no. 4, supplement. Washington, DC: Government Printing Office.
1982 "Advance report of final natality statistics, 1980," in *Monthly Vital Statistics Report,* vol. 31, no. 8, supplement. Washington, DC: Government Printing Office.
Weed, J. A.
1982 "Divorce: Americans' style." *American Demographics* 4(March): 12–17.

COMMENT

Lawrence G. Wrenn

Doctor Glick's article is packed with food for thought. The data it provides will be useful to all sorts of people: social workers, marriage counsellors, legislators, psychologists, etc. It merits close, reflective and repeated readings.

For the present, however, let me make just a couple of rather obvious comments that are particularly relevant for marriage tribunals.

First, the divorce rate in the United States will not peak until 1990. Presumably, therefore, the number of petitioners for annulment will continue to increase through the 1980s and 1990s. Consequently it behooves the Church in America (among other more important things, of course) to train more canon lawyers (cc. 1420, §4; 1421, §3; and 1435) so that our tribunals will be adequately staffed to provide a hearing for all prospective petitioners.

Secondly, America now has a very high divorce rate and has had a high divorce rate for many years. Inevitably this has produced, in a percentage of the population, a divorce mentality. When one out of every two marriages ends in divorce, many people begin to feel that marriage is not really a permanent state. What happens when such people marry? Canon 1096 says that "for matrimonial consent to be valid it is necessary that the contracting parties at least not be ignorant that marriage is a *permanent* consortium." It would seem, therefore, that an increasing number of marriages will be invalid on this ground of ignorance.

Another ground that will probably be used increasingly over the next couple of decades, as the divorce rate affects the attitudes of more and more people, is error about the perpetuity or indissolubility of marriage. Canon 1099 implies that when a person's belief about marriage as a terminable arrangement shapes his or her own marital intent, then the marriage is null. Surely that is happening with some frequency these days.

A third ground that has been influenced by the high divorce rate is the conditioned marriage (c. 1102). There is no question but that a great many people today are entering marriage with the hope that it will provide them a reasonable degree of personal fulfillment and also with the implicit understanding that they desire the marriage only on the condition that that hope be realized. Such marriages are null.

Different tribunals will, of course, tend to use different grounds. Some tribunals will use none of the three grounds suggested above but will continue to judge cases on the basis of "lack of due discretion" but with the emphasis being on the increasing transience of marriage. In order to enter a valid marriage, these tribunals will say, one must enjoy due discretion regarding "the essential matrimonial rights and duties" (c. 1092, 2⁰). These rights and duties, however, are *lifelong* rights and duties, and if they are not understood and accepted as such, the marriage is invalid.

But whatever ground is used, the divorce mentality, which is implicit in Doctor Glick's excellent paper, is bound to be a major factor in the upcoming decades.

FAITH AND THE SACRAMENT OF MARRIAGE: GENERAL CONCLUSIONS FROM AN HISTORICAL STUDY

RAYMOND C. FINN, O.P.

Synopsis of the Historical Data

The purpose of the study, which led to the writing of the dissertation entitled *Towards a Reinterpretation of Canon 1012: A Study of its Theological and Canonical Foundations* (Rome: Pontifical University of St. Thomas, 1977) was to investigate the relationship between the marriage contract and the sacrament. This relationship was enunciated in canon 1012 of the 1917 code: "Christ the Lord elevated the very contract of marriage between baptized persons to the dignity of a sacrament. Therefore it is impossible for a valid contract of marriage between baptized persons to exist without being by that very fact a sacrament." This same doctrine was repeated in canon 1055 of the 1983 code.

Besides examining the canonical and magisterial sources of this canon, an examination of their historical context leads to insight into the relationship between contract and sacrament. The essential question is not related to an independent canonical exercise but rather is intimately bound up with a continuing development of the theological understanding of the meaning of marriage as one of the seven sacraments of the New Law.

Data about the primitive church indicate that while the Church recognized a sacredness about marriage, it did not give adequate expression to this basic posture. The earliest Christians, accustomed to marriage as a secular reality, attributed the sacredness of marriage to its very essence. St. Paul, for instance, rather than offering a clear definition of marriage as a sacrament, indicates its openness to the realm of salvation. In the early centuries Christian marriage was never withdrawn from its basic context as a secular event. Nevertheless certain questions peculiar to Christians accompanied a "marriage in the Lord." The works of the great Fathers of the Church, especially St. Augustine as well as those of other early Christian writers, indicate that the primary direction of scholarship was toward the meaning of the sacredness, the sacramentality of marriage. In time (11th century) the great Christian thinkers began to speculate on when

95

a marriage came into being, relating this to when and in what the sacramentality consisted.

With Aquinas the long and problematic development of the sacramentality of marriage reached final resolution. There were dissenting voices concerning the efficient cause of marriage, the nature of its sacramentality, whether or not it conferred grace. Yet from the second half of the thirteenth century the position that marriage was a true sacrament and that it conferred grace was generally considered to be certain in the theological arena.

From the completion of the golden age of scholasticism to the 17th century there seem to have been two central points upon which dispute and discussion centered. The councils of Florence and Trent required three elements to effect a true sacramental reality: matter, form, and the intention of the minister. It is the last element which was the nub of the problem. The authors who maintained that the contract and the sacrament could be separated seized upon intentionality as the focal point and heart of their argument. It was on the basis of intentionality that their theology developed and their argument rested. A second point which came into focus was that of marriage effected by proxy—in which neither of the ministers of the sacrament are present for its celebration. However important this may be, it is of less import than the arguments bearing on intentionality. A closer examination of the requisites of intentionality— both on the part of the minister and on the part of the recipient—indicates that intentionality takes on a much greater importance with marriage since both ministers and recipients are the same, the spouses. Since this is so, the requisite intention required for the *minister* is demanded for marriage. A virtual intention is required of the recipients because of this identification.

In the celebration of marriage, in order that the sacrament be realized, the parties to the union must have an internal intention corresponding to the external ritual. Moreover, this intention must be operative in such a way as to influence, at least virtually, the sacramental reality. A germ of faith then must be present, at least implicitly, for in both ministering and receiving the sacrament the parties to a sacramental union need the minimal intention of uniting themselves to the Church—to do what the Church does.

Under the influence of Gallicanism in France (beginning in the late 17th century) the Church's competency in matters of marriage was slowly eroding. Due to the excessive nationalism in society, the process of secularization was in progress. There emerged a conflict between the Church's legislation and that of the state over marriage. The same trend was taking place in Austria (Josephinism and Febronianism). Here, the emperor claimed exclusive jurisdiction over all contracts, including the contract of marriage. In reaction, church authorities and scholars delved increasingly into the meaning of marital sacramentality and its relationship to the efficient cause of marriage. Pius VI (1775–1799), for instance, was the first pope to indentify contract and sacrament in an unqualified manner.

The most productive time in the articulation of the identity between contract and sacrament as an official affirmation of the Church was the nineteenth century, especially during the pontificates of Pius IX and Leo XIII. Practically every reference to the relationship between contract and sacrament by these popes was cast in the context of struggle between Church and state.

Moreover, in every reference to the inseparability of contract and sacrament made by the papal magisterium, some implicit acknowledgement of the faith of those entering marriage was indicated. This is especially apparent in the writings of Leo XIII wherein the pope is concerned not only with an abstract theorem concerning marriage, but is very much involved with marriages begun by the faithful.

Scholastic Reflection

To realize effectively the sacrament of matrimony an intention is required on the part of the minister-recipients to introduce themselves and their action into the compass of the ecclesial society. The Councils of Florence and Trent, and the repeated affirmations of theology, insist that the minister of a sacrament must embrace at least the generic disposition to do what the Church intends. Since the sacrament of marriage is by its very nature reserved to adults, it necessarily follows that the intentionality must respect marriage as a sacred as well as a social reality. Moreover, since marriage is a unique sacrement—it is both an *officium naturae* and a *sacramentum*—sacramental marriage must be possessed of a distinctive significance and effectiveness.

Thus at least a minimal germ of saving faith should be active for the sacrament to be realized. St. Bonaventure insisted that it is only in faith that the sacramental dimension of marriage could be discerned and distinguished.[1] For the Seraphic Doctor the sacramentality of marriage was realized in this context of living faith, and he required a proper intentional-

---

[1]"Sunt et alia, quae quodam modo ab instinctu naturae sunt—est matrimonium, in quo est maris et feminae coniunctio, . . . partem a fide, scilicet quod illa coniunctio significet coniunctionem Dei et anima." Bonaventure, *Commentarium in quatuor libros sentiarum,* (ed. Quaracchi, 1889), IV, d. 29, a. 2, q. 1.

ity, viz., being united in charity for the procreation of children, for the purpose of divine worship, in sacramental marriage.[2]

St. Albert the Great also saw the need for a defined expression of faith in order to realize the sacrament of marriage. The peculiar note of marriage as being *officium naturae* and *sacramentum* required a more active involvement on the part of the parties to marriage. The activity of the recipients is essential for its perfection, and hence its efficacy is not merely *ex opere operato* but also *ex opere operantis.*[3] Marriage demands a personal and moral decision. Because of its peculiar complexion—existing independently from the Christian dispensation as an *officium naturae* and within the New Law as a sacramental reality—the personal affirmation and recognition of its sacramental dimension is required.

In the writings of St. Thomas the intentionality of the spouses in marriage is neither overlooked nor is it minimized. The sacramentality of marriage is situated in an ecclesial context and a faith dimension is obvious. "Marriage insofar as it consists in the union of husband and wife, with the intention of generating offspring for the cult of God, is a sacrament of the Church."[4] His understanding of the sacramental axis is very much in accord with that of Bonaventure—marriage contracted in the faith of Christ is a grace-filled event and a sacramental reality. The sensitivity of the Angelic Doctor to the sacramental dimension of marriage provoked his distinguishing marriage as an *officium naturae*, *officium civilitatis*, and *sacramentum*. It is exclusively in virtue of the transforming power of Christ that marriage as *officium naturae* and *officium civilitatis* becomes co-opted into the sacramental sphere. Thus the consent initiating marriage was sacramentalized by the will to associate this community of marriage with the saving communion which existed between Christ and his Church.[5] Such an intentionality could not be conceived except in the context of faith.

---

[2]"Sed nunc tempore legis novae non tandum praestat illud remedium, sed etiam aliquod gratiae donom digne suscipientibus, utpote his qui ex caritatis consensu uniuntur ad procreandum prolem ad divinum cultum." Ibid., d. 26, a. 2, q. 2.

[3]". . . de eo quod est sacramentum et officium qui in illo est actus personalis et moralis et civilis, qui etiam fuit ante novam legem, et non trahit vim ab opere operato tantum, sed etiam ab opere operantis." St. Albert, *Commentaruim in IV Sententiarum* (Paris, 1894), d. 26, a. 14, q. 1.

[4]"Matrimonium igitur secundum quod consistit in coniunctione maris et feminae intendentium prolem ad cultum Dei generare et educare, est Ecclesia Sacramentum." St. Thomas, *Summa Contra Gentiles* (ed. Leonina, 1918–1930), lib. iv, C. 78.

[5]Edward Schillebeeckx, *Marriage: Human Reality and Saving Mystery* (New York: Sheed and Ward, 1965) 2: 326–327.

This provides more explanation for Aquinas' hesitancy to refer to marriage in a strict contractual framework. He was careful to preserve the analogical character of contract as predicated of Christian marriage, as was St. Albert before him.[6] Indeed to speak of marriage in terms of a contract necessarily requires that the nature of this contract be considered as *sui generis*.

> . . . . the nature of matrimony is entirely independent of the free will of man, so that if one has once contracted matrimony he is thereby subject to its divinely made laws and its essential properties. For the Angelic Doctor writing on conjugal honor and on the offspring which is the fruit of marriage, says: "These things are so contained in matrimony by the marriage pact itself that if anything to the contrary were expressed in the consent which makes the marriage, it would not be a true marriage."[7]

Tridentine and Post-Tridentine Response

The unique nature of marriage and the analogical application of contract to it are fundamental premises of Aquinas. For sacramental marriage both are assumed into an ecclesial reference and marriage mirrors the salvific union between Christ and his Church.

The ecclesial perspective was not absent from the Tridentine debates. Granatensis insisted that the sacramentality of marriage must be rooted in living faith and the intention to give and receive sacramentally was required from the parties to a marriage.[8]

In the post-Tridentine discussion the basic element of dissent among those authors who denied the unity of contract and sacrament was centered precisely on the intention required of sacramental minister and recipient. Vasquez insisted that an intention to enter into marriage precisely as a sacred and religious institution, i.e., an intention to do what the Church does, was an absolute requisite for sacramentality.[9] Rebellus insisted on the gratuity of the graciousness of God in all sacraments, and thus insisted

---

[6]Cf., St. Thomas, *Commentarium in IV Sententiarum* (Rome, 1570), IV, d. 27, q. 1, a. 2, d. 31, q. 1, a. 2, ad 2. St. Albert, *Comm. in IV Sent.*, IV, d. 27, a. 6.

[7]Pius XI, Encyclical letter *Casti connubii*, December 31, 1930: *A.A.S.* 22 (1930) 541.

[8]"Deinde probavit quod potest esse matrimonium absque sacramento, etiam in baptizato, qui vult contrahere et non vult recipere sacramentum; talis non suscepit sacramentum, quia non potest conferri invito." Ibid., p. 392.

[9]". . . quoad enim fiat matrimonii ratum, non pendet ex intentione contrahentium, sed eo ipso contrahitur a Baptizatis dicitur fieri ratum: ut autem sit sacramentum, pendet in ipso fieri ex intentione illa contrahentium, quam diximus." Vasquez, *De Matrimonii Sacramento*, in *Opera Omnia*, vol. VIII, disp. 2, cap. 7, num. 74.

that an intention to enter into a sacramental reality was essential to effect the Christian sacrament of marriage.[10] Pontius argued along the same lines, specifying an intention of celebrating marriage as a sacrament as an absolute with regard to the minister. He appealed to the gratuitous nature of the sacrament and to the gratuitous institution of the sacramentality of marriage by Christ and contrasted this to the notion of marriage as an *officium naturae*.[11]

Catholic theology of the sacraments supports the general lines of argumentation presented. The minimal requirement of the minister of a sacrament must encompass a virtual intention. This is evident because the minister is in the order of instumental causality and a virtual intention is not merely dispositive but causative. It is also harmonious with the teaching Church which in both the Council of Florence and the Council of Trent proposed an ecclesial dimension to all sacramental action and demanded of the minister of a sacrament that he intend to do what the Church does.[12]

It should be noted that Saints Bonaventure, Albert and Thomas also seemed to require a stronger affective posture of the parties to a marriage then was determined for the other sacraments. The importance of personal activity in the sacramental determination of marriage is made more intense because marriage is a sacrament of adults, whose free will and moral activity should be mature; and because while sacramental marriage is a unique Christian reality, marriage as an *officium naturae* continues in existence.

Ex Opere Operato

The emphasis placed on the disposition of the recipient of a sacrament parallels the insistence which the Church demands of the minister of a

---

[10]". . . significatio sacramenti mere contingenter advenit contractui naturali matrimonii; non secus atque eidem advenit esse licitum, vel illicitum, iuxta D. Thom. 26 in 4 Senten., dist. 30, art 2, ad 2um argumentum, sicut etiam lotione advenit, quod sit sacramentum baptismi, atqui lotio illa non desinit esse actio naturalis, et humana, eo quod lavans non intendit facere sacramentum; ergo nec contractus coniugalis desinet habere naturalem validitatem, quam etiam inter infideles hodie habet, esto contrahentes non intendant contrahere sacramentaliter, sed tantum naturaliter et civiliter." Ibid.

[11]". . . natura contractus matrimonii nullo modo mutata est, ex eo quod in sacramentum fuerit institutus a Christo, sed manet in sua natura consecratus est." Ibid., lib. 1, cap. viii, num. 12.

[12]"Haec omnia sacramenta tribus perficiuntur, videlicet rebus tamquam materia, verbis tamquam forma, et persona ministri conferentes sacramentum cum intentione faciendi, quod facit ecclesia: quorum si aliquid desit, non perficitur sacramentum." Denz.-S., n. 1312.

"Si quis dixerit, in ministris, dum sacramento conficiunt et conferunt, non requiri intentionem, saltem faciendi quod facit Ecclesia, anathema sit." Conc. Trident., *Canones de sacramentis in genere*, c. 11. Denz - S., n. 1611.

sacrament to intend what the Church does. Both aspects locate valid sacramental activity within an ecclesial framework—a community of believers. Aquinas in his reflection on the form of the sacrament of marriage noted "that the words by which matrimonial consent is expressed are the form of this sacrament."[13] The form of the words has a profound meaning in the theology of Aquinas, and this form is not a static reality. This *forma verborum* is interchangeable with *verbum fidei*, the word of faith.

> . . . the *forma verborum* of St. Thomas unquestionably enjoys a surplus value, precisely because the intention of the Church, to whom all the Sacraments have been entrusted, becomes evident in these sacramental words. For it is the Church alone which, in obedience to Christ, defines and preserves the soul of the sacramental rite, viz., the *significatio*. Without this supernatural meaning the Sacraments are nothing more than pure human actions.[14]

The faith of the Church is thus an integrating moment in sacramental reality. It permeates the whole being of the sacrament, so much so that the efficaciousness of the sacraments lies in faith.[15]

The insistence on this *ex opere operantis* aspect of sacramental reality, an insistence explicitly emphasized by both Saints Bonaventure and Albert with respect to the sacrament of marriage, does not denigrate from the traditional affirmation of sacramental efficacy *ex opere operato*. If anything, it enhances this tenet of sacramental theology by integrating it with the distinctive human capacity of free will.

All sacraments are effective *ex opere operato* by the positing of the act itself and in this are channels of grace independent of the sanctity and faith of the minister or recipient. This, however, must not be understood to mean that the grace conferred is absolutely and from every point of view independent of our cooperation and faith. Rather it affirms the total gratuity and initiative of God founded uniquely in Christ's work of salvation.[16] The sacraments confer grace on us not as things but as men endowed with free will, and a sacrament becomes this when the recipient in virtue of the sacrament accepts Christ freely in faith and charity.

---

[13]". . . dicendum quod verba quibus consensus matrimonialis exprimitur sunt forma huius sacramenti." St. Thomas, *Comm. in IV Sent.* IV d. 28, q. 1, a. 4.

[14]P.F. Fransen, *Faith and the Sacraments* (London: Blackfriars, 1958), pp. 14–15.

[15]"Fidei efficacia non est diminuta, cum omnia Sacramenta ex fide efficaciam habent." St. Thomas, *Comm. in IV Sent.*, IV d. 1, q. 2, a. 6, sol. 2, ad 3.

In this sense it is entirely orthodox to say that the sacrament finds its efficaciousness in our faith, not primarily, not initially, nor even fundamentally, but in the sense that the sacrament does not realize its symbolic sense or begin to achieve fully its sanctifying action until the moment when, under the continuous influence of Christ present in the sacrament, we accept him in faith and charity.[17]

A mechanistic view of sacrament and *ex opere operato* would be alien to the great scholastics and especially to Aquinas. It is unfortunate that due to the influence of nominalism a mechanistic interpretive tendency affected post-Tridentine understanding. However, Aquinas favored an intimate dynamism between *ex opere operato* and *ex opere operantis*;[18] for him the sacraments are sacraments of faith,[19] signs of justifying faith[20] requiring faith.[21] He seems to demand more of the faith of the recipient than the mere negative condition of not positing obstacles to the fruitful reception of sacramental grace.

> The *opus operatum* of St. Thomas is not opposed to the *opus operantis*, that is, to personal cooperation in faith and charity, at the level of grace, as has so often been said by post-Tridentine theologians, but at the very precisely determined level of the constitution of the sacramental sign as the authentic symbol of this active presence of Christ. The recipient of the Sacrament is, therefore, absolutely incapable of bringing about, ensuring or constituting that sacramental presence within the liturgical symbol. The same limitation applies also to the minister in as much as he is a private person. That is the exclusive power of Christ in his Church. Here we have the true significance of *opus operatum* as opposed to *opus operantis*. . . . The salvific action of Christ reaches us concretely in and through the ritual symbolical action of the Church—the *opus operatum*—and by its penetration into

---

[16]Fransen, p. 17.

[17]Ibid., p. 20.

[18]"Virtus passionis Christi copulatur nobis per fidem et fidei sacramenta." St. Thomas, *Summa Theologiae* (Ed. Leonina, 1886–1906), Ia-IIae, q. 113, a. 4 ad 3; III, q. 49, a. 3 ad 1.

[19]"Fidei efficacia non est diminuta, cum omnia sacramenta ex fidei efficiam habent." St. Thomas, *Comm. in IV Sent.*, IV d. 1, q. 2, a. 6, sol. 2 ad 3.

[20]". . . signa fidei iustificantis." St. Thomas, *Summa*, III, q. 68, a. 4 ad 3, q. 69, q. 5 ad 1.

[21]"Requiritur ipsa fides ut per virtutem passionis Christi, quae in sacramentis Ecclesia operatur, quaerat iustificari a peccatis." St. Thomas, *Summa*, III, q. 84, a. 5 ad 2.

our souls prompts us to accept him in faith and charity—the *opus operantis*.[22]

In this reconciliation of *opus operatum* and *opus operantis* the ecclesial dimension of sacramental reality is the unifying element. The sacraments are indeed efficacious signs because of their intimacy with Christ the primal sacrament and the Church which is the visible extension of Christ in history. Moreover, it is through association with the Church that recipient and minister realize sacramental perfection, intending to do what the Church does.

Contemporary Reflections

The ecclesial dimension of sacramental reality is not something new in an understanding of the sacraments. It has been observed already that this ecclesial perspective was operative in scholastic theology. In our own time, however, the ecclesial element has become a focus of renewed interest. "Characteristic of all the sacraments, deriving from the fact that they involve a proclamation of God's saving presence is the dimension of faith. The sacramental celebration is an invitation to respond in faith to the proclamation and thus enter into interpersonal communion with the community [Church] and with God the Father through Christ in the power of the Spirit."[23]

This provides a fuller context in which to examine sacramental reality. The sacraments are rooted precisely in the activity of the Church. Sacramental action is not independent of the Church which stands as the historical sign by which God wishes to sanctify man. The salvific actions of the Church are efficacious and real because of the Church's relationship to Christ.

Expressing God's salvific will and the nature of the Church the sacraments stand as unique signs of salvation. "But the sign only becomes an actual, realized event of salvation when it is freely and personally accepted."[24]

In reference to the sacrament of matrimony its sacramental definition cannot be realized divorced from an intimate association with the Church. To intend what the Church does is an empty saying without a real reference to the understanding of the community of faith. A sacramental marriage is specified as a work of the Church, a sanctifying action which demands the

---

[22]Fransen, pp. 21–22.

[23]Edward Kilmartin, "When is Marriage a Sacrament?" *Theological Studies* 34 (1973) 276.

[24]Karl Rahner, "Marriage as a Sacrament," *Theology Digest* 16 (1968) 4.

free embrace of the parties. "Marriage is essentially a commission—a task of apostolic sanctification from the partners in marriage to each other, and to the children and the family as a whole."[25]

Baptism, while essential to the Christian sacrament of marriage, is not determinative of that sacrament. "If baptism permits one to exercize the sacrament of matrimony, baptism in and of itself does not effect the sacrament of matrimony."[26] The moment of baptism does not make a Christian; Christianity must be willed and chosen. Far from being a static reality, the sacraments and Christian life are in dynamic harmony and baptism is not the term of Christian existence—rather it is the beginning.

> If sacraments specify the meaning of baptism into Christ through the Christian life, they nevertheless are precisely specifications, distinct from the sacrament of baptism itself. So, two baptized parties who contract a marriage without any reference to the activity of Christ and his Church can hardly be said to be exercizing a sacrament. Matrimony must add to baptism or else it is merely superfluous to hold that it is a sacrament.[27]

The consensus theory has become canonized in the Church's law, praxis, and theology. However, while the Western Church gradually came to interpret this consensus in terms of an identity between contract and sacrament, it is only in our century, with the promulgation of the Code of Canon Law in 1917, that a formal affirmation that the human institution of marriage cannot be separated from the sacrament where baptized persons are concerned has been espoused. However, the major proponents of the identity between contract and sacrament, Pius IX and Leo XIII, predicated this unity in terms of the faithful or Christians. There seems indicated by more than a difference in semantics and word choice. "Faithful" and "Christian" imply more than having been baptized; they bespeak an attitude of vital, no matter how minimal, congress with the community of believers. The conclusion that identifies the human institution of marriage with the sacrament does not necessarily follow from the nature of the case except where the participants recognize in the human situation, however vaguely, the place of God's special presence.[28]

Baptism of itself, without any faith-commitment, is inadequate as the

---

[25]Schillebeeckx, 1:107.

[26]Frank DeSiano, "On the Sacramental Reality of Christian Marriage," *American Benedictine Review* 24 (1973) 500.

[27]Ibid.

[28]Kilmartin, p. 283.

basis for the sacramentality of marriage. Marriage, like all sacraments, is a sacrament of faith. This is not only the faith of the Church; since adults are concerned, it is a sacrament of this faith as it is expressive of the faith of the recipient.[29]

Pope John XXIII in an address to the auditors, officials, and advocates of the Sacred Roman Rota on October 25, 1960, chose to repeat and make his own the words of Pope Pius XII.

> Speaking to a group of newlyweds on April 22, 1942, Pius XII reminded them that marriage is not only an office of nature, but for Christians it is a great sacrament, a great sign of grace and a holy thing, viz., of the marriage of Christ and the Church, accomplished with his blood for the regeneration unto a new life in the spirit for the sons of men who believe in his name. . . . The sign and the light of the sacrament, which raises the office of nature above nature, giving to matrimony a nobility of sublime honesty, which comprehends and reunites it in not only in-dissolubility, but includes everything that goes with the meaning of a sacrament.[30]

The sacramental element which raises marriage in its own nature above nature giving it a new and high value is rooted in the transformation of that nature by Christ. However this reality is perceived and confessed by those who believe in his name. The sacrament is celebrated by the Church and constitutive of the Church. It is acknowledged in faith for the purpose of giving new life to those who believe in his name. Although in and of itself the sacrament stands and signs forth the wedding of Christ and his Church, it cannot be appropriated by the parties to Christian marriage except through their intending to accept that which the Church does. The very being of someone entering Christian marriage "must be permeated with the knowledge of, the constantly renewed choice for, and the sublime acquiescence in the mystery that he and his partner effectively cause and signify, through Christ's power: the external union in love that the Savior manifests for the Church."[31]

The heart of the sacramentality of marriage is rooted in the redemptive

---

[29]Ignatius Kelly, "The Church's Understanding of Marriage," *Studia Canonica* 9 (1975) 279.

[30]John XXIII, *Ad Praelatos Auditores, Officiales et Advocatos Tribunalis Sacrae Romanae Rotae: de coniugii ac christianae familiae sanctimonia*, October 25, 1960: *A.A.S.* 52 (1960) 899–900.

[31]J. Hertel, *When Marriage Fails* (New York: 1969), p. 23.

activity of Christ who stands in relationship to the Church as faithful and saving. "The signing forth of God's rescuing act in Christ, which is the substance of the sacrament, is the signing forth of Christ's going to his death in loving obedience to the Father—of his self-giving, of his commitment of his total person to the purposes of his Father's providence for men."[32] The sacramentality cannot be discussed except in faith and cannot be embraced except by free commitment.

Marriage as a sacrament not only images the saving love which exists between Christ and his Church, but is "a sharing in the covenant of love between Christ and the Church and will manifest the Savior's living presence in the world to all men and the authentic nature of the Church."[33] As a sharing and participation it indeed is a great sacrament. Moreover, as a sharing and participation it demands an affective, free, and deliberate embrace. "It would seem theologically sound that the faith demanded to enter the marriage covenant should be a reflection of the faith demanded of an adult to enter the larger covenant of which marriage is the symbol and efficacious sign."[34] Parties to Christian marriage celebrate a human reality, an event which of its very nature is sacral. This naturally sacral dimension has been transformed through the saving activity of Christ. The natural holiness inherent in marriage is raised above its nature in Christ and this is recognized by the community of believers and lived by the spouses who enter into an intimate association with the continuing salvific action of Jesus the Lord. The profound unity between the human reality and its sacramentality in the case of baptized partners is not realized in the absence of faith. While remaining ordered to a sacramental state by the baptismal character, their unbelief prevents the actualization of this state.[35]

Reflections and Recommendations

Section one of canon 1055 (1983 code) asserts the sacramental dignity of marriage. That marriage is a sacrament in the Christian dispensation is beyond doubt. The early praxis of the Church sustained a belief in the

---

[32]Theodore Mackin, "Consummation: of Contract or of Covenant?" *The Jurist* 32 (1972) 221.

[33]"Proinde familia christiana, cum e matrimonio, quod est imago et participatio foederis delectionis Christi et Ecclesiae, exoriatur, vivam Salvatoris in mundo praesentiam atque germanam Ecclesiae naturam omnibus patefaciet. . . ." *Gaudium et spes*, 48.

[34]Jean Marie Aubert, "Foi et sacrement dans le mariage," *Maison Dieu* 104 (1970) 140.

[35]P. Palmer, "Christian Marriage: Contract or Covenant?," *Theological Studies* 33 (1972) 660.

sacredness of marriage and the great scholastic theologians vindicated this sacramental nature in their theological treatises.

Section two of this same canon posits an absolute identity of contract and sacrament between baptized persons. The absolute nature of such an identification is less defined than is the sacramental significance with which Christ has endowed Christian marriage. Such an identification was not a dogmatic position proposed by the Council of Trent and both the Tridentine debates and post-Tridentine discussion verify the divergent opinion.

Magisterial pronouncements supporting the identity of contract and sacrament are of rather recent vintage. This has been affirmed as an official posture of the Church only within the last two hundred years. This position was provoked less by a more profound study into the sacramentality of marriage, than by increasing attacks challenging ecclesiastical jurisdiction over marriage and the rising spirit of secularization which was especially pronounced in the nineteenth century.

By no means the exclusive proponents of the identity of contract and sacrament, but certainly the most influential were Popes Pius IX and Leo XIII. Their observations on the problem cannot be disentangled from nor considered apart from the broader context of ecclesiastical jurisdiction. Moreover, their reflections on the problem were always voiced in terms of marriage between the faithful, between Christians, between Catholics. The terminology implies a real association with the community of faith. The primary force of their argument focused on the sacramental reality as integral to the human institution of marriage; i.e., in sacramental marriage the sacrament is not merely extrinsic to marriage nor does it stand as an accessory to the contract of marriage. If marriage be a sacrament then the totality of marriage is sacramentalized.

The Church recognizes the existence of valid, nonsacramental marriages between the non-baptized. The question addressed is whether such a possibility exists between the baptized. Can a validly concluded marriage between baptized persons be admitted, although it be lacking in the fullness of being a sacrament?

There is a strong tradition which is supportive of such a possiblity. Duns Scotus who loudly protested the unity of sacrament and contract, admitted the possiblity of separation under certain circumstances. Cajetan and Melchior Cano favored separability and this position enjoyed considerable influence on many of the Fathers of the Council of Trent. "Even the Fathers at Trent did not make that identification although it would thereby have been far easier for them to cope with the challenge of clandestine marriages.[36] Orthodox theologians such as Vasquez, Rebellus, Pontius, Hurtado, Dicatillus, Bonacina, and Tamburini all agreed that separability of contract and sacrament was a real possibility, even for the baptized.[37] An Instruction of the Holy Office on July 6, 1817, admitted the possibility of separation of contract and sacrament by way of exception.[38] Moreover, the draft prepared by the theological commission on marriage for presentation to the fathers of Vatican Council I opposed the doctrine of absolute inseparability between contract and sacrament.[39]

An examination of magisterial texts from the nineteenth century do reveal an identity of contract and sacrament. They cannot, however, be isolated from the jurisdictional struggle which provoked them. Moreover, while the identification is made, the most cogent arguments were concerned with the identification of sacrament and contract—a position conceded even by proponents of *per accidens* separability of contract and sacrament.

Even the great scholastics such as Bonaventure, and Albert, and Thomas Aquinas who were not directly involved in the precise problem of separability demanded a proper intentionality on the part of spouses to sacramentalize marriage. The Councils of Florence and Trent insisted on a proper intentionality of the minister of a sacrament as an absolute requisite to effect a sacrament. Since the spouses themselves minister the sacrament of matrimony, and thus are acting on the level of instrumental causality, a virtual intentionality to sacramentalize must be operative. Such an intention is inconceivable outside some association with the community of faith, no matter how impoverished and vague that association might be.

Contemporary reflection on sacramental reality has insisted on an ecclesial context out of which a more complete understanding of sacrament is being developed. To speculate on the sacrament of marriage, or on any sacrament for that matter, without considering the faith of the Church and

---

[36]William La Due, "The Sacramentality of Marriage," *CLSA Proceedings* 37 (1975) 32.

[37]Cf., G. Vasquez, *De Matrimonio Sacramento*, in *Omnia Opera* vol. VIII, disp. 2, cap. 7. F. Rebellus, *De Obligationibus iustitiae, religionis, et caritatis*, pars. ii, lib. 2, q. 5. B. Pontius, *De Sacramento Matrimonii*, lib. 1, cap. viii. G. Hurtado, *Tractatus de matrimonio et censuris*, disp. 3, diff. 19. J. de Dicastillo, *De Sacramentis*, vol. III, tract. 10, disp. 2, dubit. 19. M. Bonacina, *De Matrimonio Sacramento* in *Opera Omnia*, vol. 1, Ques. 11, punctum 5. T. Tamburini, *Moralis explicatio*, in *Opera Omnia*, vol. 2, lib. viii, *de Matrimonio*, tract. 5, cap. 1.

[38]*Instructio Sancti Officii*, July 6, 1817, in *C.I.C. Fontes* 4:137–138.

[39]Eugenio Corecco, "Il sacredote ministro del sacramento," *La Scuola Cattolica* 98 (1970) 460.

the appropriation of that faith in her individual members would necessarily be incomplete.

The sacrament of marriage incorporates the totality of marriage into the sacramental sphere. In the sacrament the various dimensions of marriage are not denied but rather are elevated and unified into so great a sacrament. However, the reverse equation seems less certain. While a true sacrament permeates and includes the marriage contract, it does not seem a necessary consequence that every valid, natural marriage contract need be a sacrament.

Our investigation prompts us to propose that section two of canon 1055 remains open to further discussion and investigation. Not only pastoral reasons but also a theological and canonical investigation of the sources of this section converge to counsel a broader perspective in which the question of identity of contract and sacrament may be addressed.

In baptism one is ordered to the sacramental state. However, ordination to a state of life is not the same thing as participation in that state of life. If two baptized Catholics estranged from the Church intend marriage on the level of human covenant only, and are as yet unwilling or unable to see any deeper significance in that covenanting, must we insist in law that if such a union is to be celebrated validily, it must necessarily be celebrated sacramentally?[40] Such a position espouses a legal posture that is alien to the theology which provides its basic and fundamental inspiration.

The constant teaching of the Magisterium and the unanimous voice of theologians require a proper intentionality of the minister of a sacrament for its validity. While we ascribe an objective efficaciousness to sacramental reality it is foreign to Catholic thought to propose an automaticness to any sacrament without implicitly affirming the freedom of man to accept or reject—to sacramentalize or not—the graciousness of God manifested in sacramental being.

The present disposition of section two of canon 1055 indicates such an automatic quality. However, no sacrament is automatic, and this is true of the sacrament of marriage. The *ex opere operantis* aspect of the sacrament is not in opposition to the total gratuity and initiative of God, rather it is complementary to it.

All sacraments are "sacraments of the faith. They not only presuppose faith but by words and objects they also nourish, strengthen, and express it."[41] Marriage *qua* sacrament cannot be considered outside this dimen-

---

[40]La Due, p. 33.

[41] "Fidem non solum supponunt, sed verbis et rebus etiam alunt, roborant, exprimunt; quare fidei sacramenti dicuntur." *Sacrosanctum Concilium*, 59.

sion. As sacrament it is anchored in "a participation in the love between Christ and his Church."[42] Such a sublime sharing cannot be legislated by a legislative faculty except if it be first appropriated by the spouses in faith. As sacrament, marriage involves an ecclesial mission "to show forth to all men Christ's living presence in the world, and the authentic nature of the Church.[43] Our present legislation as manifest in canon 1055, §2 continues to favor an absolute identity between contract and sacrament, validity and sacramentality. We would suggest that such an identification, while it may be normative, need not be absolute. In a marriage between the faithful the sacrament of marriage incorporates the natural contract into itself and the total reality becomes sacramentalized. This is normative in the marriage of Christians. However, *per accidens* or by way of exception it can so happen that baptized persons may contract marriage without any reference to its sacramental being.

The present disposition of the law enunciated in canon 1055, §2 imposes sacramentality upon all baptized persons. It equates baptism and faith and fails to provide adequately for the intentionality required of the minister of the sacrament. For the Christian believer such an imposition is not necessary; one would naturally embrace the sacrament.

However, for those members of the Protestant communion for whom marriage is considered as nothing more than an *officium naturae* and whose credence cannot encompass a sacramental dimension to such a marriage, a proper intentionality to sacramentalize their marriage is absent. Rather than impose a sacramentality by legal prescription should we not recognize a natural validity to such a union? Baptized Catholics who are estranged from the ecclesial community may intend nothing more than a human conjugal covenant. Under the present law the only option open to them in terms of a valid marriage is a sacramental union. Can we legislate a sacramental covenanting devoid of Christian faith?

In the objective order marriage enjoys a sacramental dignity. This is an incontestable truth of the Christian faith. However, "truth cannot impose itself except by virtue of its own truth which wins over the mind with both gentleness and power."[44] We suggest, therefore, that section two of canon 1055 is of normative value for the ecclesial community. However, we urge

---

[42]". . . quod est imago et participatio foederis dilectionis Christi et Ecclesiae, . . ." *Gandium et spes*, 48.

[43]". . . exoriatur, vivam Salvatoris in mundo praesentiam atque germanam Ecclesia naturam omnibus patefaciet. . . ." Ibid.

[44]". . . nec aliter veritatem sese imponere nisi vi ipsius veritatis, quae suaviter simul ac fortiter mentibus illabitur." *Dignitatis humanae*, 1.
p. 49

that this section be so revised as to reflect the nuanced but real distinctiveness between *Christifideles* and those who have been baptized but whose faith has failed to mature. Because of this we suggest a revision of this section that incorporates the original language of Pius IX and Leo XIII who addressed the unity of contract and sacrament in terms of the faithful.

Such an emendation not only provides an interpretive principle faithful to the tradition, but also integrates the principles of Catholic sacramental theology and embraces the renewed ecclesial awareness promoted by Vatican Council II.

DOCTRINAL IMPLICATIONS OF CIVIL MARRIAGE BETWEEN CATHOLICS*

THOMÁS RINCÓN

I. GENERAL STATEMENT OF THE PROBLEM

Current canonical discipline establishes that everyone baptized in the Catholic Church is subject to canonical form for validity of marriage (c. 1117). On the other hand, common doctrine considers any marriage a sacrament if it is between baptized persons; for the baptized, it is not possible to have a true marriage which is not also a sacrament (c. 1055). However, two situations have arisen to complicate the question and to place in discussion both the advisability of the canonical form for validity, and the inseparability between marriage as a natural reality and as a sacrament.

The first of these situations is the disappearance of the subsidiary civil marriage system and the general adoption of the optional or obligatory systems. Regardless of the system enacted by various states, the fact is that Catholics in the optional system have the possibility of choosing *a priori* between a canonical or civil marriage, or in the obligatory system of deciding to stay in the civil marriage, or agreeing *a posteriori* to the canonical marriage. In either case, the Catholic can enter a merely civil marriage, and this is important for the purpose of this study.

Joined with this possibility it is appropriate to mention the other situation, product of a growing secularity of life which in turn influences the secularization of marriage, and pushes the effects of secularization even onto a doctrinal level. We refer to the clear fact that a growing number of Catholics opt for an exclusively civil marriage. The Italian bishops have recently emphasized this by saying that "more and more Catholics are getting married only civilly."[1]

---

*Translation by Bartholomew de la Torre, O.P., of "Implicaciones doctrinales del matrimonio civil de los católicos," *Ius Canonicum* 19 (1979) 77–158. Translated and printed with permission.

[1]Italian Episcopal Conference, "La pastoral de los divorciados casados de neuvo y cuantos viven en situaciones matrimoniales irregulares o difíciles," *Ecclesia* n. 1944 (July 28, 1979) 945.

The basic problem of all these Catholics is the same: they enter a marriage which, according to the doctrine and traditional praxis of the Church, does not exist ontologically, notwithstanding that from a civil perspective it is considered real, is accepted socially, and complies with the sociological needs of those who select it. Also, it covers at least subjectively the minimum requirements of the right to marriage. This, when properly understood, greatly smooths over, in our opinion, the dramatics with which this problem is occasionally described. In other words, many of the problems which arise regarding, for example, the principle of religious liberty, the autonomy of temporal realities and the very right to marry, although objectively real, are stated from a fictitious polemical platform, or as though in a theological or juridical laboratory. Baptized persons without faith, should they actually not have any, will care little whether the Church's magisterium, in which they do not believe, states that their civil marriage is not a marriage or that, if it is a true marriage, it is also a sacrament, a reality in which they also do not believe. Will they feel that their right to make contracts is truncated or that their consciences are violated upon having to contract a sacramental marriage? If the answer were affirmative, it would have to be concluded that those in question basically are not baptized persons without faith, since they feel their consciences moved by the judgment of the Church about civil marriage. And then, rather than a problem dealing with religious liberty or a violation of the right to marry, it is a problem of incoherence with logical practical consequences.

Leaving aside this incidental question, let us go to the bottom of the problem. For this, we consider it necessary to distinguish different situations leading to a civil marriage, as there are several doctrinal and practical implications.

A civil marriage may be entered into by those who, being canonically married, have obtained a divorce through civil law. But this is not the case we are dealing with. This case brings up the topic of indissolubility into which we do not intend to enter. We wish only to deal with those who in their first wedding opt for a civil marriage with no dispensation, excluding the canonical form to which they are obligated as Catholics. The reasons for this phenomenon of our times may be reduced to the following:

a. Many allege a lack of faith, not wanting to present a comedy, a folkloric act contrary to their present state of conscience.

b. Others have been formed to believe that they do not have sufficient faith to approach the sacrament of marriage.

c. There are always those who, despite all this, would enter into a

canonical marriage; but the many pastoral obstacles they
encounter on the way to the altar deflect them decisively to that
solution which is easier for them, the civil marriage.

d. Finally, there are those who choose civil marriage as a
previous and experimental stage, a kind of trial marriage.
They know that "for Catholics," in the recent words of the
Italian episcopate, "the only valid marriage which establishes
them as husband and wife before the Lord is the sacrament for
whose valid celebration the canonical form is required."[2]
They perceive that, in the case of a conjugal crisis, they would
be free to marry a third party.

The problem may be also seen from another perspective. Some lack faith
or do not have sufficient faith, yet due to social reasons or to family
pressure, decide to marry in the Church. For some this is not a sacrament
and for others—according to the Church's doctrine—it is a sacrament, but
received without faith and sacrilegiously. For marriage is a sacrament of
the living which requires the good disposition of the individual and, in the
first place, faith.

Based on these facts, there is a doctrinal current today which proposes to
escape such irregular situations. From the doctrinal point of view it
characterizes them as real, natural marriages. From the pastoral point of
view, it would open the doors to all the sacraments for those civilly
married, but close the doors of the sacrament of marriage to those who do
not believe they are sufficiently mature in their faith, or in their faith
regarding the sacrament of marriage. God, it is affirmed, proposes to
Catholics a marriage alternative, two marriage prospects, equally valid: the
natural for the baptized who have lost their faith or do not have a vivid
faith, and the marriage-sacrament to those who are not only baptized but
show sufficient faith to celebrate a wedding in the Lord.

To opt for the natural path, they say, is not only legitimate but is a
fundamental right of every person and, therefore, also of the baptized.
Consequently, to impede the exercise of this right, according to them, is an
injustice which would result if the thesis of a natural marriage for those
who have excluded Christ from their lives were to be rejected. A legitimate
marriage should not only be that contracted between non-believers or
between a non-believer and a baptized person with a dispensation, but
between the baptized who do not submit to the canonical form. This would

[2]Ibid.

not only be legitimate, according to one author, but also holy and blessed by God if honestly contracted.[3]

In the light of such facts and of the radical solution to which some wish to arrive, our objective is to analyze critically the doctrinal coordinates on which the present stage of the secularizing process of marriage is revolving. We are not concerned with what has originated in secular areas, but with what is sponsored to a great extent by a current of theological and canonical doctrine, certainly minor but able and tenacious when exposing its ideas, regardless of whether they contrast with those of the magisterium of the Church. For in such cases the supporters resort to the easy expedient of an ''updated rereading'' of the magisterial documents and of a contextual interpretation thereof, as we shall later discuss in more detail.

The subject presents two types of problems: those of a doctrinal nature and those of a practical or pastoral nature. Both dimensions today are worthy of study. A correct pastoral solution to the unquestionable problems involved in such irregular situations, however, depends on the answer given to the doctrinal question. This latter, then, should be the one which mainly occupies our attention, though we cannot forget that it is the pastoral question which underlies the whole discussion.

The doctrinal issue could be condensed to these questions: What is a civil marriage of a Catholic, and what reality does it have or what does it signify? May a baptized person enter into a marriage which is not sacramental? May a baptized non-believer enter into the sacrament of marriage?

The practical problem lies in knowing, on the one hand, what is the situation of such Catholics in the Church and what ought it to be, and, on the other, what the pastoral action of the Church towards them should be, considering that the Church, precisely as a mother, does not remove them radically from her bosom, but neither may she deceive them. The maternal love of the Church, according to the recent statement of the Italian bishops, ''wishes to continue being authentic because it is inseparably united with the truth.'' And, referring to the divorced who remarry, they add, ''The Church cannot deceive them, treating them as if they were not in a real situation of moral disorder.''[4]

As Professor Caffarra mentioned recently, many pastoral proposals, based as they are on false arguments, are an erroneous response to a real problem: that of evangelization in general and of evangelization with

---

[3]Cf. J. Moingt, ''Le mariage des chrétiens. Autonomie et mission,'' *Recherches des sciences religieuses* 62 (1974) 111.

[4]Italian Episcopal Conference, p. 945.

respect to marriage in particular.[5] It is true that our present controversies arise from factual observations and from the pastoral preoccupation they inspire. This laudable preoccupation is due to pastoral difficulties and is not intended to change either the doctrine nor the centuries old practice of the Church which is based precisely on that permanent doctrine. Certain authors, however, do call for the establishment of a new theology which may serve as a doctrinal justification for establishing a new law. The established law, it is said, is unfair because it is based on an erroneous theory. Therefore, it will be necessary to construct a new theology which permits new matrimonial laws according to the new symbols of the times. The secularization of life and marriage seems to be one of these new symbols, if we do not misunderstand the thoughts of certain authors.[6]

II. PROPOSED PASTORAL SOLUTIONS AND THEIR DOCTRINAL IMPLICATIONS

According to traditional doctrine and the praxis of the Church, the civil union of Catholics does not constitute them as husband and wife before the Lord, and since between the baptized there cannot be a marriage which *eo ipso* is not a sacrament (c. 1055), a civil ceremony does not constitute them as husband and wife at all. That is, they do not contract objectively, either on the ontological or on the juridical plane, a real marriage. Therefore, their union is illegitimate. But how can this be reconciled with the natural right to marry and the principle of freedom of conscience, in view of which many refuse to marry in the manner established by the Church? Or how can the problem be solved of those who, forced by family or social pressures, actually marry in the Church, but without believing in the sacrament of marriage and in the Church itself? Can those in the first case never marry? Must those in the second case necessarily unite through a sacramental marriage?

Various answers to these questions have been given in recent years. Aside from the traditional solution, there are others which we may call moderate since by themselves they do not question any traditional principle of the Church's doctrine. Implicitly, however, even these moderate postures convey doctrinal implications of a radical nature.

---

[5]Cf. C. Caffarra, "Le lien entre mariage—realité de la creation et mariage-sacrement," *Esprit et vie* 20 (1978) 353–384.

[6]Cf. J.M. de Lahidalga, "Los católicos y el matrimonio civil: ius conditum et ius condendum," *Lumen* 24 (1975) 229, 354; idem, "La Constitución del 78 como pretexto: reconsideración crítica del matrimonio civil de los católicos," *Lumen* 28 (1979) 30–95; idem, "A propósito del matrimonio civil obligatorio de la I República: el planteamiento doctrinal en la presentación de la ley," *Scriptorium Victoriense* 26 (1979) 199–200.

Other solutions have been proposed, especially in the decade of the seventies, which we call radically radical because they intend to break with all theological and canonical tradition regarding the sacrament of marriage and at the same time contradict other theological postulates on which the whole sacramental structure rests. At first glance it is easy to observe that such postures suffer from a lack of methodological precision, frequently confusing the theological, juridical and pastoral planes, calling juridically valid whatever is in reality efficacious or fruitful, and calling juridically invalid whatever may be pastorally inadvisable at a certain moment. In our opinion, what is not considered, or what is not precisely emphasized, is that the sacrament of marriage may be ontologically and juridically valid, but be ineffective at that moment as a channel of grace and even be pastorally inadvisable.[7]

Before analyzing such positions, it should be noted that both the moderates and the radicals are included within the process of secularizing marriage. This process was initiated with the Protestant Reformation, acquired virulence with the regalism of the Catholic countries, met its culminating moment during the French revolution and in the liberalism which served as its ideological basis, and crystalized into the institution of civil marriage as it is today generalized. We are now at a new stage of that process in which it is hoped to answer, through old arguments, new problems originated by the growing secularization not only of marriage but of life itself. When regalists and their theologians, for example, fought for the separation between contract and sacrament, their fundamental pretext was to achieve a juridical-political control over the institution of marriage. Today, when the same is defended and with similar arguments, aside from that same pretext, other new ones come onto the scene, such as the dissolubility of marriage in its natural dimension, or treating as true marriages those which are entered into by Catholics who freely elect the civil form or exclude sacramentality.

For the sake of brevity and inasmuch as it is well known by everyone in general terms, we will not attempt here an historical analysis of that process. However, all our present problems have such a process as their frame of reference. Their analysis thus definitely represents the uncovering of one more stage in that secularizing process, which is characterized by a deep dechristianization of thought and life, which influences theological

---

[7]Subsequently we shall refer more concretely to those authors who deny the inseparability between contract and sacrament and who have affirmed the possibility of a valid *natural* marriage between the baptized, considering faith to be a constitutive element of the sacrament of marriage.

and canonical elaborations, and which sometimes is present when making pastoral decisions.

But it would not be fair to make this introductory statement if we did not mention at the same time that a strong reaction against these secularizing theses have been felt recently in the sounder sectors of theology and of canonical science.[8]

III. MODERATE POSITIONS

A. Liberalization of the Granting of Dispensations from Canonical Form

This proposal tries to apply to non-believing or nonpracticing Catholic groups and communities, as well as to those Catholics who live in special circumstances such as in a mission country, the present discipline on mixed marriages. It is known that Pope Paul VI in his motu proprio *Matrimonia mixta* (1970), while maintaining the obligation of the canonical form as a general standard, nonetheless authorized the episcopal conferences to establish rules whereby that general law could be dispensed in the case of mixed marriages. In the following year, on January 25, 1971, the Spanish episcopal conference established that the canonical form continued to be an indispensable condition for the validity of marriage, but that when there were serious causes which make compliance with such a condition difficult, the local ordinary could dispense from the canonical form.

Could this discipline be extended to those marriages celebrated between Catholics who do not believe or do not practice? In principle no doctrinal obstacle is against the Church's deciding thus. Canon Law gives constant evidence of flexibility in this area, such as the extraordinary form, or the case of mixed marriages. Another example is the Instruction *Sac-*

---

[8]Cf. among others Caffarra, note 5, above; J. Hervada, *El Derecho del Pueblo de Dios*, III: *Derecho Matrimonial* (Pamplona: EUNSA, 1973); idem, *Diálogos sobre el amor y el matrimonio* (Pamplona: EUNSA, 1975), p. 172; idem, "Cuestiones varias sobre el matrimonio," *Ius Canonicum* 13 (1973) 11–190; P. Delhaye, commentaries on "Propositions sur la doctrine du mariage chrétien (Commission Théologique Internationale)," *Esprit et vie* 37 (1978) 497–511; E. Corecco, "L'inseparabilità tra contratto e sacramento alla luce del principio scolastico 'gratia perficit non destruit naturam'" *Communio* 16–17 (1974); L. de Naurois, "Mariage religieux et mariage civil," *Esprit et vie* 18 (1976) 241–151; idem, "Problèmes actuels sur le mariage," *Esprit et vie* 19 (1977) 33–43; F. Bersini, "I cattolici non credenti e il sacramento del matrimonio," *La Civiltà Cattolica* 127 (1976) 547–566; U. Navarette, "El matrimonio de los católicos no practicantes y no creyentes," *Sal Terrae* 61 (1973) 875–885; L. Spinelli, "Matrimonio civile e matrimonio religioso. Problemi e prospettive de iure condendo," *Iustitia* (1975) 432.

ramentalem indolem of the Congregation of the Sacraments, May 15, 1974. In response to the request of the bishops of Brazil, it was permitted that a duly prepared layman under precise and exceptional circumstances could carry out the functions of the qualified witness to marriage.

But would it be legally sound generally to regularize the civil form through an exemption? We doubt it very much, because in the first place it would not solve the heart of the question. Such contracting parties, being exempt from the canonical form, would enter into a valid and sacramental marriage and therefore continue having their anti-sacramental scruples, and in addition the civil judge would be involved in an act with religious repercussions. Furthermore, the indetermination of the concepts ''nonbeliever'' or ''nonpractitioner'' and the consequent risk of subjectivism both from the contracting parties and from the ecclesiastical authority would make inapplicable the law of the canonical form, which would be converted into a dead letter inasmuch as anyone might demand to be dispensed therefrom.[9]

In this regard mention is made of some singular cases such as of mission countries and the well-known phenomenon concerning title to real estate in Haiti. In mission lands, due to ancestral custom, there are Christians who marry first according to the use of their tribes. Since they are obliged to the general law of the canonical form just like all other Catholics, their weddings do not mean anything to the Church, and therefore they are in an irregular situation and may not accept the sacraments. The phenonemon regarding the acquisition of real estate consists in that many Catholics of Haiti do not have a civil marriage because they consider themselves Catholics, yet due to social prejudice neither do they have a canonical marriage.[10] To avoid these irregular situations, would it not be well to legalize the wedding uses of these groups of Chrisitians?

In the case of acquiring real estate, what is sought is more than an exemption from the form or the canonization of those uses; the intention is to evangelize, trying to erase those prejudices which deter them from marrying before the priest. With respect to the missions, judicious use

---

[9]If these concepts could be objectified, or as R. Navarro Valls has stated in ''Forma jurídica y matrimonio canónico. Notas críticas a las tesis canonizadoras del matrimonio civil,'' *Ius Canonicum* 14 (1974) 99, ''while the effective departure from their faith is followed by affiliation with a non-Catholic sect or formal declaration of apostasy,'' there would be no unsaveable inconveniences to sustain the thesis from the restriction of personal freedom of c. 1117 of the new code, or by the same token, of expanded exemptions from canonical form.

[10]Cf. Navarette, p. 881.

could be made of the instrument of exemption as a transitory situation, combining it with a profound evangelization in which the sacramental aspects of marriage would be highlighted and sufficient guarantee would be made for public awareness of the wedding. The reasons defending the maintenance of the canonical form in dechristianized countries are applicable, according to our judgment, in recently Christianized regions. During the first centuries the Church canonically regularized, to put it that way, many of the uses and customs of pagans, purifying them, naturally, of everything which might have contravened the Christian faith. This was in spite of the fact that in her conscience the sacred reality signifying marriage was present. The communities which are most similar to those of the primitive Church are those in missionary countries. The risk of secularizing marriage is therefore minor, in our opinion, if it is accompanied by a deep evangelization such as was brought about gradually in the primitive communities. Whatever the situation, we should not underestimate the pedagogical efficacy of going through a marriage in the form established by the Church.

B. Abolition of the Canonical Form and Canonical Recognition of the Civil Form

There are several arguments used against the present canonical discipline and in favor of deformalizing marriage. Professor Navarro Valls has echoed such arguments, criticizing them on the same level in which they are formulated by bringing up the risk of secularization which would mean a return to the old discipline, and reaffirming the still thriving values always achieved by the canonical form.[11] In addition to those of an historical nature, inspired by the desire to return to the simplicity of the first times, and those of a theological nature, already stated inside the Council of Trent, Professor Navarro Valls meets certain arguments which have gained demagogic tint in our days. I refer to the arguments of those who see at the heart of the canonical form a violation of the freedom and dignity of the human person. He also refutes the arguments of those who, on a juridical level, believe they see in the canonical form a mere formalism contrary to the spirit of canon law and to the Christian concept of marriage itself, which has always stressed the causative value of consent. In this regard and with great ability, Professor Navarro Valls has uncovered "the disconcerting contradiction which such arguments entail, since there is an endeavor to deformalize canonical marriage through the

---

[11]Navarro Valls, pp. 64–107; idem, "La expresión legal del consentimiento matrimonial canónico," *Revista General de Legislacion y Jurisprudencia* 70 (1975) 461–482.

intraecclesial elevation of a superformalized marriage structure: that of civil marriage."[12]

Although the preceding themes are important, our purpose here and now is to highlight the pastoral position, that is, all those arguments which defend the suppression of the form as a solution to the many problems arising from marriages by Catholics who do not believe or do not practice. Such arguments are summarized as follows.

1. The sacrament of matrimony is a sacrament of the living. If it is not received with the proper dispositions, and first of all faith, a sacrilege is committed. To avoid sacrilege, then, liberate them from the form.[13]

2. Once the canonical form is eliminated, marriage in the civil form would be valid, thus legitimizing the situation of those Catholics who refuse to marry before the Church while at the same time respecting their freedom. For it cannot be made obligatory for someone to receive a sacrament if he does not wish to, or if he rejects all religious ceremonial in general, a religious act may not be imposed.[14]

---

[12]Navarro Valls, p. 106.

[13]A frequent pastoral argument used to try to dissuade couples from celebrating a canonical marriage is that of avoiding sacrilege. Yet this idea makes sense only when based on the separability of contract and sacrament. On the contrary, even if sacrilege is avoided the couple are induced to live in concubinage or in a non-marital relationship which in my opinion would amount to a greater fault.

[14]Cf. Ph. Beguerie, "Problèmes actuels dans la pastorale du mariage," *La Maison Dieu* 127 (1976) 25; S. Berlingo, "De matrimonii cura pastorali ac de iure Ecclesiae in ministerio reconciliationis," *Monitor Ecclesiasticus* 101 (1976) 70–82. To find the desired balance "inter actualem deprecabilemque automatismum u.d. sacramentalem atque propositum et periculosum s.d. elitismum," Berlingo proposes as a remedy to grant bishops the right to dispense from the form.

A. Mostaza expresses himself more radically in "Competentia status in matrimonium eiusque limites," *Periodica* 67 (1978) 155–210: "Theorice nulla est difficultas in eo quod Ecclesia agnoscat etiam ut validum matrimonium civile inter catholicos canonizando leges civiles matrimoniales quae oppositae non sint juri divino, etsi propter rationes pastorales obliget suos fideles ad formam liturgicam sub aspectus liceitate."

Corecco in "L'inseparabilità" does not agree with the abolition of canonical form but rather argues for the unification of the juridical form and the liturgical form so that the nuptial blessing would manifest the mediating function of the Church.

J.M. Aubert expresses himself along a similar line in "Foi et sacrement dans le mariage. A propos du mariage des baptisés incroyants," *La Maison Dieu* 104 (1980) 116–143. For him dispensation from canonical form does not solve the pastoral problems nor does the revaluation or acceptance of civil marriage in view of the serious doctrinal difficulties this involves. Consequently, he says, there must be a search for a third way by which the presence

The answer is also clear. Canonical recognition of the civil form does not solve these problems since marriage would continue being a sacrament and would involve, as mentioned before, a civil officer in an act which, having civil formality, would nevertheless have a sacred and sacramental character.[15]

Even the supporters of the radical solutions reject this argument and uphold the present doctrinal arrangement. They say it is preferable, within the present context, to maintain the form because people would only enter a civil marriage, in which they believe, and not the sacrament, in which they do not believe. It is another thing altogether to presume that the contract and the sacrament are separable or, in other words, that the canonical form is identical with the liturgical ceremony. On this presumption, the abrogation of or an exemption from the form would be effective, because with such an exemption, there would be no sacramentalization of marriage through the liturgical rite, and thus one would have a naturally valid marriage.[16] But this assertion belongs to the group which we call radical, since it entails a total rupture with the doctrine and the traditional praxis of the Church.

C. Doctrinal Implications in Abolishing the Canonical Form

It is true that if the ecclesiastical legislator decided to eliminate the requisite of the form, returning to the situation prior to Trent, marriages between the nonbelieving or nonpracticing baptized would in principle, and saving the other essential requirements, be valid and sacramental. Neither objectively nor subjectively would such unions be qualified as irregular or as concubinage.

Would the possible good of some people—though these may be many—justify a change in the Tridentine discipline? Would the ecclesial good identifiable with the salvation of souls be protected by these means? Would a simple form for liceity consequently suffice?[17] We should not lose sight,

---

of the Church would be made essential in the formation of the sacrament, that the sacrament is the result of the collaboration of the priest and the contracting parties, and that the priest is a kind of co-minister.

Unless we are mistaken these positions are a modern restatement of the well-known thesis of Melchior Cano. What is in need of explanation is the compatibility between the thesis of absolute inseparability of contract and sacrament, and the traditional conception of the sacramentality of marriage. For more information see H. Wagnon, "La forme canonique ordinaire du mariage: abolition ou rèforme?" *Acta Conventus Internationalis Canonistarum* (Rome: Typis Polyglottis Vaticanis 1970), 702–718.

[15]Cf. Bersini, p. 564.
[16]Cf. Lahidalga, "La constitución del 78," pp. 80–82.
[17]Cf. Wagnon.

as stated by Professor Fuenmayor, "that through this requisite of the form for validity the Church intervenes—due to reasons of interest, that is because it considers the salvation of souls to be at stake—in the celebration of the marriage among its members, not being satisfied with forming simple judgments of moral value."[18]

It is frequently recalled that the public nature of marriage—a decisive factor in Trent in its fight against clandestine marriages—and the juridical assurance it entails are today guaranteed by the procedures undertaken by modern states.[19] This argument, however, is inconclusive. Undoubtedly secular ordinances with regard to the common good, which is supposed to be the inspiration for family law, guarantee a minimum public act for a marriage; but it is not less true that at the heart of such ordinances there are a great variety of marriage systems and that, in view of the great facility to change residence, the contracting party may flaunt the law of his own country and conceal his civil status in the country of his new residence.

In view of these facts it is necessary to mention that the clandestine marriage of the Middle Ages, with all its inconveniences, might very well reappear today as a new "clandestine" marriage, with different features from the former but with the same consequences, among which is the risk of a double marriage and the consequent fracture in fact of the principle of indissolubility. A clandestine marriage was valid but not demonstrable when intending a second marriage. Would not a canonical marriage celebrated in Spain in civil forum, in spite of all its formalities, run the risk of suffering all the effects of clandestinity when borders of the country are crossed? Do present international standards guarantee absolute publicity of weddings celebrated in any country? It is not easy to answer affirmatively. Hence there rises the doubt as to whether the non-obligation of the canonical form would exclude, today also, the risk of a new clandestinity in spite of the formalisms and safeguards of civil ordinances.

But the decisive arguments in favor of the canonical form, today more than ever, are determined by the doctrinal implications which a possible abolition would entail and which we formulate as follows:

1. Upon eliminating the form, the jurisdiction of the Church over marriage would be weakened at its very root.
2. Upon reducing the jurisdiction of the Church to exhortation or to a mere historical remembrance, the secularizing process of

---

[18]A. de Fuenmayor, "El matrimonio como contrato civil," *Revista General de Legislacion y Jurisprudencia* 71 (1976) 109.

[19]Mostaza, pp. 204–210; Aubert, p. 141.

marriage would hit the bottom. That is, marriage standards and marriage itself would lose even their natural values.
3. Upon secularizing the juridical form, there would be no protection for the liturgical form and the sacramental aspects of marriage.

Put another way, among the functions always carried out by the form, it is advisable today, in view of the progressive secularization of marriage, to highlight the very important role of safeguarding the jurisdiction of the Church over matrimony and of consequently protecting the very nature of the institution of marriage in its natural and sacramental aspects, as devised and desired by God. Anyone can see that we are before issues whose study in depth extends beyond our objectives. However, let us make a few observations in this respect.

1. Form and Jurisdiction of the Church

In order to examine this subject we should first methodologically examine whether the Church has proper and exclusive power over marriage between those baptized, and the juridical foundation of such jurisdiction. However, we consider this to be unquestionable *datum*, although it is still questioned today. For our purposes it is sufficient to refer to the argument from authority, drawn from the Council of Trent and from the subsequent magisterium, such as that of Popes Pius V, Pius VII, Pius IX, Lo XIII and Pius XI, etc. We have here explicit statements of the magisterium in cases where the Church's jurisdiction over marriage in Protestant or civil ceremonies is explicitly attacked.

We need some historical precision, because it is history that is appealed to in order to demonstrate a real inconsistency in the traditional thesis of the Church. In this regard, it is frequently affirmed that the Church lacked jurisdiction during the first ten centuries; that is, originally it was the secular power which exercised all jurisdiction over marriage. It is supposed that, beginning in the eleventh century, the Church started to replace the state in many areas of temporal power, but now the state has matured and secularization has advanced public life beyond the condition it had achieved in Christendom. Everything should flow back now to its primitive and original channel, that is, the Church should restore to the temporal power the regulation and control of that temporal reality called marriage, a jurisdiction which was usurped from the state in the Middle Ages.[20]

[20]Mostaza, pp. 155–210; idem, "La competencia de la Iglesia y del Estado sobre el matrimonio hasta el Concilio de Trento," in *Ius Populi Dei* III (Rome: Pont. Univ. Gregoriana, 1972). In a different sense see M. Gerpe Gerpe, *La potestad del Estado en el*

The derivative thesis denying jurisdiction to the Church requires clearing up the earlier thesis. In fact, the thesis that the Church did not exercise nor was even aware of a dominion over the marriage of Christians in the first centuries is much too sweeping and must be modified. When one glimpses the doctrinal and disciplinary sources of the Church of that period, one quickly discovers that the Church was considered competent not only to govern the conduct of the baptized in accord with divine law, but to regulate the institution of marriage itself. It is true that she frequently assumed the uses, customs and standards both of the pagan emperors at the beginning, and of the Christian emperors after them; but it cannot be denied that the Church was gradually reshaping the nature of marriage and delineating the singular features of marriage between Christians. This profound Christian transformation of marriage not only finds its source in the teaching activity of the Church, but also through its normative activity expressed in conciliar rules, in papal decrees and in custom itself as a creative source of law of great importance in the primitive Church, as is testified to by S. Augustine: "In these matters, about which the divine scriptures have not established anything certain, the custom of the people of God or the teachings of the fathers are to be followed as law."[21]

Going further into primitive sources, it is not difficult to verify the following information.

1. The Church accepted and assumed, as it may today, laws and marriage customs not incompatible with Christian doctrine.
2. The Church did not accept, nor canonize, other Roman standards which were inseparable from a pagan conception of marriage.
3. The Church legislatively expanded certain Roman standards, e.g. some of the impediments of consanguinity and affinity.
4. The Church introduced some standards which had no precedent in Roman law. They were new standards based on religious convictions, such as the new impediments of vows, of public penance, of sacred orders, the prohibition of a second marriage to clergymen, and of any marriage during the Lenten period.
5. In other cases, the Church was decidedly opposed to the standards of the established power and issued its own pro-

---

matrimonio de los cristianos y la noción contrato-sacramento (Salamanca: Instituto "San Raimundo de Peñafort," 1970).

[21]Augustine, Epistula 36: 1, 2 (*P.L.* 33: 136).

visions, showing in the clearest manner her legislative independence and an awareness of her competence regarding marriage.

Among all these standards, those referring to indissolubility are the most important. Here the Church issued her own norms or formalized divine law, punishing with excommunication those following Roman laws against her mandates formulated "not by the civil law, but by the law of heaven," as Augustine would assert. Her laws had to be obeyed by all Christians, "even if Roman laws determine otherwise," to quote Gregory Nazianzen. "And you think it is permitted for you because human law does not prohibit; but divine law does," declared Ambrose. Jerome, in his letter to Oceanus, writes, "One thing are the laws of Caesar, another are Christ's; Papinianus orders one thing, our Paul another."[22]

In the light of this necessarily brief historical reflection, it is not possible to affirm that the Church refrained absolutely from regulating the institution of marriage. Rather, it is worth noting that the Church's many interventions manifest a consciousness of power, although in that period it was not yet explicitly verbalized and certainly not in the technical terms used today to define the concept of jurisdiction. It is clear that the Church exercised not only a prophetic mission through the formulation of moral judgments regarding the value of imperial laws or the conduct of the faithful, but also the *munus regendi* through norms which bound Christians juridically, determining the lawfulness and validity of their weddings, through excommunication in its different degrees. This does not mean that there already existed a finished system of canonical marriage legislation; but it would not be difficult, compiling all the sources, to formulate a real canonical code regarding matrimony organized around the nature of marriage, impediments, consent and form.

In Trent this truth became unquestionable. The Church proclaimed its power to establish diriment impediments, and at the same time condemned those who denied its judicial power over marriage cases: "If someone should say that matrimonial causes do not belong to ecclesiastical judges let him be anathema."[23]

---

[22]Cf. T. Rincón, "La doctrina sobre la indisolubilidad del matrimonio en el primer milenio cristiano," *Ius Canonicum* 13 (1973) 106–107. Pope Leo XIII in his encyclical *Arcanum* (*CIC Fontes* III: 159) recalls the absurdity of thinking, as many do, that the Church may have usurped power over marriage from secular rulers even with their consent. He also shows how the Church has exercised this right from the beginning with standards which sometimes were opposite to those established by the emperors.

[23]Council of Trent, sess. XXIV, c. 12.

According to Professor Fuenmayor, the Church at Trent reaffirmed, as a dogmatic principle, its divine origin and consequently its jurisdiction.[24] Anathema was pronounced against those who deny the sacramental nature of marriage or its properties of unity and indissolubility, and the competence of ecclesiastic judges in marriage cases. The Council not only formally affirmed its jurisdiction; it also exercised it through the *Tametsi* decree and the imposition of the canonical form for validity.

Therefore, we will delay no longer on the subject of jurisdiction, but will move on to examine its relation with the form of marriage. As stated by Professor Navarro Valls, "Not only are categories of public contracts at stake in the subject of the canonical form, but something more profound: the maintenance of the Church's jurisdiction over canonical marriages."[25] Aside from other functions, he continues, the form "is undoubtedly a very firm bastion for the conservation of both the Church's jurisdiction as well as of the requirements for marriage delineated by Christ in its new institution."[26] All of this illustrates that the thesis which would abolish canonical form is nothing other than a tendency to abolish the Church's own jurisdiction.

It could be asked, if this were so, how one can explain the fact that for centuries the Chruch did not have any canonical form, yet not only did it not lose its jurisdiction, but gradually increased it. What is the reason for the canonical form being today, in comparison to the past, an instrument which protects the jurisdiction of the Church?

In my opinion, the reason may be found in the different secular situations into which the Church has been put. The primitive Church was inserted into a pagan world which it had to Christianize, starting with the people, and through them the institutions, among which marriage was prominent. At present the Church acts in general in a paganized environment which has been dechristianized and which she now must rechristianize. The differences are, in my opinion, important. It is not the same to have a pagan society in which the seed of Christian faith is being progressively deposited, and to have a paganized, secularized society which for centuries lived the Christian faith but which is now progressively renouncing its beneficial influences not only with regard to the supernatural, but also with regard to the human and the social orders as well. The difference lies, in my opinion, in that the Christian values which the

---

[24]A. de Fuenmayor, "El matrimonio y el Concordato español," *Ius Canonicum* 3 (1963) 283.

[25]Navarro Valls, "La expresión legal," p. 478.

[26]Ibid.

Church tries to instill need a greater protection in the present situation than they did previously. In former times, the Christian postulates which the Church offered to a society that was pagan were accepted or rejected by it. The basic interest of the pagan society was to protect its own cultural patrimony, while the Christian patrimony as such did not suffer any detriment, although Christians suffered persecutions. Today, on the contrary, it is the paganized society which can drag its secularization into the Christian institutions and structures. That is, our institutions themselves—in this case marriage—can suffer the same fate as society in not mediating the reviving influence of the Church. Today it is the society which tries to influence the Christian patrimony, secularizing it. This different and indeed inverse situation strongly motivates the Church to use every possible means to protect marriage, an institution dangerously exposed to total secularization. Without doubt, the dike against this current secularizing of marriage is constituted not only by the prophetic word of the Church evangelizing in a multitude of ways, but also by her normative and jurisdictional power over marriage, which she holds by divine right and not by delegation from a temporal power.

2. Form and Secularization of Marriage Norms

This jurisdictional power would turn little by little into a simple relic of the past if it were not protected by the canonical form for validity. To be married in the Church, therefore, is something more than a simple formality. It also means to be married by the Church, that is, to be married according to the regulations of the Church, which is the authentic guarantor of natural law. It means, finally, to uphold the normative power of the Church over the marriage of the baptized. Not to be joined substantially because not done before the Church entails the possibility of marrying before a secular entity with the risk of originating a union which is not precisely that of marriage according to the plan of God.

In theory, it is true that the *kind* of marriage is one thing and its *form* is another, as when a canonical marriage follows a civil ceremony. But it is not less true that in fact the criterion for knowing whether a marriage is canonical or civil is none other than its form. Therefore there are authors who define the nature of marriage, civil or canonical, by its form. When the ceremony is civil (although it is canonized), it is immediately thought that the applicable law and the competent judge is the civil one.

No wonder Professor Fuenmayor states: "If the Church accepted as sacramental the civil unions of Catholics—leaving harmless and without vitality the doctrine of inseparability between contract and sacrament—the role of the Church would be practically reduced to nothing. The hypothesis that civil marriage should be substantively canonical, as has been rightfully said, 'would suppose a clear regression in time, which would forget the fundamental reasons underlying the Church's jurisdiction over marriage,' summarized in the need for marriage to be, through juridical determinations, adjusted to the demands of the natural and divine law. These demands are unknown, to a greater or lesser extent, by a large proportion of civil marriage systems.''[27]

In other words, the canonization of the civil form would first require the Church to surrender to the State jurisdiction over marriage, even though afterwards the secularized juridical structure would not always measure up to the requirements of divine, natural and positive law. One need only think of divorce laws to wonder if what is regulated today by many States may really be called marriage, or whether it is the mere living together, more or less lasting, of a couple which one day decided to share certain things, and not always strictly conjugal ones. As Professor Lombardia recently stated, "State ordinances are not permeated with the principles of natural law,"[28] and therefore it is an unavoidable task for the Church to have tutelage over marriage. This tutelage would be impossible if only a power of moral judgment is granted to the Church.

In conclusion, in our opinion the form has today the fundamental function of protecting the jurisdiction of the Church, while it protects, consequently, the natural institution of matrimony. Moreover, by protecting natural marriage, the form is safeguarding the only possible natural basis for the sacrament. Therefore there are not only juridical, but theological reasons as well, which urge the maintenance of the Tridentine discipline. A denaturalized marriage would be a non-marriage, and when there is no marriage there can be no sacrament. The pastoral problems of Catholics married civilly, while they are real, yield before the importance of preserving those substantial values.

IV. RADICAL SOLUTIONS AND THEIR DOCTRINAL IMPLICATIONS

Whether the canonical form is maintained or eliminated, the fundamental problem purdures. Other ways, then, should be taken in order not to leave those married by the civil form in a blind alley or before an unsolvable dilemma: whether to contract a sacrament or not to marry at all.

---

[27]Fuenmayor, p. 109.

[28]P. Lombaría, "El matrimonio en España, cara al futuro," in *Instituciones canónicas y reordenación jurídica* (Salamanca, 1979), pp. 70–71.

For some, one such alternative to solve that dilemma consists in having the Church give a natural value to civil marriage so that the baptized can elect a real non-sacramental marriage, a marriage which is a natural institution or even a sacrament of nature, which is not therefore a sacrament of the new law.[29]

According to these proposals, what happened in the history of salvation as a whole should happen in the personal history of the human couple. Natural marriage should have that consistency which the sacrament of nature had, until through faith (not through baptism) those married enter into the mystery of Christ and the Church. Thus it happens that natural marriage (of which the civil ceremony is an expression) is the initiation of a path to be followed until the sacramental plenitude is obtained through faith. Between one state and the other, according to one author, there is an interval of reflection and experience in which the Church should not be absent. This is why the Church should be pastorally present from the start at the celebration of nonsacramental marriages through the use of appropriate rites, including a blessing. This first sacrament of nature would be like the prelude and preparation for the sacrament of the new law.[30]

If I refer to this dimension of the radical statement it is because there are several authors who, upon admitting the validity and consistency of natural marriage, consider that such a marriage has not acquired its ontological plenitude until it becomes a real sacrament once the obstacle of the lack of faith is removed. So Bernhard, faithful to his idea of the existential consummation expressed in another context, states that the sacrament of marriage, more than a static reality, is a dynamic reality which permits evolution and progress. Consequently, he says, a distinction should be made between the plenitude of the sacrament and other sacramental species and states which are more or less developed.[31]

Other authors have compared natural marriage—basically a civil marriage—with the catechumenate, without being aware that the problem is different because it is a case of marriage between baptized.

---

[29]Cf. Moingt, pp. 71–116; Lahidalga, "La constitución del 78," pp. 78 ss; J. Manzanares, "Habitudo matrimonium baptizatorum inter et sacramentum: omne matrimonium duorum baptizatorum estne necessario sacramentum?" *Periodica* 67 (1978) 35–71; Mostaza, "Competencia status," p. 197; J.M.F. Castaño, "De quibusdam difficultatibus contra formulam c. 1012, §2," *Periodica* 67 (1978) 269–281; J.M. Diaz Moreno, "La regulación canónica del matrimonio," *Pentecostés* 13 (1975) 227–252; idem, "Reflexión jurídica sobre la pastoral de las uniones irregulares," *Estudios eclesiásticos* 53 (1978) 291–320.

[30]Cf. especially Moingt, pp. 112 ss.

[31]Cf. J. Bernhard, "Competentia Status in matrimonium, Introductio," *Periodica* 67 (1978) 152.

Manzanares has also defended the validity of civil marriage in its natural dimension. He claims that as long as it contains everything ethically necessary for a real marriage, it does not lack value with regard to salvation, although lack of faith is something contrary to Christ's redemption. According to him, one could even talk about a certain natural generic sacramentality, but not of a real sacrament of the new law, an effective symbol of grace. Notwithstanding, such a natural marriage will not obtain its ontological perfection unless it is through the real sacrament, once the obstacle of lack of faith is removed.[32]

Addressing the same issue, Lahidalga—the author who deals with this subject most frequently—states that the civil marriage of Catholics is a non-sacramental valid marriage, although it is sacramentalizable since baptism gives the capacity for sacramentalization. For the sacrament, however, is not the result of some baptismal automation, but depends on the intention and will of the contracting party: the passing from a sacrament of nature to a sacrament of the new law is a personal option of the baptized. The civil marriage of Catholics, therefore, is a legitimate marriage such as that contracted between the non-baptized, but having a difference: that of the non-baptized is only remotely sacramentalizable, and that of the baptized is immediately sacramentalizable due to the radical capacity granted by baptism.[33]

As may be observed, serious doctrinal difficulties are hidden in these statements. We shall deal with the following:

1. Separability of contract-sacrament;
2. Undervaluation of the baptismal character;
3. Overvaluation of the rite and of sacramental intention in marriage.

Everything might be summarized by saying that this doctrinal current is strongly affected by an extrinsic conception of the sacramentality of marriage, new in its pastoral motivations but as old as that already formulated by Duns Scotus in the fourteenth century. Let us go, then, to the analysis of these questions. We shall try to unify the matter by tracing all problems to the fundamental question of the inseparability between marriage and sacrament. Once this central issue is cleared, it will be easy to solve the collateral themes already noted as well as others which will be appearing during the course of the exposition.

In fact, the undervaluation of baptism with regard to the sacrament of

---

[32]Manzanares, p. 70.
[33]Lahidalga, ''La constitución del 78,'' p. 86.

marriage may only take place when it has not been well understood that the sacramentality of marriage is inserted ontologically—and therefore inseparably—into the nature of marriage. The same occurs when the sacramental rite and intention are given constitutive worth, introducing an extrinsic value—and therefore, separable—in the formation of the sacrament of marriage considered only as a sacrament with no regard to its nature as a marriage.

V. Inseparability of Contract-Sacrament

A. Historical notes

1. A Preliminary Clarification

We cannot elude the historical statement of the problem, because it is on an historical basis that the present theses are intended to be sustained. Moreover the reiterated doctrine of the Church in this regard is evidently situated within an historical context. There are those who intend on that basis to invalidate today that doctrine since it does not correspond to the cultural coordinates of present times. A critical and updated rereading of these magisterial teachings, their precise contextualization or, as one author says, a study of their cultural totality, are essential requirements for a good hermeneutic.[34]

Furthermore, there are few authors who do not introduce this theme historically when dealing with it. But something unaccustomed occurs which I wish to emphasize: in general they start their history of this theme when it starts to be debated formally. It seems logical to do this, but with the condition that the earlier evidence be presented, according to which during many centuries, concretely until the fourteenth century, they taught and lived the doctrine of inseparability by connaturality, because contract and sacrament were included in the same Christian conception of marriage. It would suffice to mention two facts. The first was given by an author who is a strong defender of separability. According to him—and I believe this happened—Christians in the first centuries were married like everybody else—"civilly," we would say today. At the beginning the greater part of pagans who converted to Christianity were already married. Afterwards, those who were already Christians married as everybody else. The cere-

---

[34]R. Rincón, "Identidad real entre contrato y sacramento en el matrimonio de los bautizados," *Pentecostés* 15 (1977) 37–75.

monies were identical. Their marriage was a terrestrial, secular reality, but "lived in the Lord."[35]

On the other hand, the same author states—and this is one of the fundamentals of the separationist thesis—that it is not baptism but the will, the intention or the free option of the baptized which converts the natural union into a sacrament.

In the light of these two assumptions, a forceful question arises. How many pagans, married and afterwards converted into Christianity, and at the same time, how many Christians who married, had the sacramental intention to use their baptismal capacity to convert their marriages into the sacrament?

I leave the answer in suspension, although it is my belief that if the premise is right (of the need for an option of the baptized to elect between natural marriage or sacramental marriage), Christ would have indeed instituted the sacrament of marriage, but the sacramental reality would have begun to exist in the concrete only after many centuries of the history of the Church. Do not argue from what happened with the other sacraments about which for centuries there was no reflective awareness that they were effective symbols of grace, because the problem is a different one. In fact, not for lack of awareness of the sacramentality as a theological concept, neither baptism nor the Eucharist failed to exist, because people did not have a conscious and theological awareness of their sacramentality. But those sacraments as well as others did require a rite for their constitution, and the rite already implied an intention expressed in some formula. Now then, marriage is not comparable with the water of baptism nor with the bread of the Eucharist. No rite having a constitutive value was then required nor is it required now. It is sufficient to contract a real marriage in whatever form—if there was none established, as in the first centuries—for that union to be elevated through the action of Christ to a sacrament. If this were not so, few marriages—at least during the first centuries—would have been sacramental, few Christians would have had avilable that current of grace which is also the sacrament of marriage. At present innumerable marriages between Christians would not reach the status of a sacrament because of the lack of an option or of a clearly sacramental intention.

Though I can but briefly refer to it here, I have been able to investigate many centuries of the history of Christian marriage. The result of this investigation is summarized in that the significant factor penetrates so intimately the entire structure of marriage that marriage and sacrament

---

[35]Lahidalga, "La constitución del 78," p. 70.

never appear as two realities accidentally and extrinsically overlapped. The sources, from the patristic to the most juridical, present us with marriage as a natural reality but full, even from its origin in paradise, of the dimension of a sign; this is true whether the sources interpret marriage prophetically, or whether when the signified mystery, the union of Christ and the Church, has been made objectively present (potentially or in act) by baptismal incorporation.[36] Think, for example, of the famous medieval polemic of the *"consensus-copula."* This polemic can be understood only in the context of the significative function of marriage. In summary, the factors which cause marriage, the intimate structure of marriage, the supreme law which orders it and gives it sense, the foundation which is not unique though it is ultimate and does illuminate and reinforce the essential characteristics of unity and indissolubility, is the sacramental significance which saturates from the inside the whole of the marriage reality as such. To speak, then, of a separability of the sacramental or significiant factor of marriage in the ninth century or in the thirteenth century, would be the same as denaturalizing the very nature of marriage, which is a symbol and a mystery, or a significant mystery and a producer of grace by the action of Jesus Christ, which is actualized when the human couple through baptism has been elevated ontologically to the order of Redemption.

After this qualification of an historical nature, let us see the most important milestones of the polemic with which we are dealing.

2. Classical Theologians Denying Inseparability

In my opinion, Duns Scotus is the first of all the theologians to deny inseparability. Moreover, he is the father of all subsequent currents, since his doctrine on the sacramentality of marriage represents the germ from which all postures contrary to inseparability will be born, including those in our days. With Tejero it may be said of the *Doctor subtilis* that "neither at the time of demonstrating that marriage is a sacrament, nor when explaining the nature of its sacramental being, nor when manifesting the effects related with the sacrament, does he consider the nature of marriage as a sign."[37] For him the sacrament was "something added, something which God 'attached to the matrimonial contract.'" Note that the concept of annexation is not the same as the concept of elevation employed by the

---

[36]Cf. T. Rincón, "Siglos IX al XIII," in *El Matrimonio Misterio y Signo* (Pamplona: EUNSA, 1971); cf. also E. Saldon, "Siglos I a S. Augustín," ibid.; E. Tejero, "Siglos XIV–XVI," ibid.; idem, "La sacramentalidad del matrimonio en la historia del pensamiento cristiano," *Ius Canonicum* 14 (1974) 11–31.

[37]Tejero, "Siglos XIV–XVI," p. 46.

magisterium and included in c. 1055. For the *Doctor subtilis*, marriage is one thing, the contract of marriage another, and the sacrament something else again."[38] This conception of sacramentality is in open and radical contradiction to the doctrinal postulates of previous developments.[39]

Perhaps as a consequence of this extrinsic conception of sacramentality, Duns Scotus arrived at a conclusion which has served as an argument from authority for those defending separability: for sacramentality to be produced a form is necessary, that is, a sensible sign perfectly audible. Among dumb people, consequently, there may be a valid marriage, but due to a substantial defect of form, it cannot be sacramental.[40] Nothing is more logical than the requisite of a sensible and audible factor when sacramentality is understood as an extrinsic superimposition on the reality of marriage.

One century later, Cajetan (1468–1534) added one more situation: marriage contracted by proxy. It is possible to execute a contract by proxy, as it is possible to carry out judicial acts through the same means, but neither is marriage in that case a sacrament of the Church, nor could the sacrament of penance be either.[41]

Gabriel Vázquez (1549–1604) is one of the more cited authors in this respect. For him, the sacramentality of marriage, states Tejero, consisted exclusively in its capacity to cause grace. "Any other aspect of the sacramental symbol . . . instead of being ignored, is positively demolished by the author."[42]

> The signification attributed by Vázquez to marriage is not real signification, but a relation of similarity, which leaves marriage sunken in its own self, without participating in the union of Christ

---

[38]Duns Scotus, *In IV Sententiarum questiones subtilissimae*, dist. XXVI, q. I, n. 16; cf. Tegero, "Siglos XIV–XVI," p. 48.

[39]Consider, for example, the matrimonial doctrine of Hincmar of Rheims in the ninth century, of the authors of the school of Laon in the twelfth century, of Hugh of St. Victor, of Peter Lombard, of the great canonists of the twelfth and thirteenth centuries such as Rufino and Hostiensis, etc. For all of them the sacramental significance is such a part of marriage that even the debates on the nature of marriage, when marriage comes about, and the essential features of the bond, are not totally understood if they depart from the revealed data that marriage has been configured in itself as a mysterious sign of God's love for humankind, a love which acquires its fullness in the incarnation of the Word or in the union of Christ with His Church. Cf. T. Rincón, "Siglos IX al XIII"; idem, "Relevancia jurídica de la significación sacramental del matrimonio," *Ius Canonicum* 9 (1969) 465–488.

[40]Cf. Caffara, p. 354.

[41]Ibid.

[42]Tejero, "Siglos XIV–XVI," p. 483.

with his spouse. The value itself of the memorative signification has been killed—first cause of our sanctification. Consequently, Vázquez has also killed the value of the *res et sacramentum*, abandoning the conjugal institution to its own natural being. In other words: we are in line with Protestant thought, in spite of Vázquez' care lest his words be so considered.[43]

For the purpose of our subject, the principal part of his thought lies in the accidental nature which he gave sacramentality. If sacramentality is a mere accident superimposed by Christ without affecting substantially the reality of marriage as such, the consequence extracted by Vázquez was that neither baptism nor the intention to marry suffices to produce the sacrament. The reality of marriage is identical in the baptized and in the unbaptized. If there is no intention for the sacrament, what the baptized achieve is as valid as whatever the non-baptized do, but this would not be a sacrament.

As is well known, the Spanish author Melchior Cano is the theologian who presented, according to the expression of Tejero, the most sacralized vision of the sacrament of marriage. Prescinding from its signification, the only thing which he emphasized is that the sacramentality of marriage necessarily requires the intervention of the priest as the minister of the sacrament, faithful to his idea that all sacraments—including marriage—demand a sacred rite, a religious ceremony. Through this means it is difficult to explain the real identity between marriage and sacrament.[44] That is, through a different path, even opposite, Melchior Cano comes to the same conclusion as previous writers. This is because at the bottom there is a common meeting point between them: the noncomprehension that the sacramentality of marriage—signification and grace—is ontologically included in the reality of marriage itself.[45]

3. Defenders of Inseparability

a. Robert Bellarmine (1542–1621)

As stated by Caffarra, the contribution made by Cardinal Bellarmine is without doubt the most decisive historically with regard to our subject,

---

[43]Ibid., p. 492; Caffarra, p. 355; Corecco, "L'inseparabilità"; L. Acevedo, "Controversia sobre la inseparabilidad del contrato y el sacramento en el matrimonio cristiano," *Franciscanum* 19 (1977) 231–299.

[44]Cf. Tejero, "Siglos XIV–XVI," p. 294; Caffarra, p. 258; Corecco; Acevedo.

[45]For this same reason we did not previously understand the contemporary position of Corecco, Aubert and others (see note 14).

since the teaching of the Church is generally based on it. His thesis is clear: "Among Christians, no legitimate marriage is celebrated which is not at the same time a sacrament."[46]

> Marriage is a sacrament of the Church: for among Christians a legitimate marriage contract is not separated from the sacrament of marriage, for every lawful contract of marriage is by this very fact a sacrament of marriage. Therefore to judge that a contract of marriage is lawful is to judge that the contract is a sacrament: but to judge the sacraments pertains to the Church.[47]

But I do not wish to ignore something that I also consider decisive in understanding this problem. I refer to the consideration of sacramentality of marriage not only *in fieri*, but also *in facto esse*. Regarding this, the thought of Bellarmine is very clear:

> The sacrament of marriage can be considered in two ways. First, while it is coming into being. The other, in its abiding reality, after it has come into being. Matrimony is like the Eucharist which is a sacrament not only when it is confected but even while it remains: therefore as long as the spouses are alive, their marital society is a sacrament of Christ and of the Church."[48]

b. Tómas Sáchez (1550–1610)

His thought is similar to that of Bellarmine and may be summarized by the following points. Following Pedro de Ledesma, Sánchez concludes that those baptized, when marrying, cannot exclude sacramentality "because by the institution of Christ the sacrament and the contract are inseparably united."[49] Baptism is a necessary factor for sacramentality. The unbaptized, except in a broad and improper sense, are incapable of the sacrament because baptism is the door of the sacraments. Nevertheless, marriage between the unbaptized, once they are baptized, becomes a true sacrament "because when they are baptized, that marriage represents the union of Christ with the Church for the contract perseveres and is made indissoluble by the faith of Christ."[50]

Perhaps the most important contribution of Sanchez is that of emphasiz-

---

[46]Cafarra, p. 356; cf. also Corecco, Acevedo.

[47]Tejero, "Siglos XIV–XVI," p. 455, note 213.

[48]Ibid., p. 358.

[49]Ibid., p. 471; cf. Caffarra, p. 358.

[50]Tejero, "Siglos XIV–XVI," p. 471; cf. Caffarra, p. 358.

ing the *in facto esse* (i.e., the societal aspect) of marriage and the sacrament, making his the doctrine of Bellarmine matching the sacrament of marriage with the Eucharist, which not only is a sacrament while it is coming into being but also while it remains. Sanchez also makes his the doctrine of St. Thomas Aquinas on the *res et sacramentum* applied to marriage.[51]

4. Council of Trent

The inseparability of contract-sacrament and the priest's benediction as a form of the sacrament were discussed at the Council of Trent with reference to the condemnation of clandestine marriages, that is, as possible reasons for such a condemnation and for the establishment of a form for validity.

Recent authors of separationist theses have mentioned such debates and seek support in the authority of those fathers who in these debates had theses similar to their own. A curious importance is given by them to the doctrine of the Archbishop of Granada, Pedro Guerrero, who affirmed with all clarity the separability: "There can be matrimony without . . . the sacrament even for a baptized person who wishes to contract marriage but does not wish to receive the sacrament because it cannot be conferred against one's will."[52]

The truth is, as underlined by Caffarra, that these explanations and reasons were present only in the beginning. Ultimately only the reason of personal inability passed: they could prohibit clandestine marriages, disqualifying the persons. The attempt to establish and justify the power exercised by the Church on the basis of the distinction between contract and sacrament was rejected. If it is true that Trent did not define the question and did not condemn its authors, it is also true that it opened the way or suggested the direction which would be followed later by pontifical teachings, invoking explicitly the Council of Trent.[53] This conclusion of Caffarra is clear, because the disqualification of the contracting parties to marry if they do not follow the prescribed form, entails an incapacity for the sacrament, considering that the existence of the latter is based on the

---

[51]Cf. Tejero, "Siglos XIV–XVI," p. 472, note 259. I insist that it seems to me a significant fact that both Bellarmine and Sanchez formulated their doctrine on the sacramentality of marriage, which would be subsequently held by the papal magisterium, from the perspective not only of sacrament *dum fit* but also *dum permanet*. At the present time all of the accent is placed on the *in fieri* which may be the key to the deviations from this matter.

[52]Cf. Lahidalga, "La constitución del 78," p. 53; Manzanares, p. 37.

[53]Caffarra, pp. 359–361.

real existence of marriage. As is stated by Cardinal Bellarmine, to judge whether a marriage between Christians is legitmate (i.e. real) is to judge at the same time if it is a real sacrament.

5. Legalism and Liberalism: Doctrine of the Pontiffs

Cafarra[54] distinguishes two phases within this period: the first covers the seventeenth and eighteenth centuries, during which the doctrinal bases are laid in an attempt to justify the legislative and judicial authority of the State over marriage. Such bases are the separation between the real, natural and political contract, and the sacrament. It pertains to the State to regulate the contractual dimension, and to the Church the religious-sacramental. The second phase of this period, which corresponds with the nineteenth century, is characterized by the creation of the juridical institution of civil marriage, whose historical journey we shall not go over since it is well known. We note only the fact that together with the regalism of the previous phase coincident with the previous regime, a new ideological factor comes onto the scene, clearly operative in the French revolution and in the history of civil marriage. We refer, as is obvious, to liberalism.

It is true that regalism, in its different historical forms, as well as liberalism intend ultimately to extract from the Church all jurisdiction over marriage; but they do it from a doctrinal platform which will provide the Church the occasion to formulate doctrinal principles concerning the sacramentality of marriage—principles which extend the historical occasion by becoming permanent doctrine.

Modern authors[55] consider as an irrefutable fact that all the pontiffs of this period confirmed the traditional doctrine of the Church, concentrating at first (Pius VI, Pius VII) on making clear the legislative and judicial competence of the Church over the marriage-sacrament understood as a single reality. The later popes continued to condemn the doctrinal bases on which regalists and liberals sustained their intention to detach the Church

---

[54]Ibid., p. 361.

[55]J. Arias Gómez, "Doctrina católica sobre la indisolubilidad matrimonial," *Scripta Theologica* 10 (1978) 291, follows the same line as the statement that "some modern authors, looking for a papal opinion, turn to the doctrine of Benedict XIV as an authority in trying to resurrect the theory of the separability between contract and sacrament already considered by the ordinary magisterium." The opinion of these authors—J.M. Díaz Moreno, A. Mostaza, and J. Manzanares specifically—was based not on a papal document but on a scholarly writing of Prospero Lambertini while he was bishop of Bologna and not Sovereign Pontiff. "But what is more," continues J. Arias, "Benedict XIV himself, in a brief which is actually a papal document, written in the last days of his pontificate, March 1–9, 1758, entitled *Paucis abhinc*, recalled explicitly the doctrine of inseparability." (*CIC Fontes* II, n. 11, p. 575.)

from jurisdiction over marriage as a reality separable from the sacrament; at the same time they formulated in a positive manner the true theological and canonical doctrine on marriage of the baptized.

Pope Pius VIII in the encyclical *Traditi humilitati* (May 21, 1829) marked a fundamental, theological turning point.[56] Marriage, according to the Pope, is not a terrestrial but a sacred reality elevated by Christ to the dignity of a sacrament and endowed with celestial gifts, just as grace perfects nature. That is, the marriage-sacrament relation finds its foundation doctrinally in the relation between nature and grace, between the order of creation and the order of redemption.

In our opinion, although this pontiff's doctrine is very important, it does not seem a novelty in Christian thought. It is precisely an explicitation of what has been latent for centuries in genuine Christian doctrine on marriage.

In a previous work we wrote that "marriage may be considered as a typical example of the relationship between the natural and the supernatural, between the order of nature and the order of grace. The existence of man has always been marked, *de facto*, by its elevation to the order of grace, since no man of pure nature has ever existed. This theological situation of man is logically reflected in the natural institution of marriage: it is a natural institution, but is framed within the fact of supernatural elevation. If to this we add that such a supernatural elevation has always been determined by a peak, transcendental happening, such as the Incarnation of the Word, we shall be in a condition to understand marriage in Genesis, since it was originally projected to represent Christ and the Church."[57] We expressed these ideas according to the reflections which exegetes such as Rabanus Maurus made when connecting the ordinary marriage of our first parents with the mystery of Christ and of the Church, which has been a constant of Christian thought.

a. Pius IX

This great pontiff repeatedly faced the regalist and liberal theories, dismantling the doctrinal bases on which they had relied for a long time, specifically the doctrine favoring the separability of contract and sacrament. This Pope's teachings were patent on many occasions. We shall mention some of the most significant documents.

In the apostolic letter *Ad Apostolicae Sedis* of August 22, 1841, many

---

[56]Caffarra, p. 370.
[57]T. Rincón, "Siglos IX al XIII," p. 53.

errors and falsehoods contained in the works of Juan Nepomuceno Nuytz were condemned. The letter stated "there are many falsehoods asserted" about marriage. Among the errors it highlighted the following: "that it cannot be demonstrated with any proof that Christ elevated matrimony to the dignity of a sacrament; that the sacrament is only an accessory to the marriage contract from which it can be separated, and that the sacrament itself consists only in the nuptial blessing. . . ."[58]

On September 9, 1852, in a letter addressed to King Victor Emmanuel, while again vindicating for the Church the jurisdiction over marriage, the Pope noted important ideas on the sacramentality of marriage:

> It is a dogma of the faith that matrimony has been elevated to the dignity of a sacrament by our Lord Jesus Christ, and it is a doctrine of the Catholic Church that the sacrament is not an accidental quality added to the contract, but is the very essence of matrimony so much so that the conjugal union between Christians is not legitimate if there is no matrimonial sacrament but a mere concubinage.[59]

In the allocution *Acerbissimum* of September 27, 1852, he again expressed himself in similar terms, after having condemned those who despise the dignity and sanctity of the sacrament of marriage, proposing it as a merely civil contract:

> No Catholic is or can be ignorant of the fact that matrimony is truly and properly one of the seven sacraments of the evangelical law, instituted by Jesus Christ Our Lord. It necessarily follows that among the faithful there cannot be a marriage which is not at the same time a sacrament and that any other union between Christian men and women outside of the sacrament, even made in force of civil law, is nothing other than base and disgraceful concubinage, repeatedly condemned by the Church, and further-more, the sacrament can never be separated from the conjugal convenant and only the Church has the power to regulate those things which in any way pertain to marriage.[60]

---

[58]*CIC Fontes* II: 869. Translation by Michael Byrnes in *Matrimony*, edited by the Monks of Solesmes (New York: St. Paul Editions, 1963), p. 105 (hereinafter cited as "Byrnes").

[59]*CIC Fontes* II: 869 (Byrnes, p. 107).

[60]*CIC Fontes* II: 877 (Byrnes, p. 110). All these errors are subsequently gathered in the Syllabus (*CIC Fontes* II, nn. 66, 73, pp. 1007 ss).

b. Leo XIII

In the well known letter *Ci siamo* addressed to the episcopate of the ecclesiastical provinces of Turin, Vercelli and Genoa, Pope Leo XIII sanctioned not only fundamental Christian principles, but also those elementary natural rights which were also abrogated in Italian legislation:

> The conjugal union is not the work or invention of man; God Himself, the supreme author of nature, from the beginning of creation ordained such a union for the propagation of the human race and the constitution of the family. In the order of grace, he willed this union be ennobled more by imposing on it the divine seal of a sacrament.[61]

Afterwards, the Pontiff reminded bishops of the ultimate reason upon which civil powers rely in order to steal from the Church her jurisdiction over marriage, which reason is stated in the concept "of the dissociation of the contract from the sacrament" and in the belief that what corresponds to the Church is "only the insertion of a ritual blessing." But for the conscience of sincere Catholics, none of these reasons is valid since they are based on a dogmatic error repeatedly condemned by the Church:

> . . . that is, the reduction of the sacrament to an extrinsic ceremony and to the condition of a simple rite. This is a doctrine which overthrows the essential concept of Christian marriage, in which the bond, sanctified by religion, is identified with the sacrament and constitutes inseparably with it but one object and one reality.[62]

The encyclical *Arcanum* (1880) of Leo XIII constitutes a whole treatise on Christian marriage. With respect to the subject with which we are dealing, it is probably the most important document. We have selected some of its main ideas:

1) According to the Pontiff marriage is not only a sacred thing, *sua vi, sua natura, sua sponte*, but on its natural, inner reality a trace of sacramental signification is already impressed. Here the Pope echoes Christian tradition, which has seen in all marriages, including those of the non-baptized, a sign at least potentially of the Incarnation of the Word or of the union of Christ with the Church.

2) Before the regalists the Pope proposed without equivocation the doctrine of inseparability.

---

[61]*CIC Fontes* III: 132 (Byrnes, p. 128).
[62]*CIC Fontes* III: 133 (Byrnes, p. 128).

3) For the reason mentioned below, the same can be said of any theory—even that not circumscribed to that time—which imagines a relative or accidental inseparability, since it is the contract itself, entered into according to law, which has been elevated to the dignity of a sacrament. More precisely, it is the same conjugal union, in which marriage consists, which contains *in se et per se* the sacramental signification and grace, in view of the elevation of Christ and not of the choice of men.

> For Christ Our Lord added to marriage the dignity of a sacrament, but marriage is the contract itself whenever it is lawfully concluded. Marriage is a sacrament, however, because it is a holy sign and cause of grace, showing an image of the mystical union between Christ and His Church. But the form and image of this wedding are shown in that very bond of the greatest conjoining by which a man and a woman are bound together, which bond is nothing other than the marriage itself. Hence it is clear that among Christians every true marriage is, in itself and by itself, a sacrament, and that nothing can be further from the truth than to say that the sacrament is an added ornament or an outward endowment which can be separated and torn away from the sacrament arbitrarily by man.[63]

In the letter *Il divisamento* (Febraury 8, 1893) Leo XIII reiterates the same doctrine with these words:

> It is a dogma of faith that the marriage of Christians was raised by Our Lord Jesus Christ to the dignity of a sacrament, nor can this dignity according to Catholic doctrine be treated as an accidental quality added to the matrimonial contract, but rather it is intimately essential to it, so much so that the very contract became a sacrament by divine institution.[64]

c. The Draft for the Decree of Vatican Council I

E. Corecco has recently demonstrated how a preparatory commission, in charge of wording the *schemata* which would be submitted to the deliberations of Vatican Council 1, gave much attention to the subject of inseparability between contract and sacrament.[65] In his detailed study,

[63]*CIC Fontes* III: 159–160 (Byrnes, p. 150).

[64]*CIC Fontes* III: 393 (Byrnes, p. 179).

[65]Cf. E. Corecco, "Il sacerdote ministro del matrimonio?" *La Scuola Cattolica* 98 (1970) 427–476; idem, "L'inseparabilità."

Corecco shows us the revisions the draft underwent, especially in relation to the problem of whether or not to define absolute inseparability. The last edition of the *schema*, although it was not discussed in a conciliar assembly and did not receive the definitive sanction of the council, was published by *Mansi* and therefore we know that it consisted of an introduction, three chapters, and six condemnatory canons.[66]

The first chapter, entitled "The Elevation of Matrimony to the Dignity of a Sacrament," contains substantially the doctrine on inseparability which the pontiffs, especially Pius IX, had sanctioned. The second chapter deals with the power of the Church over marriage, and the third with the goods of marriage.

Regarding the canons, the tenor of the two first are as follows:

> Canon 1. If anyone says that Christ did not raise marriage to the dignity of a sacrament and that Christian men and women can have a union which is a true marriage but not a sacrament, let him be anathema.
>
> Canon 2. If anyone says that the sacrament of matrimony is not itself the marriage contract when it is made by the consent of Christians, but is something accessory to the contract and separable from it, or that among Christians there can be a true marriage which has merely civil force, let him be anathema.

As is known, this *schema* did not receive any conciliar approval and therefore it literally has no other value than the private authority of its authors. But the simple fact that the possibility was stated for a dogmatic definition means at least that inseparability was a truth deeply established in the Church's conscience.

B. The Subject Today

The clarity of papal teachings caused the inseparability between marriage and sacrament to be for many years a truth implicitly admitted by all Catholic authors. As is known, this doctrine was definitely enshrined in canon 1012 of the 1917 code. It was again ratified by Pius XI in the encyclical *Casti connubii*, who clearly stated that the notion of sacrament is so intimately connected with marriage that no true marriage can be established between the baptized without it also being a sacrament.

Because of such a repeated papal position, there have been those who have qualified it as a doctrine *proxima fidei*, or at least as Catholic doctrine

---

[66]Mansi, vol. 53, pp. 719–721.

or theologically true.[67] But aside from the theological qualification it may deserve, it seems clear that what the solemn magisterium did not define has been constantly ratified by the ordinary magisterium.[68] This magisterial judgment has been sufficient for the doctrine of inseparability to become part of the patrimony of Catholic doctrine, from which it will be difficult to part in spite of the seriousness and urgency of the pastoral reasons invoked. Corecco is right when he affirms:

> A similar reversal of doctrine cannot be motivated by pastoral reasons alone, since a theological doctrine cannot be open to discussion unless the discussion is based on rigorous theological principles.[69]

Nevertheless it is a fact that for several years, and especially during the decade of the seventies, this doctrine has been subject to increasing debate particularly in light of the draft for the new law on marriage, which is identical to canon 1012 of the 1917 code and, consequently, maintains the traditional doctrine on inseparability. Some requested elimination of this canon to leave the door open to discussion;[70] others wanted it radically modified in order to make it compatible with the thesis of separability.[71]

---

[67]Bishop Castillo Lara stated the following in a presentation made February 19, 1977 at the International Congress held at the Gregorian University: "Canone 242 confirmatur doctrina catholica de inseparabilitate contractus et sacramenti. Coetus plane noverat disceptationem hac de re, et praesertim gravem quaestionem pastoralem et doctrinalem de frequenti fidei defectione in contrahentibus, tamen opportunum duxit non recedere a doctrina Magisterii, quae a quibusdam theologis habetur 'proxima fidei' vel 'theologice certa.' Hac de causa voluit perscribere ad litteram canonem 1012 C.I.C. Neque hoc modo impeditur suscepta investigatio theologica, sed tantum significatur mutationes inducendas non esse in re tam delicata et tam gravi pro Ecclesiae vita, donec Magisterium publice sententiam suam ediderit." *Communicationes* 9 (1977) 190.

[68]Cf. E. Lio, "Unicità del matrimonio," *L'Osservatore Romano*, January 10, 1976, p. 2.
[69]Corecco, "L'inseparabilità."
[70]Cf. Manzanares, p. 71.
[71]Cf. *Communicationes* 9 (1977) 122 where mention is made of proposed reforms and the response of the consultors: "Quidam sive ex Episcoporum Conferentiis sive ex Studiorum Universitatibus quaestionem fecerunt utrum omnis contractus matrimonialis inter baptizatos sit 'eo ipso sacramentum' etiamsi partes contrahentes fide careant. Quare votum fecerunt vel ut quaestio profundius investigetur, vel ut canon compleatur per clausulam 'servatis iis quae ad validam sacramentorum receptionem requiruntur,' vel ut dicatur 'inter christifideles' loco 'inter baptizatos,' vel ut canon penitus deleatur.

"Consultores unanimiter fatentur non esse nostrae Commissionis hanc quaestionem dirimere et usque dum quaestio theologica ab organis competentibus non solvetur alio modo, necesse est ut leges fundentur in praesuppositis theologicis communiter admissis. Ideoque Consultores censent canonem minime esse mutandum."

In this sense it would be a radical change, not only of discipline but also of Catholic doctrine, to substitute the *inter baptizatos* of canon 1012 with *inter credentes* or *inter christifideles*, making the sacramentality dependent not on an objective fact like baptism but on a necessity of subjective faith without knowing well what degree of faith is needed or what the criterion to determine the effective existence of faith could be. A change of this nature is impossible, states Corecco, "without damaging all of the Catholic theological system," especially the principle of *ex opere operato*.[72] However, the polemic continues, and it is necessary to analyze critically the doctrinal foundations upon which it is intended to sustain the thesis of separability.

C. Critical Analysis of the Arguments Against the Traditional Thesis

1. The Theological Tradition

The defenders of the thesis of separability should first state, so that no harm is done to the magisterium which has defended the thesis of inseparability, that it is a matter historically debated and that the authors who supported the thesis of separability have never been condemned by the Church. Looking through history, the theologian finds a favorable theological tradition and based on it we do not see why the subject should not be open to debate.[73] Consequently, the discussion will investigate whether the particular cases invoked by theologians such as Duns Scotus, Vazquez, Rebello, etc., to defend separability—marriage among dumb people, among those absent or through a proxy, etc.—apply today to another particular case, that of marriage among non-believers, and whether this enables at least a relative separability.[74] This distinction, it is argued, basically prevented Vatican Council I from deciding in favor of the dogmatic definition of inseparability as presented by the draft of the preparatory commission mentioned above. The council would have condemned the thesis defending absolute separability, leaving open the question of relative separability, a position defended by an important theological sector which had not been condemned by the pontifical magisterium, nor does it appear that it was inclined to do so at Vatican Council I.

It is not my intention to say this theme is closed to all theological discussion. The power to say this, in one or the other sense, rests only in the magisterium of the Church. The Commission for the Revision of the

---

[72]Idem.

[73]Manzanares.

[74]On one occasion it is referred to as separability "per accidens." Cf. "Le mariage des baptisés non-croyants," *La Maison Dieu* 132 (1977) 156–162.

Code is under the magisterium and preferred to follow the traditional doctrine. However, I cannot resist making some observations in this respect.

a. The fact that a subject has been debated at some time in history does not mean it should always be so, since a magisterial intervention—although not solemn—may have settled the question. Nor is it of importance that at certain councils, some of the fathers have defended the most curious theses. Their value may remain unauthorized if the council has pronounced against it.[75]

b. It is true that Duns Scotus, Vazquez, etc., have not been expressly condemned by the magisterium, but we doubt very much that they have not been condemned implicitly if we look at the meaning and spirit of the papal documents. When Pius IX condemned the errors of Nuytz or the errors contained in the *Syllabus*, he condemned not only the regalists but any theory which considered the sacrament as something accessory, extrinsic or superadded to marriage. I do not know whether the popes were aware of the doctrine of Duns Scotus, but his thought on the sacrament as "something added" does not differ much from what the popes condemned.

c. The artificial distinction between absolute and relative separability is only, in my opinion, a dialectical subtlety to defend separability without adjectives and to avoid going to the heart of the question. Because from the moment in which, in only one case, sacramentality were separable from marriage, it could never be affirmed that marriage is a mystery connected intrinsically with the mystery of Christ and of the Church. Here is what would happen with the indissolubility of the conjugal, sacramental and consummated union: such indissolubility could never be affirmed of marriage once one sole and unique exception were introduced. From the moment in which a case is admitted for the separability of marriage and sacrament, admission should be made of the separability of both realities without any distinction. If, on the contrary, it is understood that sacramentality is incorporated intrinsically into the reality of marriage, forming a unique and elevated entity, no exception may be made to this principle, just as there is no exception to the principle that all the baptized carry within themselves indefectibly the baptismal character, regardless of whether their life is with or against Christ.

---

[75]Not all traditions are Tradition in the precise theological sense, argues Naurois, "Problèmes actuels," pp. 33–43; in turn he himself asks if inseparability had not been explicitly affirmed until lately, would it not be because the possible separability had not been conceived of.

2. Value of the Papal Magisterium

It is certain that the papal magisterium at a determined moment favored inseparability, but to this it may be answered that such a determination should be interpreted in its own context, which was none other than that of the political fight between State and Church about jurisdiction over marriage. Since the present problem is totally defferent, it is not correct to extend to it the doctrine of the nineteenth century; it is indispensable to reinterpret, reread the magisterium in the light of present problems.[76]

There are always those who assert that papal declarations "are motivated directly or indirectly by questions of a political-ecclesiastical nature" and that "they may not be considered as strictly theological."[77] From this is drawn the necessity to contextualize and reread them.

There exist even more radical positions. Another Spanish author refers to the compulsory civil marriage of the first Spanish republic. He qualifies the Spanish liberals of the Constituent Courts as predecessors of Vatican II on the issues of religious liberty and the secularization of marriage. This is nothing else, for this author, than the application to marriage and to its juridical regulations of what Vatican Council II calls "the autonomy of temporal realities." Therefore, facing this progressivism of the liberals, the backwardness of the Church stands out starkly. The author not only intends to reinterpret in a new context the doctrine of the nineteenth century, but even to say in plain language that the Church of the nineteenth century was wrong and that it is necessary to rectify her course.[78]

This easy recourse to the rereading and reinterpretation of magisterial decisions conceals behind it a new pretext for presenting the debate and for avoiding a deep study of what the sacramentality of marriage is, in accord with a genuine comprehension of the authoritative voice of the popes and independently of all possible and sometimes real pastoral problems. There is no question that the conflict of jurisdiction between State and Church caused the magisterium to start taking doctrinal positions, but a close reading of the papal documents qualifies as unacceptable the claim to reduce the value of its teaching to a mere contemporary formulation deprived of permanent theological significance. Obviously the magisterium was opposed to those who intended to take from the Church its jurisdiction over marriage, but as the regalists based their pretensions on a false doctrine of marriage, the Pontiffs simultaneously condemned the

---

[76]Manzanares.
[77]R. Rincón, p. 57.
[78]Lahidalga, "A propósito del matrimonio civil obligatorio," p. 199.

falsity of the doctrine and formulated positively the true doctrine on Christian marriage. More concretely, the popes condemned those who denied the Church's jurisdiction while condemning the doctrinal bases on which regalist and liberal pretensions were supported. These doctrinal bases are summarized in the conception of the sacramentality of marriage as something extrinsic, overlapped, accidental or accessory and, therefore, separable from the reality of marriage. But the magisterium did not entrench itself in a purely negative posture of condemnation; the Church formulated the guidelines for a positive elaboration of the sacramental nature of marriage. As Prof. Caffarra has very rightly said:

> It is precisely against this manner of looking at it that the magisterium has issued pronouncements beginning with Pius VI, by rejecting every form of extrincisim, safeguarding as well the central revealed truth, affirming both the absolute and gratuituous transcendance and the immanence of the sacramentality, rejecting all extrinsicism "in se and per se" (in the words of Leo XIII).

That this papal thought, continues the same author, "no longer has the same meaning today gives rise to the judgment, in my humble opinion, of superficial theological thought."[79]

> Although controversy then had been the occasion for its declarations, the intention of the magisterium was to recall the fact that the separability thesis cannot be reconciled with the original idea from revelation on marriage, and that for this reason the juridical consequences upon which these declarations had been drawn was no longer acceptable. The question had not been, therefore, in the first place, a conflict of competence but a point of Catholic doctrine (as explicitly declared formerly by Popes Pius VI and Leo XIII).[80]

3. Religious Freedom and the Autonomy of Temporal Realities

Vatican Council II consecrated these principles and some intend to argue from them in favor of the thesis of separability. Their arguments run as follows.

The dignity of human persons, as well as that of nonbelieving or nonpracticing Catholics, demands that they be free to opt for a marriage according to their conscience. Such a requirement would not be complied

[79]Caffara, p. 378.
[80]Ibid., p. 383.

with if a civil marriage, when elected, could not be real or sacramental. On the other hand, every terrestrial reality, including marriage, should be configured autonomously, that is aside from any religious connotation, if those interested so decide. All of which is incompatible with the thesis of inseparability, which therefore amounts to a throwback to an earlier time of Christendom which has now been overcome.[81] Inseparability implies that the baptized do not have freedom of choice: either they marry sacramentally or they do not marry at all.

Anyone can note that these are not demonstrative arguments for the thesis of separability, but that they presuppose it *a priori*. It is on the basis of such presumption that the *ad casum* concepts of the dignity of the human person are formed, and of the autonomy of earthly realities. Actually, they begin with the fact—which has not been demonstrated—that the baptized man is free and capable of opting between contracting a marriage sacramentally or only naturally. Based on that possibility—I insist that it has not been demonstrated as real—the consequence is drawn that any obstacle to this freedom of election supposes an attempt on the dignity of the human person and breaks the conciliar principle of the autonomy of terrestrial realities. The consequence is logical, but not real because, in our opinion, the premise on which it is founded is not true. The truth is that marriage follows human nature and this has only existed concretely in the history of salvation. The order of pure nature has never existed. Therefore a regression from the order of redemption to the order of creation is unthinkable.[82]

---

[81]For Lahidalga ("La constitución del 78," pp. 46–48) the traditional doctrine and discipline mean that certain things are not taken seriously, including the dignity of the person, the autonomy and consistency of temporal realities, and the protection of religious freedom. According to Mostaza ("Competentia status," p. 209) the present canonical legislation takes into account neither the *ius connubii* nor the *ius ad libertatem religiosam*. Manzanares (p. 48) also mentions as arguments for the separability thesis the protection of the right to marry and the principle of religious freedom as well as the legitimate autonomy of the secular culture of the conjugal society.

According to Aubert (pp. 116–143) there are notable differences in the manner in which marriage was contracted in a Christian society and in a secular world. As to the need for faith, for example, religious indifference at an individual level was compensated by a sociological dimension of faith sustained by institutions and generally accepted. Along these lines, R. Rincón (pp. 54–55) holds that the concept of identity of sacrament and contract does not have the same sense today as it did when society could be called Christian. Cf. among others, R. Didier, "Sacrement de mariage, baptême et foi," *La Maison Dieu* 127 (1976) 106–138; L.M. Chauvet, "Le mariage, un sacrament pas comme les autres," *La Maison Dieu* 127 (1976) 64–105; Beguerie, pp. 7–33; Moingt.

[82]This is literally the thesis of Corecco, synthetically expressed in the debate following the work of Manzanares cited earlier.

As argued by Cafarra, "to decide to depart from this economy to return to an economy of pure creation is to fall into non-being." To affirm the effective possibility of election between a natural or a sacramental marriage implies an affirmation that man is ". . . fundamentally neutral, freely faced with two economies and he can imprint a dynamism and sanctify creation outside of Christ: without doubt, this thesis is substantially Pelagian."[83]

A consequence of these theological considerations is that the concepts of the dignity of the human person or of the autonomy of earthly realities cannot be understood at the margin of the economy of salvation, where the council situates them. Christ is the ultimate reference of all human dignity; Christ is the ultimate goal of all right ordering, including earthly realities, and especially of that earthly reality called marriage, intrinsically raised to the level of a sacrament. From this it follows that the thesis of separability, instead of protecting the dignity of the human person, favors precisely the contrary, its degradation, because the nature of things is degraded when they are separated from their ultimate destiny. In the same manner, an absolute autonomy of the reality of natural marriage, instead of allowing for its dignity, provokes precisely its degradation.

It may be useful to conclude this brief critical meditation with some words of Prof. Caffarra, intended expressly to denounce the erroneous concept of freedom contained in the thesis of Vazquez and Rebollo and not yet overcome because of a certain body of Christian thinkers:

> The notion of freedom as "libertas indifferentiae" and of man as essentially neutral in relation to God, a neutrality which emerges as a decision of his liberty, is a notion which is for all practical purposes common to the scholastics; it has introduced one of the gravest contaminations into Christian thought; our case is one of the clearest proofs of this.[84]

4. Faith as an Essential or Conditioning Element of Sacramentality

The relationship between faith and the sacramentality of marriage is the central aspect of the subject we are analyzing. For that reason it has been abundantly treated in recent teaching. This is logical, considering that the problem of lack of faith has been the primary stumbling block in the entire present problem concerning the connection between sacrament and contract, as shown by the proposals for modification or suppression of the

[83]Caffarra, p. 379.
[84]Ibid.

present canon 1012. We already noted before how these proposals intended definitively to have sacramentality depend not on the objective act of baptism, but on the more subjective aspects of faith, completely modifying all the traditional doctrine; for this latter reason the corresponding commission for the revision of the code did not deem it prudent to introduce any modification: "until now this theological question has not been solved by competent bodies in any way, thus it is necessary that the laws be grounded in theological presuppositions commonly accepted."[85]

All the proposals for revision, including those less radical, have as background their opposition to what is usually called "sacramental automatism," without really knowing what such an expression means, although in many cases it is nothing more than an euphemistic manner of rejecting *ex opere operato*. But as not all statements reflect the same doctrinal coordinates, it is necessary to distinguish and analyze them separately.

In fact, along side the traditional approach to the question which considers faith as a requirement of efficacy and not of validity, there is a school of thought which presently understands that faith is such an essential requisite that, without it, it is impossible for the sacrament to be born, even though the contracting parties may give birth to a real marriage with regard to the natural institution. What decides, finally, whether the conjugal pact constitutes only marriage or the sacrament as well, is not the objective fact of the spouses being baptized, but the sacramental intention which presumes faith. Thus faith is elevated to the rank of a constitutive element of the sacramentality of marriage. According to this theory, in its most radical form, even for one possessing faith it is possible to opt (taking intention into consideration) between entering a natural marriage or a sacramental marriage. But without faith, the option would be impossible: non-believers could only attempt a real marriage, but not sacramental.

This first approach is the one supported by defenders of separability. According to them, marriage has two dimensions which are different, separable, and autonomous: the natural and the sacramental. From there it is concluded that it is not the objective fact of baptism, but the subjective act of faith, which assumes one or the other dimension. That is, marriage is *per se* a natural reality which is not automatically sacramentalized. This is done through a free option of the contracting parties, through the faith expressed in the consent, through the will to found their union on the mystery of Christ and the Church.[86] It is because of faith that the marriage

---

[85]*Communicationes* 9 (1977) 122.
[86]Cf. Moingt, pp. 107–110.

contract becomes a valid matter for the sacrament.[87] But lacking faith—and even with it—the fact of baptism does not deprive those baptized of their free disposition in the domain of natural existence in which marriage is also inscribed; grace does not eliminate the natural power of union in marriage.[88] In summary, since the act of marrying is a voluntary act, presuming that sacraments are signs of faith and that marriage, before anything, is a natural reality, it may only be intended as sacrament through faith,[89] at least in the present context of the secularized world which is different from the times of Christendom in which sociological faith compensated to a certain extent for the lack of individual faith.[90] To these reasons others are added which are derived from a concept of marriage as a mission which should not be ignored, but places absolute responsibility on those who marry sacramentally. These other reasons are derived from a concept of matrimony as an ecclesial ministry, for whose exercise faith is needed, since it is not possible to act as a minister on behalf of someone in whom one does not believe.[91]

In light of this presentation of the question, I consider it opportune to mention that these reasons cannot be used as valid arguments in favor of the thesis of separability, as seems to be insinuated. Rather, they are or seem to be the consequence of an undemonstrated thesis, or a desire to see reality other than it is. If the presumption of separability were real it might be asked if it would not be reasonable, anthropologically or ecclesiologically, for faith and sacramental intention to be compulsory in order that the natural entity of marriage be assumed intentionally as sacrament. But strictly speaking, for the argument to be valid, it would first have to be demonstrated that the two dimensions of marriage—natural and sacramental—are separable and with an autonomous existence according to the desire of the contracting parties; it would have to be proven that Jesus Christ did not intrinsically elevate to a sacramental level the natural reality itself of marriage, but that he simply ordered that specific graces be conceded to those who upon marrying made a sacramental intention. Finally, the error would have to be avoided of comparing marriage, in all respects, with all the other sacraments of the New Law. This is historically what caused a delay in the theological configuration of the sacrament of marriage, and it continued to be, in our opinion, one of the greatest

---

[87]Cf. Chauvet, pp. 104–105.
[88]Cf. Moingt, pp. 112 ss.
[89]Cf. Manzanares, p. 269.
[90]Cf. Aubert, pp. 130 ss.
[91]Cf. Manzanares, p. 269.

obstacles to the comprehension of its specific sacramental meaning. Patristic and medieval theology soon understood (with the Gospel in hand) and established doctrinally the sacramentality of baptism and the Eucharist; but it took longer to establish marriage as an efficacious sign because, we think, when applying the same sacramental categories, they did not fit marriage well. The action of the minister when acting over the bread of the Eucharist or over the water in baptism is not the same as when he is acting over the natural reality of marriage. Those sacraments require "the confection of the rite (consecration, ablution) inasmuch as the rite is not the ordinary action of daily life: baptism is not the daily cleaning of a person, converted into a sacrament; the Eucharist is not the daily food which produces the grace *ex opere operato*." But this confection of the rite "is not necessary nor is it given in marriage. The sacrament of marriage is not a sacred action in form of reality of ordinary life; it is that very same ordinary reality which *ex se* has been converted into a sacrament."[92] Actually, bread needs to be consecrated; the ablution with water needs the words by which the form is expressed, and these obviously require a sacramental intention. But not so marriage which, without any imposed or additional factor, is in itself, with regard to natural reality, elevated to a sacrament by the will of Christ.

While underlining that sacramentality resides in marriage itself, we also come across a latent and erroneous statement of the sacramental meaning of marriage. One author says, for example— and the idea is latent in other authors—that between the sign (the community of life and love) and what it signifies (the union of Christ with the Church) there is a relation which is either measured by faith or is not given at all. Without faith every possibility of symbolism disappears; without faith the sacramental event is not in order, not does it become a personal communication or encounter between God and man.[93]

In our opinion the error of these affirmations lies basically in these two things: first, that marriage is confused with married life; second, following on the first, that the sacramental signification is situated not in marriage as such, but in the life of the spouses, therefore mistaking sign with testimony.[94] Thus when the author mentioned refers to the "impossibility

---

[92]J. Hervada, *El Derecho del Pueblo de Dios*, III, pp. 165–166.

[93]Cf. R. Rincón, p. 69.

[94]"Conjugal life, however, is not a sacrament because it has neither a reason for a sign nor sacramental efficacy. The matrimonial dynamism is not marriage but rather its vital realization. For this reason the life of the spouses and the fact that they live according to their condition as Christians and to the demands of Christian marriage is not the sign of the union of Christ and His Church. The sign is the union of man and woman as soon as they constitute

of symbolism,'' this should be understood as the impossibility of testimony, but not the lack of the sacramental symbol, insofar as this lies in the bond or in the *res et sacramentum* in the Thomistic view.

Obviously, to accept this conclusion implies accepting that between the symbol—marriage, an elevated natural reality—and the thing symbolized—the union of Christ with His Church—there is a real relation, not merely a symbolic one. On the other hand, to think that natural marriage can become a sacrament only in view of an act of faith and according to the will of those interested would mean depriving marriage of its rich mysterious content and would convert it into an empty image. This was stated by M. J. Scheeben, the great theologian of the nineteenth century, when commenting on the *magnum sacramentum* of the letter to the Ephesians:

> The sense in which marriage should be understood as such a great mystery depends evidently on the manner in which the relationship it has with Christ and the Church is defined. Such a relationship may be conceived as merely symbolic or as real. In the first case the Apostle would present marriage according to its natural being as a symbol of the supernatural unity existing between Christ and the Church; marriage itself would not be mysterious, it would only be an empty image to make us perceive by intuition a mystery which is far removed: the unity of Christ with His Church; before the mystery, there would be the sacrament of a mystery, and a sacrament without any content. Such would be marriage among those who are not Christians. On the other hand, Christian marriage has a real, essential, intimate relationship with the mystery of the union of Christ with His Church; marriage is rooted therein, with this it is organically related; thus marriage participates in the being and the mysterious nature of that union. It is not simply a symbol of this mystery or a model of something outside of itself, separated from itself, but marriage is a copy of the union of Christ with the Church. The copy comes from such a union, is founded on it and is penetrated by it, since marriage not only symbolizes this mystery, but it represents it, because, in marriage, this mystery makes evident its activity and efficacy.[95]

---

marriage. Conjugal life is an answer to the demands of marriage which are derived from marriage as a mystery. It is then testimony and not a sacramental sign.'' J. Hervada, ''Cuestiones varias,'' p. 83.

[95]M. J. Scheeben, *Los misterios del cristianismo*, 3rd Spanish ed. (Barcelona, 1960), pp. 636–637.

The same author denounces the posture of those theologians who espoused opinions similar to those of many modern authors who condemned the popes of the nineteenth century. The eminent professor of Cologne said in this respect that

> some theologians understood by the sacramentality of marriage not a new, special and mystical way of being . . . ; they thought that marriage between Christians or sacramental marriage is distinguished from marriage contracted between those not baptized only because Christ, through a positive order—which does not touch the essence of the alliance—joined special graces to the former in order to obtain the end more easily. In such a case the supernatural sanctity of marriage would rest only on the grace obtained when marrying; it would not lie within marriage itself as such, and would only be an exterior addition, which according to circumstances might be lacking; the marriage alliance as such would not have a supernatural character; the contracting parties would not realize a sacramental act; and thus the act itself of entering into marriage would not be interiorly and essentially a sacrament; only the benediction given by the Church on behalf of Christ would be considered a sacrament.[96]

We have taken the liberty of quoting this long passage inasmuch as we understand that in Scheeben's statement lies the key to understanding the present confusion of those who make the sacramentality of marriage depend on an act of faith, without which it would not be a sacrament but still be real marriage contracted as a natural institution.

To end this criticism of the first approach to the relationship between faith and the sacrament of marriage, we cannot ignore another latent error in those statements which affect sacramental theory in general and marriage in particular. We refer to that veiled intent of putting the divine activity in the background and making human initiative more prevalent.[97] Sacraments are made the actions of man and not mainly the actions of Christ. This is clearly seen in marriage, when its sacramental existence is made to depend on the faith of the contracting parties. In classical terminology, *ex opere operato* is deemphasized, in order to give essential relevance to *ex opere operantis*, thus directly attacking the entire Catholic sacramental system. Today nobody doubts that it would be pastorally advantageous to accentuate the *ex opere operantis* in order that a greater

[96]Ibid., p. 628.
[97]Cf. Naurois, p. 37.

sacramental efficacy be added to validity. But this does not mean that the two levels should be confused and that the subjective factor be given an essential character, which it does not hold. Vatican Council II, in spite of having accentuated the pastoral aspects of participation of the faithful in the sacraments, did not forge a rupture with the traditional system. Therefore it is difficult for us to understand, in a Catholic sense, the thesis which posits faith as an element constituting the sacrament.[98]

A second approach to this question consists in considering faith not as a constituent of the sacrament but as a possible requisite for validity since, without faith, the sacramental intention is vitiated or weakened. In other words, faith is joined with intention and the latter with the sacrament. A minimum requirement in every sacrament is the intention of doing what the Church does. It is concluded that in marriage, also, there is a lack of an essential requisite when there is no sacramental intention, which would be even less likely to exist when the contracting parties have no faith. All this is held without failing to support continually the traditional thesis of inseparability. Therefore, if the sacrament should be impossible, it would also be impossible for marriage to be born.

Once again, the serious pastoral problems of nonbelievers are what inspire this new theological thinking, which tends to reappraise the faith of those who approach the sacrament in accordance with what Vatican Council II noted. In effect, the Constitution on the Sacred Liturgy says in n. 59 that the sacraments ''not only presuppose faith, but by words and objects they also nourish, strengthen and express it. That is why they are called sacraments of faith.'' This same idea passed subsequently into the *Ordo celebrandi matrimonium* promulgated by the Apostolic See on March 19, 1969, in the following terms (n.7): ''Pastors should first of all strengthen and nourish the faith of those about to be married. The sacrament of matrimony presupposes and demands faith.''

Based on these texts, one school of thought has tended to see in faith, as a subjective reality, an essential requisite for validity. But to arrive at such a conclusion we would have to know whether both the council and the rite of marriage are to be taken at a theological level, or rather, have been intended for a more pastoral context which seeks better and more fruitful participation in the sacraments, particularly in the sacrament of marriage, through a faith which is ever more alive.

Some episcopal conferences in recent years have also promoted theological reflection in order to solve at the doctrinal level the serious problems frequently presented by those who approach marriage without the neces-

[98]Cf. Chauvet, p. 105.

sary faith. But a close reading of these episcopal documents emphasizes that the bishops are situated strictly at the pastoral level. That is, they do not enter into the question of the effect the lack of faith has on the validity of the sacrament of marriage. Indeed, there are standards according to which a nonbeliever must be dissuaded from a religious ceremony. Nevertheless, as mentioned before, a marriage may be inadvisable pastorally without implying its nullity.

For example, the French episcopal conference reached these pastoral conclusions. Worried by the serious pastoral problems arising from a lack of faith, the conference requested a group of specialists to study carefully the theological and pastoral problems implied in the lack of faith of many baptized parties. In 1977 a group of specialists published a paper on the work performed and mentioned some of their conclusions, among which the following are worth noting.

1. The paper of the French episcopal conference does not enter into the question of whether the lack of faith impedes validity of the marriage sacrament.

2. The traditional answer to this question, from the twelfth century to our own day, has been negative: the lack of faith does not invalidate the sacrament. After mentioning some historical data[99] the paper adds:

> In such a perspective the faith of the spouses is not constitutive of the sacrament but, for a valid sacramental marriage, it is necessary at least, according to Prevostin, that there be an intention (on the part of the spouses) to do that which the Church does, or, more precisely, to contract a true marriage and at the same time not to exclude that which the Church considers sacramental.

[99]P.M. Gy, "Le sacrement de mariage exige-t-il la foi? La position medieval," *Revue des sciences philosophiques et théologiques* 61 (1977) 437–442, gathers the most important medieval testimonies such as that of Innocent III: "Nam etsi matrimonium verum quidem inter infideles existat, non tamen est ratum; inter fideles autem verum et ratum existit, quia sacramentum fidei, quod semel est admissum, numquam amittitur; sed ratum efficit coniugii sacramentum, ut ipsum in coniugibus illo durante perduret. . . ." Here is another, from William of Auxerre: "Cum enim fidelis fit infidelis, licet blasphemet fidem, tamen, quia aliquid habet de fide, non solvitur matrimonium. Habet sacramentum fidei, scilicet baptismum; caracter enim inseparabilis est, et per baptismum consecratum est corpus eius ad hoc ut sit templum spiritus sancti, unde non vilificatur membrum fidele, quod tamen adhuc retinens consecrationem baptismi." There is also the more explicit statement of St. Thomas: "Ad quintum dicendum quod matrimonium sacramentum est, et ideo, quantum pertinet ad necessitatem sacramenti, requiret paritatem quantum ad sacramentum fidei, scilicet baptismum, magis quam quantum ad interiorem fidei." Thus the Angelic Doctor concludes that a sacramental marriage contracted with a heretic is valid, although that contracted with a catechumen having the true faith would not be true matrimony.

3. In spite of everything, this traditional theology does not invalidate present attempts to highlight more ". . . that the faith of the Church (to which the intention is attached) enters into the constitution of the sacraments, and of which the liturgy is a confession of faith."

The paper recognizes that in recent years many theologians have been inclined to think that faith is necessary for the sacramentality of marriage. But such attempts have been met with serious reservations by many other theologians who insist on safeguarding, in the case of marriage, the objectivity of the sacraments defined by Trent. In view of this, the note concludes thus:

> Nevertheless accepting as a given the thesis that the faith of the spouses is not constitutive of the sacrament and that, for sacramental validity the only thing required on their part is the intention to do what the Church wants them to do, then there is reason to wonder if the absence of a declaration of faith could not impede or vitiate the necessary intention.

Afterwards the paper goes into the subject of separability or inseparability, leaving the question open of whether it is possible to speak of separability *per accidens*—to which we referred previously—in the case of the baptized who disavow both their faith and marriage as a sacrament in that faith. Such a thesis, they say, would have in its favor a certain analogy with a marriage contracted in disparity of cult,[100] which is today admitted to be nonsacramental.

We will leave aside this reference to relative or *per accidens* separability, which we have previously called separability without adjectives. However, it is clear that the group of French theologians and canonists, without daring to contradict the traditional doctrine and even affirming it formally ("the faith of the spouses is not constitutive of the sacrament"), intends to connect the problem of the lack of faith with that of the lack of the necessary intention. They wonder if the first will not damage the second in some way.

The International Theological Commission recently faced the same problem, but it embraced without equivocation the traditional thesis of the inseparability of marriage and sacrament among the baptized.

Regarding the relationship between faith and the sacrament of marriage, the thought of the Theological Commission is as follows: on the one hand, it reaffirms the traditional doctrine that marriage, as all the other sacraments,

---

[100]"Le mariage des batisés non croyants," pp. 156–162.

. . . ultimately confers grace in virtue of the action of Jesus Christ performing it and not only through the faith of the one receiving it . . . faith is presupposed as a dispositive cause of the fruitful effect of marriage but validity does not necessarily imply the fruitfulness of marriage.[101]

On the other hand the Commission intended to give an answer to the new theological difficulty and to the serious pastoral dilemma presented by baptized nonbelievers. The Commission sought a middle way between the rejection *simpliciter* of sacramentality and baptismal automatism. The key to the problem lies in the intention of not doing what the Church does:[102]

Ultimately the true intention is born from and nurtured by a living faith. Therefore where there is no vestige of faith as such . . . and no desire for grace and salvation is found, then a real doubt of fact arises, whether the above-mentioned general and truly sacramental intention is present, and whether the marriage contracted is valid or not. As it was noted, the personal faith of the contractants does not constitute the sacramentality of matrimony, but without such personal faith the validity of the sacrament is weakened.

In view of the scientific rigor with which the International Theological Commission acts, it is certain that the statement made regarding the connection between faith, intention and sacramentality of marriage was preceded by serious reflection on the problems surrounding the new approach. Therefore we do not doubt the seriousness of this statement. We

---

[101]The Latin version of the theses of the International Theological Commission is found in "Propositiones de quibusdam questionibus ad matrimonium Christianum pertinentibus," *Gregorianum* 78 (1978) 453–464. English translation from *Origins* 8/15 (September 28, 1978) 235–239.

[102]Ph. Delhaye, commenting on the thesis of the I.T.C., formulates the question thus in *Espirt et vie* 37 (1978) 503: "Il a semblé à la C.T.I., à la suite de longues discussions dont trouve ici un certain résumé, qu'une double question se posait. Une première se situe au niveau des faits: quand et comment peut-on savoir si le jeune homme et la jeune fille qui demandent un mariage religieux, ont vraiment la foi ou l'ont perdue? Une second question est plus doctrinale: peut-on dire comme l'ont fait certains publicistes: 'pas de foi, pas de mariage' ou, au contraire, peut-on faire jouer un certain 'automatisme': il y a eu baptême, donc le seul mariage possible est sacramentel?"

Further on he indicates the key which is, according to him, the middle way: "La clé du problème est dans l'intention, l'intention de faire ce que fait l'Eglise en offrant un sacrement permanent qui entraîne indissolubilité, fidelité, fecondité." For the existence of a valid sacramental marriage, "il faut le baptême et une foi explicite qui, tous deux, alimentent l'intention d'insérer un amour conjugal humain dans l'amour pascal du Christ."

could formulate, however, a series of questions which are not entirely answered in the summary though they were discussed at length, as indicated by the General Secretary of the Commission.[103]

The first question presented to us deals with the possibility that there is no faith, *nullum vestigium fidei*, remaining in a baptized person. We wish to know whether faith has to be interpreted only as an accepted gift or also as a gift infused and in some manner bound to the baptismal nature.[104] In this last presumption, the problem would disappear because in any baptized person there would always be a *vestigium fidei* sufficient for the valid reception of the other sacraments. But the first presumption suggests another series of questions of a practical order: what would be the criterion to discern the degree of faith necessary to enter into the sacrament of marriage and to determine whether or not there is a vestige of faith, and who would be entitled to issue a judgment in this respect?[105] I do not believe this has an easy answer and therefore in fact it would also be difficult to evade the theological and juridical insecurity which would afflict the validity of marriage. A new factor of nullity would have to be added to the invalidating elements of the conjugal pact, because the lack of faith would be a serious *dubium facti*. But how would this new *caput nullitatis*, consisting in the lack of faith be demonstrated? Traditionally, the question was solved by appealing to the exclusion of sacramentality through a positive act of will which implied exclusion of marriage itself, presuming their inseparability. But from this new perspective the problem seems different, since nullity would come from the mere fact of a lack of faith, which implies an absence of a sacramental intention.

Another question is how the natural reality of marriage as such can be elevated to a sacrament and transformed from the inside by Christ's action, when a truly sacramental intention is what is required. Starting from the

---

[103]See the previous note.

[104]See the statements of William of Auxerre and Thomas Aquinas cited above, note 99. In the context of these texts it is opportune to ask if faith is to be understood as the response of man to God or as the call of God to man through baptism, the sacrament of faith.

[105]In the aforementioned commentary, Delhaye, Secretary General of the I.T.C., has similar questions: "Est-il si simple de porter, en toute sérénité, un jugement sur l'existence ou la non-existence de la foi? Qui a vraiment juridiction pour la faire?"

In this sense Naurois in "Problèmes actuels," p. 36, is more convincing. For him it is easy to say that the Church may not accept a sacrament when there is no living faith. But the criterion is not to discern the faith nor to depend on the person who makes this judgment. From this it is clear than any such judgment would be necessarily arbitrary. Moreso, there is the intolerable result of having the inquiry into the faith made in the internal forum with consequences in the external forum.

thesis of inseparability, the traditional doctrine has taught that the intention of the contracting parties was directed only to giving concrete existence to the marriage, that it was enough to marry for the marriage-sacrament to be effected provided the contracting parties were *in actu* elevated objectively by baptism to the supernatural order and so incorporated into the economy of redemption. But requiring a sacramental intention in the same way as for the other sacraments clouds the fact that marriage, as an institution of nature, itself represents the union of Christ with the Church. That is, if we do not misunderstand, the statement of the Commission obscures to a certain extent the same thesis of inseparability which it defends with so much force.[106] It is not strange, therefore, for those who defend at all costs the thesis of inseparability to require faith and a sacramental intention in order to make a sacrament out of the natural reality: the natural institution, with its own entity and autonomy, needs to be considered a sacrament not by virtue of the action of Christ, but by the option of the contracting parties expressed in the sacramental intention, as happens in the other sacraments. But is the action of the ministers over marriage identical to that of the ministers over other sacraments?

In this same line of thought, we wonder what is the role played in fact by baptism in the sacramentality of marriage. Leaving aside whether the baptized live their baptismal convenant or not, as soon as the sacrament is validly received the person becomes objectively—ontologically—included in the mystery of Christ, in the environment of redemption; the baptismal character accompanies that person perpetually. Hence, though the argument against a certain automatism is justified at the pastoral level, it is less justified at the theological level, that is at the level of reality: either you are baptized or you are not. But if you are validly baptized, it is not possible

---

[106]"In altri termini, poché il sacramento è inseparabilmente congiunto al vero contratto, per amministrare e recibere validamente il sacramento del matrimonio non si richiede l'intenzione interna circa la sacramentalità, cioè quell'intenzione che si referisce al contenuto intrinseco del rito voluto interiormente come un'azione santa, religiosa, sacramentale, ma è sufficiente l'intenzione interna circa il contratto, la quale in relazione alla sacramentalità del matrimonio è intenzione puramente esterna, limitata alle sole formalità esterne del medesimo. . . . A diversità degli altri sacramenti, nei quali, come se'èdetto, la posizione del segno può essere ordinata per altri fini—per esempio per servizio liturgico—nel matrimonio il segno è lo stesso contratto valido, dal quale, secundo la voluntà di Christo, è inseparabile la ragione di sacramento."

Subsequently the same author writes: "La mancanza di fede, per se stessa, non è causa di invalidità del sacramento del matrimonio tra battezzati. Invano si cercherebbero nel Codice di diritto canonico o nella guirisprudenza ecclesiastica un capo o una sentenza di nullità motivati dalla mancanza di fede." Bersini, pp. 556 and 558.

not to be, and no subsequent event, no future act of the will can change the ontological status of the baptized, not even lack of faith.

In this latter assumption, the only thing to which the contracting parties may arrive is to exclude the sacramental dimension in the pact, but since they do not have the power to remove the baptismal character which essentially marks them, such an exclusion would have relevance for sacramentality only if it produced nullity; in the absence of marriage, there would obviously be no sacrament.

On the other hand, if the exclusion of sacramentality is brought about not through a positive act of the will, but it is rather the lack of faith which makes impossible the sacramental intention, which is in turn required essentially to give birth to the sacramental bond, a radical incapacity to marry would be produced in nonbelievers; they would lack *jus connubii*, since because of lack of faith they could not "celebrate" the sacrament, and because of their being baptized, they would be unable to enter into a natural marriage. The thesis of inseparability would necessarily lead to this conclusion, assuming the stated premises. This does not occur in the traditional version of the problem, inasmuch as the exclusion of sacramentality, which effects an exclusion of marriage itself, implies an act of the will by which the contracting party decides freely not to excercise the *jus connubii* as established by the Church.

In conclusion, we estimate that in this difficult problem there are still obscure areas which need greater light and require a serene and deeper reflection, taking care lest the urgency to solve pastoral problems deflect us from the true doctrine.

D. The Thesis of Inseparability

1. Recent Teaching: the International Theological Commission

With regard to the traditional doctrine exposed vigorously by Bellarmine, Thomás Sánchez, Scheeben, etc., and assumed afterwards by the magisterium, clear voices have been raised in recent years in favor of the thesis of inseparability. They have inspired an investigation of theological and juridical fundamentals, and have therefore weakened the arguments for the contrary thesis which had spread among certain sectors on the strength of serious and circumstantial pastoral problems.

Since we have analyzed critically the bases on which the thesis of separability rests, the moment has come to present the most modern thought about the ultimate reason for inseparability, with the aid of some of the most qualified exponents of such thought. The open polemic must have at least the advantage of stimulating and deepening reflection on what the sacramentality of marriage is and what it means, just as happened in the golden century of canonical and theological science when, for other reasons, the task had to be undertaken to establish doctrinally the dogmatic assumption of the sacramentality of marriage.

We highlight in the first place the vigorous defense of inseparability made by the International Theological Commission. In view of the confusing doctrinal panorama observed in numerous writings, the prestigious Theological Commission, after long deliberations on the subject, presented to the public in 1977 a series of proposals or theses about certain doctrinal questions referring to Christian marriage.[107]

Regarding the subject we are discussing, some theses have great importance, covered under the generic title "On the relation between matrimony as created reality and as a sacrament." Therefore I believe it advisable to transcribe literally some of those theses, to which only a brief comment will be added, considering that in the following paragraph we shall present the thought of Professor Caffarra, one of the members of the International Commission and therefore an authoritative interpreter of its proposals.

As its title indicates, the intention is to see the existing relation between marriage as a natural institution and as sacrament, and to extract the consequences. But note from the beginning that the relationship is not established between contract and sacrament. Rather, it considers marriage as such, in its double dimension, natural and sacramental. I do not know if this was an explicit decision on the part of the Commission; but it is clear, in my opinion, that this is the best path, or maybe the only one, to make understandable the relation applied to marriage between the order of creation and that of redemption, between the order of nature and the order of grace.

Belonging to the order of creation, what is transfigured into a sacrament, without changing its essence, or what is elevated to the order of redemption is not primarily the act of contracting the marriage, but marriage itself, its essence, its characteristics, its objectives. It is in this sense that the *in fieri* of marriage is sacramentally affected and not inversely.

Assuming this, let us analyze the following proposals.

> 1. Since all things were created in Christ, through Christ and in view of Christ, marriage as a true institution of the creator, becomes a figure of the mystery of union of Christ, the groom, with the Church, the bride, and, in a certain way, is directed toward this mystery. Marriage celebrated between two baptized

---

[107]Cf. Latin version in *Gregorianum* 78 (1978) 453–464.

persons has been elevated to the dignity of a real sacrament, that is, signifying and participating in the spousal love of Christ and the Church.

In this proposal there is a rich doctrinal content, to which the most genuine Christian thought of all times, and especially of the classical times of theology and canon law, bears testimony. Marriage belongs to the order of creation; it is an *institutum naturae*. But it is from its origin and potentially a sacrament, inserted in the history of salvation, that is, in the history of the alliance of God with man. Now then, when reaching the fullness of time, this radical orientation representing the union of Christ with the Church is actualized. This is what constitutes its elevation to the dignity of a sacrament properly so called: formerly it was potentially a sacrament or a sacrament of the old law; today it is a sacrament of the new law. Without changing the natural essence it has become a new reality as redeemed humanity is a new creation. For this same reason, just as a potentially redeemed person starts to be a new creature through baptism, the sacramental newness of marriage is made actual whenever the united couple, in whom marriage consists, has been incorporated into the mystery of Christ through baptism.

> 2. Between two baptized persons, marriage as an institution willed by God the creator, cannot be separated from marriage the sacrament because the sacramental nature of marriage between the baptized is not an accidental element which could be or could just as well not be, but is rather so tied into the essence of it as to be inseparable from it.

In this second proposal the thesis of the inseparability between marriage and sacrament, between the created reality and the elevated reality, is clearly and unequivocally affirmed. It is a consequence of the previous proposal, although a new reason is added in line with that expressed by the papal magisterium. In fact, the sacramentality of marriage between the baptized is not something attached extrinsically. It is not something accessory or accidental, but something instrinsic, which penetrates to the essence and which transfigures marriage without changing it in the same manner as grace perfects nature without destroying it.

> 3. Thus between baptized persons no other married state can exist really and truly which differs from that willed by Christ in which the Christian man and woman, giving and accepting one another freely and with the irrevocable personal consent as spouses, are radically removed from the "hardness of heart" of which Christ

spoke (cf. Mt. 19:8) and, through the sacrament, really and truly included within the mystery of marital union of Christ with his Church, thus being given the real possibility of living in perpetual love. As a consequence the Church cannot in any way recognize that two unbaptized persons are living in a marital state equal to their dignity and their life as "new creatures in Christ" if they are not united by the sacrament of matrimony.

In this proposal two supplementary conclusions are established. (a) Between the baptized, there is no conjugal status which is not sacramental. (b) Consequently, in the case of the baptized, the Church cannot recognize as a real marriage a union or conjugal status which is not sacramental.

It is easy to arrive at such conclusions when all the foregoing is understood. Marriage has suffered the vagaries of human nature. Just as humanity has never existed in the state of pure nature, neither has marriage ever been outside the status of elevated, downfallen and redeemed humanity. The baptismal event actualizes the last stage and gives it the character of irreversibility. Marriage between the baptized can not mean anything else but the marriage-sacrament. The Church may impede a marriage between two baptized persons, may stipulate limits for the exercise of *jus connibii*; but if they really marry, she may not impede it from being a sacrament.

4. The strength and the greatness of the grace of Christ is extended to all people, even those beyond the Church, because of God's desire to save all men. They shape all human marital love and strengthen created nature as well as matrimony "as it was in the beginning." Men and women therefore who have not yet heard the gospel message are united by a human covenant in a legitimate marriage. This legitimate marriage is not without authentic goodness and values, which assure its stability. These goods, even though the spouses are not aware of it, come from God the creator, and are included, in a certain inchoative way, in the marital love which united Christ with His Church.

This thesis confirms the potentially sacramental value of any legitimate marriage. Although the spouses are unaware of it, a real marriage of the nonbaptized is also inserted into the dynamics of the history of salvation, just as all men, called to salvation in Christ, are incorporated potentially into the present economy of salvation.

It cannot be concluded from this that baptized nonbelievers are in a worse situation than the non-baptized because they are unable to enter into a true natural marriage. This conclusion might be legitimate if the lack of faith was considered in itself as a radical incapacity to contract the sacrament of marriage. But in the traditional version of the problem, baptized nonbelievers, by being able to contract a real sacrament of marriage, once other essential requisites are complied with, would have only to remove the obstacle of lack of faith for the sacramental grace to display its efficacy. Those not baptized, although their marriage is real, with goods and values connected potentially with the espousal of Christ and the Church, can never receive sacramental grace unless through baptism they are incorporated into Christ.

> 5. It would thus be contradictory to say that Christians, baptized in the Catholic Church, might really and truly take a step backward by being content with a non-sacramental marital state. This would mean that they could be content with the "shadow" when Christ offers them the reality of his espousal love. Still we cannot exclude cases where the conscience of even some Christians is deformed by ignorance or invincible error. They come to believe that they are able to contract marriage without receiving the sacrament.
>
> In such a situation, on the one hand, they are unable to contract a valid sacramental marriage because they lack any faith and lack the intention of doing what the Church wishes. On the other hand they still have the natural right to contract marriage. In such circumstances they are capable of giving and accepting one another as spouses because they intend to contract an irrevocable commitment. This mutual and irrevocable self-giving creates a psychological relationship between them which by its internal structure is different from a transitory relationship.
>
> Still this relationship, even if it resembles marriage, cannot in any way be recognized by the Church as a nonsacramental conjugal society. For the Church, no natural marriage separated from the sacrament exists for baptized persons, but only natural marriage elevated to the dignity of a sacrament.

Various questions are contemplated in this proposal. In the first place, the previous theses are ratified with regard to inseparability and the irreversibility of the baptismal character. There cannot be a natural marriage between the baptized without it being a sacrament since the mere possibility would entail a contradiction. Every such marriage has been elevated by Christ to the dignity of a sacrament and when it passes into concrete existence through the mediation of the baptized couple, the offer of the spousal love of Christ, the definitive offer of salvation, cannot be produced. Still, what happens when two Christians due to ignorance or invincible error think they can contract a marriage that is not sacramental?

The answer of the Commission has a double aspect which should be delineated. On the one hand, an incapacity to "celebrate" the sacrament validly, located in the negation of faith and the negation of the intention of doing what the Church does, is affirmed. On the other hand, considering the natural right to marry, the possibility is stated of satisfying this right through a mutual and irrevocable union consisting of a psychological relationship in the manner of a marriage, but not recognizable by the Church as a real nonsacramental conjugal association since the two dimensions are inseparable.

In other words, if we do not misinterpret the thought of the Commission, when due to a lack of faith the offer of Christ is rejected, one of two things may happen: (a) either the marriage itself is rejected because it is not thinkable without its sacramentality—we would then be in a typical case of simulation; (b) or such rejection would mean not an incapacity to marry, nor a simulation of the conjugal pact as such, but an incapacity to accept the sacramental offer of Christ. In this latter supposition, there are also two interpretations: either the traditional one, which recognizes that the rejection by a free man of the salvific action of Christ renders His offer fruitless; or that which appears to derive from the meaning of the decisive words, "they are incapable of validly celebrating the sacrament of matrimony," in which case the lack of faith would not only block the saving efficacy of the offer of Christ, but the offer itself would not be made. This is to erase the *ex opere operato* of the sacrament, that is the conception of sacramentality as above all an action of God.

If this interpretation were true regarding the need of faith for the sacrament of marriage to be valid, then, in our modest opinion, the intrinsic relationship between baptism and the sacramentality of marriage would be ineffectual, and the reason for upholding the thesis of inseparability would be dissolved. For the elevation by Christ of the natural institution to a sacrament would be conditioned by a subjective factor, faith; while baptism, although it ontologically constitutes man in a new status within the economy of salvation, would have only a subsidiary efficacy in converting the conjugal bond into the *res et sacramentum*; i.e., into that new sacramental state to which marriage is elevated when the united couple is objectively inserted into the mystery of Christ.

On a more technical plane, this interpretation would mean that, to the known chapters of nullity affecting the conjugal pact as such—diriment impediments, consent and form—a new chapter would have to be added which would not affect marital consent but the sacrament; all of which entails so radical a change in the conception and regulation of marriage between Christians, that it compels at least a certain reserve regarding hasty conclusions which endanger substantial values, jealously guarded by Christian tradition.

In the last two proposals, the Commission stands up against some erroneous pastoral objectives which, by their very nature, endanger the thesis of inseparability:

> 6. It is therefore wrong and very dangerous to introduce within the Christian community the practice of permitting the couple to celebrate successively various wedding ceremonies on different levels, even though they be connected, or to allow a priest or deacon to assist at or read prayers on the occasions of a nonsacramental marriage which baptized persons wish to celebrate.

It would also be erroneous and dangerous to reevaluate the dignity of civil marriage in such a way that in the eyes of Christians it appears as a real and legitimate union:

> 7. The Catholic faithful should be adequately instructed that these official formalities, commonly called civil marriage, do not constitute real marriage for them except in cases when through dispensation from canonical form or because of a very prolonged absence of a qualified church witness the civil ceremony itself can serve as the extraordinary canonical form for the celebration of the sacrament of matrimony (cf. canon 1098 [canon 1116 in 1983 code]). For non-Christians and often even for non-Catholic Christians this civil ceremony can have constitutive value both as legitimate marriage and as sacramental marriage.

2. The Theological Juridical Bases of Inseparability

a. Marriage follows human nature

Professor Hervada has based part of his reflection about the sacramentality of marriage on this axiomatic principle, and on it he also bases the inseparability—not the identity—between the natural institution and the sacrament. Marriage follows human nature because its values, requirements and intrinsic constitution "are not dimensions imposed *ab extra*" but "arise from the very structure of human existence (therefore their author is God the creator) and for this reason they depend on the state—original, fallen, redeemed by grace—in which human nature is found, to the degree such a state is attributable to the creative divine will and not—as in the case of fallen nature—to the destructive human will."[108]

Starting from this principle, it is sufficient to know the stages through which the history of humanity has passed, to know which have also been the stages of marriage. It is sufficient to know the status of the couple joined in marriage to infer the actual level on which their conjugal union is verified. In principle, theology has taught that the state of pure nature has never existed. Thus a marriage without any supernatural dimension "is as much a hypothetical institution as the state of pure nature."[109] On the other hand, just as Christ is the Redeemer of mankind, of all human beings, and everyone is called to participate *in actu* in the redemption, so also "every marriage is ordered and called to be a sacrament by the design of God,"[110] and every marriage revolves within the orbit of the economy of salvation. This does not mean that the so-called legitimate marriage is in any strict sense a sacrament—an effective sign of grace—since for this it is required that the persons joined be incorporated into Christ through baptism; that is, that redemption be actualized in them. If the persons contracting marriage are baptized, the marriage itself is also elevated to the condition of sacrament. It is accommodated to the status of redeemed nature, to the new person arising from baptism—and this even on the assumption that baptism takes place after a marriage, as the Church has constantly taught. "In fact," writes Hervada, "redemption, just as it supposes the elevation of the human person by grace to be a son of God, also supposes the elevation of marriage, the principle of generation, to a superior condition. And in the same manner that man as son of God is nature and grace, a sacramental marriage is a natural reality enriched by a supernatural dimension. In both cases, without identifying nature and grace, the supernatural presupposes, integrates, heals, lifts and enhances the natural."[111]

Sacramentality thus understood, it is impossible to infer that it is something added exteriorly to the natural reality of marriage:

> In the same manner that for a Christian to be a son of God does not represent an outer addition to his human nature, but that the Christian, son of God, is the person himself healed, lifted and enriched by grace, so also is the sacrament of marriage the same marriage enriched by sacramentality. And as in the Christian, son of God, there is nature and a supernatural factor, so the marriage-

[108]Hervada, "Cuestiones varias," p. 139.
[109]Ibid., p. 168.
[110]Ibid., p. 169.
[111]Hervada, *Dialogos sobre el amor y el matrimonio,* p. 161.

sacrament comprises the natural institution and the supernatural dimension, in one inseparable unit.[112]

If the couple is Christian, the sacrament is not separable from marriage because just as marriage is inherent to the human person, so is it configured to fit the condition in which the person is. But not only is inseparability inferred from this postulate; in our modest opinion, the traditional thesis, that a lack of faith does not impinge in any way on the validity of the sacrament unless indirectly, that is by provoking a positive and voluntary rejection of marriage itself, is also based on it. For the sacramentality of marriage arises from the fact that the couple is ontologically inserted into the mystery of Christ by the character of baptism, and not because of the intention of the contracting parties.

This positive manner of understanding sacramentality as a corollary of the principle that marriage corresponds to the level with the state of nature in which the contracting parties or those married are found, has its justification in the oldest tradition of Christian thought. A well-known text of St. Leo the Great in the sixth century already views marriage with this perspective: "Whenever the couple's society has been so constituted from the beginning that besides the joining of sexes it contains in itself the 'sacramentum' of Christ and the Church."[113]

Analyzing the biblical exegesis of some authors of the ninth century, we came to the following conclusions in another work:[114]

1. Marriage at its original institution already was a type or figure of another, mysterious, future reality. This illuminates or explains better the moral and institutional symbolism we mentioned before: when God impressed on marriage a mysterious meaning beyond the limits of its own nature, He logically had to give it certain characteristics similar to those of the mysterious reality it concealed.

2. From the historical fact that marriage was instituted in order to symbolize the union of Christ with the Church, it may also be inferred that every legitimately contracted marriage entails that symbolism, since it is radically immersed in the same nature.

3. The prophetic vision intimately connects the moment of the

---

[112]Ibid., p. 173.

[113]Leo the Great, Epistula 167, IV (Mansi VI: 402).

[114]T. Rincón, "Siglo IX al XIII," p. 56. We refer to the following exegetes: Haymon, Rhaban Maur, Pascasius Radbert, Angelomo, etc. Cf. E. Tejero, "La sacramentalidad del matrimonio en la historia del pensiemento cristiano," Ius Canonicum 14 (1974) 11–31.

institution of marriage with the complete realization of the mystery of Christ and of the Church. However, this does not prevent the distinction, the clear differentiation, between the two moments: a first moment of radical ordination to symbolize that union, and a second moment of present and effective signification. Those who through baptism are presently incorporated into the mystery of Christ and the Church, join the double moment into one. Marriage between the non-baptized, on the other hand, is still at the institutional moment, although open to the historical-Christian completeness if it is therein immersed.

4. Finally we believe that from the citations given above, we can infer that its signification was already seen as a constitutive element in the institution of marriage. It is worth nothing that the significance referred to is exclusively the union of Christ with His Church; although the institution occurred prior to original sin, our authorities deal with the historical fact of redemption and leave aside the hypothesis of an unfallen humanity.

The great theologians of the thirteenth century have also left us affirmations that a sacramental significance was present in some way at the very institution of marriage from its origin; that therefore this significance affects every marriage, including that contracted between the non-baptized; that marriage strictly follows the history, the destiny and the states passed through by human nature; and that in the fullness of time through the Incarnation of the Word, marriage acquired *in actu* the sacramental significance to which it was radically ordered *ab origine*, and was thus converted into a channel of grace and salvation. Here are some examples.

For Hugh of St. Cher, ". . . the marriage of Christ and the Church had been prefigured in paradise in Adam and Eve, begun in faith and in the promise of the patriarchs and the prophets, consummated in the assumption of a human nature."[115]

In the thought of St. Bonaventure, it is also clear that God, when He instituted marriage in paradise, sealed it with the essential character of the significance of the union of Christ and the Church which will always be an immutable element, inseparable from the reality of marriage. Therefore, he affirms that the unbaptized contract the sacrament, although in an incomplete and imperfect form, because there is no significance *in actu* but *aptitudine tantum*.[116]

St. Albert speaks very clearly of two or three marriage institutions corresponding to the different status of nature:

> Nothing should prohibit marriage from having two or three kinds of divine institution: first as an institution of nature itself, another as an institution of fallen nature, and a third as an institution of redeemed nature in Christ; and thus marriage is a sacrament of the innocent of the old and new laws.[117]

The Angelic Doctor also consistently considers marriage according to the different state of nature in which it was instituted: before sin, after sin, and as a "sacrament of the new law. In the state of innocence, it was instituted not as a sacrament but as a function of nature. Consequently, however, it foreshadowed something in relation to Christ and the Church: just as everything else foreshadowed Christ."[118] From this he concludes that marriage between the non-baptized is in some way *sacramentum habitualiter*, although *non actualiter*.[119]

This historical analysis brings into relief the enormous relevance acquired by the significant dimension of marriage. It is clear that, like the other sacraments, marriage is an efficacious sign: it signifies and produces grace. Therefore, the causative dimension of grace cannot be forgotten. However, unlike the other sacraments, in marriage the significant aspect has its own specific weight in virtue of which the transfiguration of the natural institution is based, as well as the whole of the conjugal order. For example, indissolubility is rooted in the bond; it acquires greater strength for being a sign of that indestructible union of Christ with His Church, brought about by the hypostatic union. Therefore it is imperative that the study of the sacramentality of marriage not lose sight of this dimension of sign. It was precisely with Scotus, if I am not mistaken, that this perspective first got unfocused, giving rise to the extrinsicist conception of sacramentality which impoverished the reality of marriage by depriving it of its mysterious and significative value.

b. The idea of "elevation"

In the statement of sacramentality made in the foregoing paragraph, the idea is already implied that marriage as a natural reality has been elevated

---

[115]Hugh of St. Cher, *Opera Omnia in Universum Vetus et Novum Testamentum*, t. III (Lugduni, 1669), fol. 66, v. Cf. T. Rincón, "Siglo IX al XIII," p. 266.

[116]Cf. T. Rincón, "Siglo IX al XIII," pp. 302–313.

[117]Albert the Great, *In IV Sententiarum*, dist. XXVI, art. V. Cf. T. Rincón, "Siglo IX al XIII," p. 330.

[118]Thomas Aquinas, *Summa Theolgiae* III, q. 61, a. 2 ad 3.

[119]Idem, *Supplementum* q. 59, a. 2 ad 1.

by the redemption of Christ to the condition of a sacrament in the strict sense, in the same manner as a human being, without changing the natural being, is converted by baptism into a new creature.

This idea of elevation, aside from being an expression used by the papal magisterium and synthesized in c. 1055, is possibly the richest category in theological consequences concerning the structure of Christian marriage, as E. Corecco has very justly stated. The idea of elevation means "that marriage, as a natural reality, rooted in the economy of creation, is fully realized in the sacrament, in the same way that the economy of creation is fully realized in that of salvation."[120]

In the abstract, the elevation to a sacrament is produced by the fact of redemption. The institution of marriage, just like the economy of creation, is inserted effectively into the new economy of the covenant of Christ and the Church. But it is the concrete event of baptism which actualizes the redemption in each case and which likewise inserts natural marriage into the sacramental economy of the new covenant.

Just as the order of the creation is not destroyed by the order of redemption, but is rather perfected in the sense of the scholastic principle "grace perfects and does not destroy nature," so also does the elevation to a sacrament not destroy the natural dimension of marriage; on the contrary, it is that same natural reality which is lifted up, which "receives a new light and is enriched with new values,"[121] which is converted not into an empty symbol, but into a mystery full of effective significance, into a sacred and holy thing. Scheeben then had every reason to say that the nuptial blessing and the intervention of the priest was not required *for* the marriage to be holy, but *because* it was holy.[122]

Within the idea of elevation so understood lies the identity between marriage and sacrament, and as a consequence their inseparability. Corecco writes:

> Natural marriage, as a reality rooted in the economy of creation, is the same reality that the sacrament is in the economy of salvation . . . the principle of elevation postulates, within the internal dynamics of the economy of salvation, that of identity and inseparability of the sacrament from the contractual marriage.[123]

[120]Corecco.
[121]Hervada, "Cuestiones varias," p. 60.
[122]Scheeben, pp. 642, 645.
[123]Corecco.

There are three principal practical consequences which flow from the preceding doctrinal exposition and which are brilliantly stated by Professor Corecco, in substantial accordance with the thought of Professor Caffarra, to whom we shall refer below:

1. For a Christian, a return from the economy of salvation to that of creation is impossible, because this simply does not exist except with regard to reality elevated and assumed within the history of the new covenant. In the same sense

> It is no longer possible for a baptized married couple to leave aside their sacramental marriage and return to a natural law marriage, since the latter no longer exists as a reality filled with liberating and salvific meaning except as a sacrament.

2. Consequently, those who exclude the sacrament with a positive act of the will,

> decides to place their marriage outside of the economy of salvation, without being able to create as an alternative, a natural law marriage which still possesses a valid and salvific significance. The marriage becomes theologically invalid and as a consequence juridically non-existent.

3. Although the exclusion of sacramentality by a positive act of the will may make a supposedly natural marriage null and non-existent, the mere lack of faith does not directly attack the validity of the sacrament:

> This explains why the Church has always regarded, even until today, the marriage between baptized Catholics as a sacrament, independently of the fact whether or not the parties regard it a sacrament in the strict sense. The objective existence of the sacrament does not depend on the subjective faith of the individual.[124]

c. The relation to Christ of everything created

Our intention is to summarize in this section the thought of Caffarra, one of the authors who has recently studied the subject of inseparability more profoundly from both an historical and a systematic point of view. As a member of the International Theological Commission he was able to get to the roots of the above-mentioned published theses when he undertook the task of explaining some of them, namely those dealing with the relation-

---

[124]Ibid.

ship between marriage as an institution at creation and marriage as a sacrament.

His main objective is to determine the theological foundation on which the impossibility of a nonsacramental marriage between the baptized lies. He does not expressly consider the relationship between baptism, faith, and the sacrament of marriage. This is in accord with his belief that the solution to this second problem does not solve the first one, since even on the assumption that a lack of faith impedes the valid celebration of the sacrament, the fact of being baptized would still prevent a couple from contracting a natural marriage.

The idea which gives structure to his thought, orients his theological reflection and inspires his conclusions regarding marriage, is the ordination of all creation to Christ. Therefore his exposition is made in two stages. First he discusses the theological question about the relationship between creation and redemption, between nature and grace. The theological conclusions extracted from this reflection are applied in a second stage to marriage, created institution and redeemed reality. Professor Caffarra notes that the present polemic has arisen, and not by coincidence, just when the theological problem of the relationship between nature and grace is being debated anew.[125]

Regarding the general theme, his basic premise is that Christ is the Alpha and Omega of all creation, the ultimate reason for all created things. He fully develops an expression with which one of the thesis of the International Theological Commission begins: "everything has been created in Chrsit, through Christ, and for Christ." Looking at things from this perspective—and at humankind in the first place—makes us see in terms of classical theology that nature was from the beginning elevated to the supernatural order, and that consequently the status of pure nature has never existed.

With reference to this last consequence, Professor Caffarra makes an interesting disquisition which is worth highlighting since it explains and clarifies many present attempts to structure marriage as a natural reality without any reference to sacramentality, thus favoring the existence of two marriage realities, different and separable. In summary, the author asks the following: granted that only the states of elevated, fallen and redeemed nature have existed, is it possible for a theologian to speculate about a creation without grace, to think about the hypothesis of a state of pure nature?

The answer is affirmative but with the important qualification that the

---

[125]Caffarra, p. 375.

reflection always remain at an abstract level, or in other words, that what is a mere hypothesis not become a thesis, elevating to reality what is nothing more than a mere possibility. God could have created the world in another form, but by revelation we know that the only existing reality is the elevated reality, the creation ordered to Christ, aimed at the historical plenitude of redemption and at the eschatological plenitude, when all things will be restored in Christ. Therefore, the risk lies in "considering as real that which remains within the realm of possibility (a creation which does not call for communication *ad extra* of the divine life in Christ and which should consist in itself), and as a possibility that which in fact is the unique existing reality (creation as communication of the trinitarian life)."[126]

Summarizing his thought, the author mentions three fundamental theses which we quote in full in view of their brevity:

1. Man (and therefore also marriage as a human reality) was created in fact in view of the alliance with God in Jesus Christ by the gift of the Spirit.
2. Man (and therefore also marriage) is therefore susceptible to be finalized toward this same alliance.
3. Man, (and therefore marriage) is truly realized in this alliance with God.[127]

As is obvious in these conclusions, the application of these general conclusions to marriage as a human reality is clear and logical. Professor Caffarra continues here the oldest and most genuine tradition of Christian thought about the sacramentality of marriage, as we mentioned before.

In agreement with this constant Christian tradition, we accept the affirmation that marriage, as part of creation ordered to Christ, cannot theologically have more than one real sense: "Marriage was in fact instituted in view of the participation in Christ in the alliance with God."[128]

This is the only existing reality. It does not contradict the transcendency and gratuity of the elevation, nor does it compromise the intimacy which exists between sacramentality and the created institution but rather establishes and explains it. On the contrary, it is the extrinsicist conception of sacramentality which the papal magisterium has condemned and which seems to be the inevitable consequence of taking as real what is merely

[126]Ibid., p. 376.
[127]Ibid., p. 377.
[128]Ibid.

possible. If, in fact, natural marriage really existed as something by itself, in a state of pure nature as it were, there would be two marriage realities and the sacramental reality would logically be constituted as something added. As Scheeben already complained, it would consist merely in a positive order given by God (an extrinsic factor) by virtue of which an effective sign of grace would be added to the natural reality.[129]

But the truth is that two marriages do not exist, any more than two creations or two human natures. There exists only one marriage which, like humankind itself, has passed through the stages of the history of salvation and has always been ordered to signify the union of Christ with His Church. Right from the days of earthly paradise in which marriage was instituted, states St. Bonaventure, marriage represented this mysterious union, since even then God anticipated the Incarnation of the Word. Even under the hypothesis that man had not sinned, he adds, "the sacrament would not be void of signification."[130]

One must conclude that if the human couple is incorporated into Christ through baptism, the only marriage they can contract is the sacrament, since it is the only one existing: "to decide to depart from this economy in order to return to an economy of pure creation is to fall into non-being."[131] And in the case of marriage, such a decision "produces absolutely nothing."[132]

This is so to such an extent, states Caffarra, that asking the Church to recognize as a real, nonsacramental conjugal union one that is contracted by two baptized persons, is to ask for an ecclesial impossibility:

> For the Church, the decision to marry "naturally" and not "sacramentally" can signify only one thing: the decision to marry outside of the economy of salvation which is the only one in which the Church can and must recognize marriage.[133]

---

[129]Scheeben, p. 628.

[130]Bonaventure, *Opera Omnia*, t. IV, *Commentaria in IV Lib. Sententiarum*, dist. XXVI, a. 2, q. 1 ad 3.

[131]Caffarra, p. 379, note 22.

[132]Ibid., p. 378.

[133]Ibid., pp. 379, 381.

This present study was already prepared when the book *Problèmes doctrinaux du mariage chrétien* (Louvain-LaNeuve, 1979) came into my hands. It includes the works of Delhaye and Caffarra which are cited above. I only wish to add the clear position of Caffarra regarding the thesis of inseparability, p. 82: "Cela étant, la these de l'inseparabilité, nous semble devoir être tenue au moins comme 'doctrine catholique,' et, à notre humble avis, comme n'étant plus sujette à la discussion des théologiens. D'un côté, elle se rattache étroitement, selon l'analogie de la foi, aux vérités de foi, et, d'autre part, elle a été constamment enseignée par le Magistère Pontifical de Pie VI à Leon XIII, avant d'être introduite dans le Code de Droit Canonique (c. 1012)."

E. Conclusion: Criteria for a Correct Understanding
of the Sacramentality of Marriage

In summary, our analysis of the theses defending separability have lead us to the following critical judgments.

1. Regarding the sacraments in general, there is a more or less explicit rejection of *ex opere operato*, a rejection which in the case of marriage is especially significant when the aim is to have sacramentality exist not among the baptized as in canon 1055, but rather vaguely among believers or among the Christian faithful. Aside from introducing a factor of insecurity which is not easily surmountable, this entails in my opinion a frontal attack on the whole sacramental system.

2. There is seemingly no awareness that the sacrament of marriage is a truly effective sign of grace in a manner specifically different from that of the other sacraments so that sacramental categories are not applicable to matrimony in an indiscriminate and univocal manner. Its specificity lies in that matrimony is the only sacrament whose substratum is a natural reality complete in itself, that is not modified substantially by its elevation to a sacrament. It is the natural reality itself which is made a sign without another rite having to concur, as is the case with the water in baptism or with the bread and wine at the Eucharist. According to St. Bonaventure,[134] marriage in itself "is capable by nature and signifies by institution." The divine design of elevating it to a sacrament does not pass through any sacred rite.

3. The significative factor is unknown or undervalued, accentuating instead the causing of grace. This is historically the doctrinal position of Scotus. The sacramental significance which saturates the whole natural being of marriage is decisive for understanding why the Supreme Pontiffs have consistently rejected the extrinsicist conception of the sacramentality of marriage. The significative value of marriage is also the element of the traditional doctrine which renders the accusation of automatism unrealistic.

4. As a consequence of the foregoing, the *in fieri* aspect of sacramentality is accentuated almost exclusively, practically ignoring the classical Thomistic doctrine of the *res et sacramentum*. From this flows a tendency to give utmost importance to the sacramental intention of the contracting parties-ministers, as if the elevation of marriage to a sign of the union of Christ and the Church depended on it. This ritualist conception also exhibits a propensity to make of the rite, as in the other sacraments, a constituting factor of sacramentality. It is true that the religious rites which in the present discipline of the Church usually accompany the act of

---

[134]Bonaventure, dist. XXVI, a. 2, q. 1.

contracting a marriage have a definite pedagogical as well as catechetical value in showing the contracting faithful that what they are going to create is not only a natural bond, but also a Christian mystery filled with significance and grace. The rites also enhance that efficacy which is *ex opere operantis*, that is, they help make the salvific action of the sacrament more fruitful. But in no way does the sacramentality of marriage depend on a sacred rite in the same sense as ablution with the water at baptism needs to be ritualized in order for it to cease being a merely natural reality—a washing for corporal cleanliness—and come to be effectively a mystic ablution and a spiritual cleanliness.

In summary, in the first place, what is in question is not so much the subject of separability or inseparability, but the concept itself of the sacramentality of marriage. The thesis of separability is nothing more than the corollary of what we consider an erroneous statement about what matrimony is and how it specifically differs or not from the other sacraments. The ground for its specific difference has been explained above, when we exposed the theological-juridical foundations of inseparability. In fact, it may not be affirmed of any other material reality serving to support the other sacraments, that it is a reality which accompanies the historical journey of human nature, or that it is a reality in itself elevated, or that in itself it is a created reality intrinsically ordered to the redemption. Only marriage is a self-standing created reality which acquires the plenitude of significance and of saving effectiveness when the couple is incorporated to Christ through baptism.

In the view of this negative evaluation, we consider it opportune to formulate, in conclusion, certain criteria for understanding the true extension of the sacramentality of marriage and, consequently, of the thesis of inseparability.

1. A Methodological Presupposition: Marriage as a Permanent Sign

Throughout these pages we have made constant reference to this subject inasmuch as we consider it of utmost importance when understanding the sacramentality of marriage and because we believe that nevertheless this approach is not very general among those students of matrimony who follow the methodolocical line based on canon 1055, §2 of the current code, which expressly refers to the inseparability of contract and sacrament. Regarding the new code, one amendment proposed substituting the word *foedus* for *contractus*, but to this the consultors were opposed since they understood that the word *contractus* indicates marriage *in fieri*, while *foedus* can mean marriage *in facto esse*. In any case, ''the word 'contract' should not be entirely suppressed because in this canon it refers to marriage as a natural reality which is raised to the dignity of a sacrament; therefore marriage as an institution of nature is already a contract."[135] This proves to what extent the conception *in fieri* of marriage is established in the canonical mentality when dealing with its natural as well as sacramental aspects. This approach does not at all favor, in my opinion, the thesis the consultors sustain in substance and to which we adhere.

There is little doubt regarding the historical fact that before Scotus authors situated the sacramental sign mostly *in facto esse*. The best exponent is the Angelic Doctor who, distinguishing between *sacramentum tantum*, *res et sacramentum*, and *res tantum*, accentuates the *res et sacramentum*, that is the bond, to the point that, for the Angelic Doctor, consent is not the immediate cause of grace but the cause of the bond: ". . . so the outward acts and the words expressive of consent directly effect a certain tie which is the sacrament of matrimony; and this tie by virtue of its divine institution works dispositively to the infusion of grace."[136]

On the other hand, if sacramentality were to reside fundamentally in consent, it would be difficult to develop the concept of sacramental significance and its intrinsic connection with the whole conjugal order, especially with the notes of unity and indissolubility which are essential properties of the bond. But in that age old tradition, marriage itself is what is constituted as the mystery and the sign of that permanent and indestructible union of Christ with the Church.

It is perhaps that Thomistic and age old context which best explains the luminous words of Pope John Paul II:

> Certainly, every sacrament includes a participation in the nuptial love of Christ for His Church. But in matrimony, the modality and content of such a participation are most proper. The spouses participate in Christ's spousal love precisely as spouses, the two of them, as a couple, and to such an extent that the first and immediate effect of marriage (*res et sacramentum*) is not supernatural grace itself, but the Christian conjugal bond, a communion between the pair which is typically Christian because it represents the mystery of the Incarnation of Christ and its mystery of union.[137]

---

[135]*Communicationes* 9 (1977) 121.

[136]Thomas Aquinas, *Supplementum*, q. 42, a. 3 ad 2.

[137]John Paul II, Discourse to CLER and FIDAP, November 3, 1979, DP-368, *Palabra* (1980).

As is known, a doctrinal current was initiated by Scotus which accentuated exclusively matrimony *in fieri* even from the sacramental point of view. The results of this approach have already been mentioned in these pages. On the other hand, the great defenders of inseparability—Bellarmine, Pedro de Ledezma, Sanchez, etc.—stressed that sacramentality, just as in the Eucharist, is not produced in marriage only *dum fit* but also *dum permanet*. These classical authors are very clear that although grace is produced at the initial moment if there is no obstacle to impede it, the sacramental significance is as permanent as marriage itself.

In modern times Hervada has carefully studied this question and has distinguished two relevant aspects: marriage as *signum rei sacrae* and marriage as *signum efficax*. According to the first aspect, "the representation of the union of Christ with the Church is not part of the conjugal consent, but of the marriage, or in other words of the bond (according to the doctrine of St. Paul, which is peacefully admitted by the tradition). The state of union between a man and a woman is, then, a sign of a sacred thing (*signum rei sacrae*), and this significative nature of marriage is the root and foundation of its sacramentality in the proper sense."[138]

Regarding sacramentality in the proper sense, that is as an effective sign, (*signum efficax*) of grace, "our view should include the unity between matrimony *in fieri* (the consent) and the matrimonial *esse* (the bond) because among other reasons, the consent is in every case a sign and a cause of grace with regard to the bond it originates, since it is in the bond where that primary feature of mystery and sign (of the union of Christ with His Church) resides, on which the sacramental nature of marriage is founded, as we have seen."[139]

According to Hervada, the classical distinction between *sacramentum tantum*, the exterior act or conjugal consent, the *res et sacramentum* or bond, the *res contenta*, that is grace, and the *res non contenta* or the union of Christ with His Church, refers to this unity.

In summary, the conjugal pact (contract, *in fieri*) is undoubtedly a sacramental factor since it is the sign and cause of the bond, as well as being a sign and a cause of grace. But the reduction of all sacramentality to this *in fieri* dimension, while it impoverishes the significative power of marriage, prepares the way methodologically, without intending it, for the thesis of separability and the situational concept of the sacrament of matrimony. This is the reason why we would have preferred that the new canon (c. 1055) substituted for canon 1012 of the 1917 *Codex* would

---

[138]Hervada, *El Derecho del Pueblo de Dios*, III, p. 151.
[139]Ibid.

simply have put *matrimonium* in place of *contractus*, just as we speak of inseparability between marriage and sacrament. In our modest opinion, there can be no fundamental opposition to this terminological change, because at bottom what has been elevated to the dignity of a sacrament is the marriage as natural institution and not only the marriage contract.

2. Sacramental Categories Applicable to Marriage

The univocal application of all sacramental categories to marriage is another factor of confusion. As already explained before, it took a while before the concept of sacramentality in the strict sense was applied to Christian marriage, although the notion of a sacramental significance is already present in the most primitive sources. In our opinion one of the reasons for this historical fact lies in the univocal and therefore unsuccessful application to marriage of the sacramental categories in use for the other sacraments. For example, during the twelfth century it was a universally admitted doctrine that the sacraments produce what they signify; they were effective signs. But in the sacrament of marriage there was a difficulty: although a sign of the union of Christ with the Church, it could not produce what it signified. As is well know, to obviate this difficulty it was decided to make a distinction between *res contenta* (grace) and *res non contenta* (the union of Christ with His Church). Theology and canonical jurisprudence should now devote themselves to clarifying the other sacramental categories, whose univocal application to marriage makes a clear comprehension of inseparability difficult if not impossible.

Such is the case, for example, with sacramental intention, to which Hervada refers in these terms:

> This characteristic of marriage explains why an intention need not be directed specifically toward the confection of the sacrament. The intention of marrying is the only necessary intention. For example, if a sacramental intention is not added to the ablution, if there is only the intention of making an ablution, obviously there is no baptism, for the reason mentioned above. But in the case of marriage there is no need for a special, sacramental intention other than the will to marry; the institution of matrimony is radically instituted as a sacrament, and therefore such a special sacramental intention, although very laudable and fitting, is unnecessary. The contractual intention is, by divine institution, a sacramental intention.[140]

[140]Hervada, "Cuestiones varias," p. 85.

Nor for F. Bersini "is the internal intention regarding the sacramentality required, that is the intention that refers to the intrinsic content of the rite, desired interiorly as a holy, religious and sacramental act. What is sufficient is the internal intention regarding the contract which in relation to the sacramentality of marriage is intentionally purely external, limited by the external formalities alone of the same."[141]

The same may be said of other categories frequently applied to the sacrament of marriage, like those of confection and administration. Are they applicable to marriage in the same sense as to the other sacraments? Hervada again answers negatively: the contracting parties are the real ministers, but they do not confect nor administer the sacrament "in an unequivocal sense, such as these terms are predicated of the other sacramental actions. If, as is customary, by *confection of the sacrament* we understand the realization of the rite or sacred action through the application of the form (words) to the matter (rite), and if by *administration*, the application of a sacrament to a subject, then it does not seem correct to apply these terms in the same sense to marriage."[142]

For one reason, this sacrament is not made actual by any rite; it is sufficient to give existence to the marriage for the created bond to be, by divine institution, a sacramental bond. In my opinion, the thesis of inseparability can only be understood this way.

3. Reevaluation of the Significant Factor of Marriage and its Connection with Baptism

"The sacramentality of marriage," Pope John Paul II said in the aforementioned speech, "can be understood only in the light of the history of salvation. Now then, this history of salvation consists in the history of the covenant and union between Yahweh and Israel first, then during this time of the Church awaiting the eschatological fulfillment, between Jesus Christ and His Church. . . . This marriage constitutes, then, simultaneously a memorial, an actualizing and a prophecy of the history of the covenant. "It is a great mystery,' said St. Paul."[143] With these words, the Pope refers without doubt to the profound sacramental significance with which marriage is adorned in the present stage of the history of salvation: a commemorative, demonstrative and prophetic significance, according to

---

[141]Bersini, p. 556.

[142]Hervada, *El Derecho del Pueblo de Dios*, III, p. 165.

[143]John Paul II (see note 137). T. Rincón, "Revelancia jurídica de la significación sacramental del matrimonio," *Ius Canonicum* 9 (1969) 465–488; J. Tejero, "Significación sacramental y orden jurídico del matrimonio," *Ius Canonicum* 10 (1970) 137–160.

classical terminology; a representation of the "mystery of the Incarnation of Christ and of its mystery of union."

We have taken this text from the present Pontiff to indicate with it that marriage not only produces grace, but that it is also constituted as a significative mystery which penetrates and operates on the whole conjugal order. It is difficult to understand the doctrine of inseparability between marriage and its sacramentality when the effect of grace is given almost exclusive attention and the theological and juridical dimension of sacramental significance is practically neglected. We honestly believe that there are few themes like this in which the theological and canonical perspectives are called upon to complement one another. When explaining above the fundamentals of inseparability, we intentionally called them theological-juridical bases. We also discovered the same fundamental argument in various but supplementary authors, some juridical and some theological. Perhaps this broader vision of sacramentality holds the key to understanding why faith or a lack thereof is not a decisive factor for the sacramentality of marriage between the baptized, although circumstantially its salvific effectiveness would be affected.

All this is clear, of course, once it is admitted that "defection from the faith does not rupture the relationship of the baptized to the Church, which is founded in the baptismal character, which remains forever."[144] In other words, as the sacramental significance of marriage is better appreciated, so also are the profound dimensions of the sacrament of baptism, dimensions which do not disappear regardless of the moral conduct or the psychological state of the baptized.[145] This is a new key for understanding the profound significance of the sacramentality of marriage. Since this latter can be understood, according to John Paul II, only in the light of the history of salvation, it will be necessary to know what role is played by baptism in the insertion of humankind in that history of salvation from the ontological point of view, that is, regardless of the manner in which the baptismal commitments are existentially lived. Fears of magic or automatism have nothing to do with the profound truth that at the baptismal font a new creature is born, through baptism the order of redemption is made actual and concrete in each person, incorporation into the Church is indefectibly consummated. Therefore, every time that a Christian couple establishes a real marriage, such marriage is situated "in the time of the Church" even if they are unaware of it or do not want it, and therefore it is unthinkable that their marriage not be a sign of the "mystery of the

---

[144]Bertrams, p. 267.
[145]Navarrete, p. 268.

Incarnation of Christ and of its mystery of union.''[146] This is not automatism, at least in the derogatory sense with which this term is normally used; it is simply a mystery, as that indelible sign we call the baptismal character is a mystery, or as the recapitulation of all things in Christ is a mystery, although people are unaware of it or are opposed to it.

This has been the understanding shown by the Church's praxis through the ages when accepting as sacramental, from the moment in which the spouses have received baptism the natural— legitimate—bond contracted in infidelity; the Church has never required that such a marriage have a new *in fieri* or any special rite or be initiated by an act of faith, but only that infused faith be received in baptism. What has simply occurred is that this marriage, through the action of Christ applied by means of baptism, has ceased to be a merely potential sign, passing on to be *in actu* an effective sign of the union of Christ with the Church, that is, a sacrament in the strict sense, a sacrament of the new covenant.

[146]John Paul II.

THE ROLE OF LOVE IN CHRISTIAN MARRIAGE

John R. Connery, S.J.

In our society marriage is the result of a love relationship between a man and a woman. To us this seems perfectly natural, and even necessary, and we are inclined to conclude that it was ever thus. A little study of history, however, will show that love did not always play this role in marriage. A study of other cultures will also show that it does not play the same role in all societies even today. To understand the development that has taken place it will be helpful to take a brief look at the history of marriage, especially in the Judaeo-Christian tradition, with particular attention to the role love has played in this development. It will be possible due to the brevity of the paper, to consider only those works that played a more influential role in this development. The study hopes to show that despite cultural changes and differences love has always occupied a key position in Christian marriage.

EARLY CHURCH

If we look at the early chapters of Genesis, we will find there the foundation of the Judaeo-Christian concept of marriage. Genesis tells us that God created woman to be a suitable companion to man.[1] Augustine comments that this was not just to fulfill the social needs of man, since these could have been provided for by the creation of another man.[2] God provided man a unique kind of companion. This companion, a woman, would be taken from him, and therefore be of the same species, but she would also be different. The differences would make a kind of intimacy possible that would surpass all other human relationships, even that between parent and child. They could be two in one flesh. For this kind of union a man would leave his parents. In another passage in Genesis the couple are blessed with the power to increase and multiply.[3] Thus, attention is called to the procreative aspect of sexual creation. Although these passages are primarily aimed at a description of creation, they do

---

[1] Gen. 2:19.
[2] *De Genesi*, Lib. 9, c. 5 (*PL* 34:796).
[3] Gen. 1:28.

reveal to us the meaning of sex and marriage, including both the unitive (love) and procreative aspects of marriage and the conjugal act.

The above description is of marriage as it came from the hands of God. When the early Fathers and theologians discussed it, however, they had to consider it also in light of man's sin. This would make a difference. Before the Fall, marriage was aimed at procreation. After the Fall it served also as a *remedium*, a relief for concupiscence.[4] St. Augustine tells us that before the Fall man had the same control over his sex faculties that he had over the other members of his body.[5] They were under the control of his will and he could determine their movements. In that state charity rather than concupiscence would have initiated sexual activity. After the Fall the will did not have the same control over the sex faculty. Sexual reactions and desires occurred apart from it and even against it. They could not easily be controlled. In providing a legitimate outlet for sexual activity, marriage would offer relief from this concupiscence.[6] After the Fall, then, marriage served the goal both of procreation and of relief from concupiscence.

St. Augustine said that marriage also provides a kind of natural society for those of opposite sex.[7] This would obtain particularly in the case of older people, especially those who had lost their children, or those who had no children. Charity would govern this kind of relationship. Augustine is obviously speaking here of the companionship aspect of marriage referred to in Genesis, that is, of a love relationship between husband and wife. He is thinking particularly in terms of their relationship apart from sexual activity. As mentioned above, however, he says that charity would have inspired even sexual activity before the Fall. So he did not limit the rule of charity to the non-sexual aspects of marriage. What did concern him, however, was the influence concupiscence might have after the Fall, particularly on the marriage act. It might introduce a certain ambiguity into the act and interfere with the role charity should play.

Although the Fathers spoke of marriage as an *officium*, at least in respect to procreation, it was not considered of universal obligation, except at the beginning of history, or perhaps during times of catastrophe. In other words, one was ordinarily not obliged to marry for purposes of procreation. John Chrysostom would say that although marriage was instituted for

[4]*Contra Julianum Pelagianum*, c. 25, n. 57 (*PL* 44:732).
[5]*De peccato originali*, c. 35, 40 (*PL* 44:405).
[6]*De bono conjugali*, c. 3, n. 3 (*PL* 40:375). Augustine also considered marriage and the marriage act a healing institution because, besides providing an outlet for concupiscence, it gave couples a consciousness of parenthood. This consciousness would help to moderate their sex desire.
[7]*De bono conjugali*, c. 3, n. 3 (*PL* 40:375).

two purposes, as far as need was concerned, since the world was already populated, and since belief in the Resurrection has overcome death and the need to have offspring as survivors, procreation is not a necessity.[8] The only thing that would make marriage a necessity would be the problem of chaste living.

But during the whole period of the Old Testament marriage was considered by the Jews to be the natural choice. Marriage and procreation were highly regarded, and barrenness was considered a curse. There is no clear evidence that the Jews ever made fertility a condition for a valid marriage, as did other cultures in the past, and even today, but they did prize it highly. It was only with the coming of Christianity that celibacy became an accepted way of life. This was undoubtedly due to Christ's own example, as well as the subsequent urgings of Paul. But while Paul encouraged the celibate life, in no way did he condemn or discourage marriage. He told the Corinthians explicitly that becoming Christians would not require them to give up either married life or marriage relations.[9] He urged husbands to love their wives, giving them as a model the love of Christ for his Church. He even advised that marriage would be better than celibacy for those who could not handle the problem of concupiscence. So, while he urged others to remain as he was, he did not condemn marriage in any way but gave it a Christian dimension.

This was not true of much of the pagan world of the time. By many marriage was considered an evil institution, and precisely because of its relationship to procreation. Dualist philosphers, who considered matter evil, thought that procreation involved imprisoning free human spirits in evil bodies. Since this occurred in marriage, and specifically in the marriage act, they condemned both. The Church had to continue to insist that marriage and procreation were good.

At the other end of the spectrum were the philosphies that canonized pleasure. Such philosophies, or their abuse, reinforced natural tendencies toward pleasure, and rebelled against the restrictions the institution of marriage placed on the sexual appetite. Christianity had to steer a middle path between these two extreme philosophies. Against the Manichaeans, etc., it had to insist on the goodness of marriage and the marriage act. Against the Epicureans it had to emphasize the need to limit and restrict the role of pleasure in human activity, especially sexual pleasure.

A key figure in this controversy in the early Church was St. Augustine. To him there was no doubt that procreation was a good, and that it was one

[8]*In illud, propter fornicationes*, 3 (*PG* 51:213).
[9]1 Cor. 7:1–11; 25–28.

of the elements that made marriage and the marriage act good.[10] The *bonum prolis* was one of the goods of marriage. On this point he was on much more solid ground than he was in dealing with pleasure. As already mentioned, he saw the desire for sexual pleasure as the effect of original sin, and as sinful in itself, if pursued. Before the Fall, presumably, charity would have directed sexual activity toward procreation.[11] After the Fall, the desire for pleasure might dominate the marriage act. To Augustine this would be sinful. The intention to procreate makes sexual activity permissible, that is, a legitimate expression of charity or love.

Some have exaggerated the position of Augustine in this regard and argued that he considered sexual activity in marriage sinful unless engaged in with the intention of procreation. This is not true. Augustine, following Paul, recognized the obligation of a marriage partner to consent to a reasonable request for conjugal relations.[12] Augustine could do this because he held that besides the *bonum prolis* there were other goods in marriage. In this case it would be the good of fidelity (*bonum fidei*) that would be achieved in consenting to sexual relations. In consenting to a request the spouse would be showing fidelity to his or her marriage commitment. So, it was really only when sex was sought for the purpose of pleasure that it would be sinful. Even in this case it would not be seriously sinful unless means were used to prevent offspring or unless the person would have had sex whether it was with his or her spouse or not. In either case the party responsible would be acting like an adulterer, whose only goal is pleasure.

When one speaks of fidelity in the sense of being faithful to a *debitum*, the language comes closer to justice than love or charity. But from what St. Augustine has already said about charity in reference to the relations between spouses, I think one can argue to love or charity as the ultimate source of this response to a *debitum*. So whether the goal is procreation or fulfilling a commitment (*debitum*) I think one could argue that in the mind of Augustine, it is genuine love that is, or at least should be, the initiating factor.

More explicitly related to love is the third good of marriage of which Augustine speaks, the *bonum sacramenti*.[13] He is referring to the unbreakable commitment that spouses make to each other. That this commitment is one of love and is unbreakable follows from the fact that it is to be a sign of

---

[10]*De nuptiis et concupiscentia*, c. 17, n. 19 (*PL* 44:424).

[11]*De peccato originali*, c. 35, n. 40 (*PL* 44:415).

[12]*De bono conjugali*, c. 6, n. 6 (*PL* 40:377).

[13]*De nuptiis et concupiscentia*, c. 10, n. 11 (*PL* 44:420).

the love of Christ for his Church.[14] St. Paul had spoken of marriage as a great mystery, referring to the relationship between Christ and his Church. He also advised husbands to love their wives as Christ loved the Church. The word *sacrament* when used by Augustine does not have the technical meaning we are familiar with, nor even the simple meaning of sign found in some of the early Fathers. In Augustine it seems to refer both to the indissolubility of the marriage bond and to the meaning of marriage as a sign. Since these two are intimately united, that is, since the indissolubility flows from the fact that the marriage is meant to symbolize the indissoluble love of Christ for his Church, both meanings seem to be present. It would also seem clear that he saw the sign not only in the marriage itself, that is, in the marital consent and commitment, but also in the conjugal act, which is the consummation of that commitment. It is a mistake then to assert that Augustine and his followers did not see marriage or the conjugal act as an expression of love. If it were not, it could hardly be considered a sacramental sign.

The good of the sacrament (indissolubility) is undoubtedly related to the good of the offspring. And the same is true of the good of fidelity. Human offspring need a permanent and exclusive relationship between father and mother. Theoretically, a man and a woman could make a marital agreement that would be permanent and exclusive without a love relationship. It should be obvious that Augustine was not speaking of this kind of agreement. It seems clear that he was speaking of a permanent and exclusive love relationship. Such a love relationship was necessary not only for the good of the offspring but for the good of the spouses as well. Without it marriage could hardly exercise a healing function or provide the kind of mutual help the couple were looking for.

As pointed out, however, Augustine spoke most explicitly of this love relationship in reference to the sign value of marriage. It was because of this relationship that it could function as a sign. The love of Christ for the Church was to be the model for marital love, and by patterning their love on this model a married couple could be a sign of this love to their world. But it was not simply that it might serve as a sign that it was called for. It was because it was an inherent need of marriage, as mentioned above. Briefly, then, we can say that although in the early history of Christianity the emphasis may have been on procreation and the function of marriage as

---

[14]Eph. 5:25–39. The religious symbolism of the marriage relationship is not something original with Paul. Throughout the Old Testament the marriage relationship was seen to symbolize the covenant between God and Israel. This is found first in Hosea in reference to his own marriage, and then in Isaiah (5:1–7), Jeremiah (2:20–25) and Ezechiel (16).

a relief for concupiscence, the love aspect of marriage was not at all neglected.

There is a tendency to assume that in a culture, such as prevailed for centuries, where marriages are arranged by parents, and to a large extent with a view to offspring, a love relationship between the two parties would not be considered important. While recognizing the problem two people who may never have known each other before, might have of establishing a love relationship at the beginning of marriage, John Chrysostom insists on its importance.[15] He first recalls Paul's mandate to spouses to love each other as Christ loved the Church. Like the latter, marital love should be without reserve. The relation between the two mandates was clear since Christ loved the Church as his own body. Looking at the actual cultural situation, Chrysostom finds an element of mystery in the fact that two people who may never have seen or known each other must from the first day of their marriage prefer each other to all their friends or relatives, even their parents. But he never hesitates to affirm this obligation. Whether, given what seemed to be a serious handicap, the love relationship developed in that society the way it should have is another question. But it is quite clear that the Fathers considered it basic to the marriage relationship.

SCHOLASTICS

For the most part the medieval scholastics built their treatises on marriage around St. Augustine, and his three goods of marriage. This is certainly true of St. Thomas.[16] He does, however, depart from Augustine in his appoach to the subject of pleasure. He does not see pleasure or the desire for pleasure as wrong in itself, as Augustine seemed to do.[17] St. Thomas followed Aristotle in this respect and related the morality of pleasure to the morality of the act to which it was attached. If the act was bad, the pleasure was bad. If the act was good, the pleasure was good. Since the marriage act was good, Thomas had no problem with consent to the pleasure connected with it. But while he did not consider the pleasure of the marriage act as bad, he would not allow it as the goal of the act. This would be contrary to the whole nature of the act, and therefore sinful. In the divine plan, pleasure, while attached to certain actions, was never meant to be the total reason for performing them. Spouses who performed the marriage act solely for pleasure would be acting contrary to God's plan. Later theologians will say that spouses could be accused of having relations

---

[15]*Quales ducendae sunt uxores*, n. 3 (*PG* 51:230).
[16]*S.T., Suppl.*, q. 49.
[17]Idem, a. 6.

solely for pleasure only if they violated the proper goals of the conjugal act, e.g., through contraception, adultery, etc.

Even among the scholastics of the Middle Ages the role of love in marriage may not have been given the attention we would expect today. It would be a mistake, however, to claim that it was neglected. To the scholastics of the Middle Ages, as well as to St. Augustine, married people were to love each other as Christ loved the Church. There can hardly be doubt that this love would extend itself to and be expressed in every aspect of their married lives, not excluding their sexual relations. Although these relations were to be aimed at the *bonum prolis* or the *bonum fidei*, they must ultimately derive from this love since it was basic to the relationship.

Even admitting all this, one may still ask why more is not said about love by the scholastics in their treatises on marriage. The answer may be contained in the understanding medieval theologians had of charity or love. In the tradition they followed love was not something limited to marriage or a marriage partner. It was to be shown, at least to some degree, to everyone, and was to be expressed in all our relations with our neighbor. Christian love must be universal, in the sense that no human being may be excluded. This means at the least that one may never think, wish or do evil as such to another; hating another human being or harming him are never permissible. The opportunities of going beyond this minimal charity are, of course, innumerable, and the depths of a person's charity will be measured by the extent to which he takes advantage of them. But any further obligation in charity to the neighbor in general will depend on his need and a person's ability to relieve that need without serious hardship to himself. More specific obligations will depend on the relationship one has with the other person. Some of these relationships do not depend on our free will, e.g., parent-child obligations, brother-sister obligations, etc. Such obligations may even involve some other virtue, e.g. piety. Other relationships we enter into freely. The love of friendship, for instance, is taken on freely; one chooses one's friends. It is not always clear what specific obligations arise from friendship, but they go considerably beyond the general obligation to love one's neighbor.

Conjugal love comes closest to the love of friendship. It differs from other kinds of friendships because it has a sexual dimension. This is what makes it unique—its relation to sex, and consequently to procreation. It is this dimension, basically, that requires that conjugal love be exclusive and permanent. Ordinary friendships may be terminated by prolonged physical separation or some other circumstance that might make it difficult to sustain a friendship. Also, although there may be a limit to the number of friendships one can maintain simultaneously, there is no reason why one cannot have more than one friend. But conjugal love must be permanent and exclusive. It is a total commitment of a man and a woman to each other.

It is because of its unique nature that conjugal love goes beyond that of ordinary friendship and involves a commitment of justice. Conjugal love, then, has a dimension which other kinds of love do not have. It is this dimension to which medieval scholastics devoted their attention. Actually, St. Thomas in his treatise on charity does deal with the love husbands should have for their wives, but when he deals with marriage he concentrates on those aspects which make marriage different from other expressions of love.[18] A serious mistake is made, however, when one concludes from this concentration that the love relationship is not important. The truth is that it is precisely on the love that exists between husband and wife that the justice commitment is founded. It may be true that in cultures where marriages are arranged by parents this commitment or consent may be made before a real love relationship is developed. But even in these cultures the obligation to develop this relationship is assumed at the time the commitment is made. If it is not included, it would be difficult to see how marriage could be a sacrament, that is, a sign of the love of Christ for his Church. This understanding is really basic to Christian marriage.

Had St. Thomas spoken only in terms of love in reference to marriage, his treatise might not have been very enlightening. The specific nature of marital love would not have received adequate treatment. Also, while love is a necessary element in all human relationships, it is not in itself a reliable guide. Love tells us to do good to our neighbor, but it does not tell us in a particular instance what is good. For instance, the fact that a sexual act is inspired by love does not guarantee its goodness. There are other clear requirements. It was with these requirements of conjugal love that scholastic theologians were concerned.

One medieval theologian, Hugh of St. Victor, speaks very explicitly of the love relationship in marriage.[19] The explanation of this may be the fact that he is concerned about the marriage of Mary and Joseph. The issue is that of the virginal marriage. Since the ordinary concept of marriage is centered around sexual relations, one has to inquire about the authenticity of a marriage of two people who rule out such relations. Hugh adopted the common position that this was a marriage in the true sense of the term. His argument was that the basic consent in marriage is to a union of minds and

---

[18]*S.T.*, 2–2, q. 26, a. 11.
[19]*Dogmatica*, Pars Undecima, *De sacro conjugio*, c. 3 (*PL* 176:481).

hearts, a *foedus dilectionis*. He sees carnal union and procreation as something that flows from this union, but not as essential. Marriages can be, and are, without children. Marriages can also be without carnal relations. As long as the love commitment mentioned above is present, a true marriage can exist. It is this relationship that is basic to marriage. He even says that it is the principal reason why God instituted marriage.[20] Hugh sees in marriage a double sign. The union of minds and hearts in the basic commitment is the sign of the union of God with the soul. Carnal union is the sign of the union of Christ with the Church. I am not sure that all theologians would agree with Hugh's explanation of the virginal marriage, but I doubt that anyone would question his general principle that love is basic to marriage.

If one had any doubts about the role of love in marriage in the Church thus far, they would be dispelled by examining the various liturgies of the times.[21] In the readings (Eph. 5:23–27, Matt. 19:1–11, and John 2:1–11), the prayers and the hymns, strong emphasis is put on this role. The indissolubility of marriage is indeed the focus of the reading from Matthew, but the liturgy goes beyond it to the plan of God underlying it. It is the intimate love relationship made possible by the sexual creation of man that makes conjugal love indissoluble.

A constant factor in all these liturgies is the attention given to Old Testament models of conjugal love and union: Abraham and Sara, Isaac and Rebecca, etc. Stress is also put on the symbolic meaning of marriage in reference to the covenant between God and Israel in the Old Testament, and Christ and the Church in the New Testament. The basis for this symbolic meaning is again the intimate love relationship that should characterize marriage. Finally, marriage is presented as a prefiguration of the heavenly wedding. It is here that love will be perfectly fulfilled.

Certainly procreation is given a place in these liturgies, and an important place. But the context is always that of an intimate love relationship. Marriage is never presented as a mere procreative contract between two people (or their parents) with no love relationship between them. Procreation is presented rather as the fruit of their love.

CATECHISM OF COUNCIL OF TRENT

The Catechism mandated by the Council of Trent, the so-called Roman Catechism (1566), is the next document that should be consulted regarding

---

[20]*De Beatae Mariae Virginitate*, c. 1 (*PL* 176:864).

[21]For an excellent treatment of this topic, see Aimé-Georges Martimort, "Contribution de l'histoire liturgique à la théologie du mariage," *Esprit et vie* 88 (1978) 132–135.

the role of love in Christian marriage.[22] While admitting that the needs of procreation do not in a developed society make marriage obligatory, it does list several reasons why man and woman should be joined in marriage. What is the difference in the Catechism is the fact that the natural desire for companionship with the opposite sex is made the first reason for marrying. What is hoped for is the mutual help the spouses can give to each other in bearing the ills of life and the weakness of old age. The second reason given is the desire for offspring, not so much to have heirs as to increase the number of true worshipers of the Divinity. The catechism also says that this is the only reason why God *created* marriage, and concludes from this that married people who by medicine either prevent conception or cause an abortion are guilty of a most heinous crime. The third reason for marriage given by the Catechism was occasioned by man's fall from grace. Marriage would heal his concupiscence. In giving him a legitimate outlet for sexual relations, marriage will protect him from his own lust. The supposition, however, is that the act of intercourse be legitimate in the sense given above. Otherwise, it will be an expression of lust rather than a remedy against it.

One will recognize the Augustinian influence in this treatment of marriage. What is different is the ordering of reasons for marriage, at least the place given to companionship or mutual assistance in marriage. Augustine while recognizing that it had a place did not assign it any particular priority. Some theologians gave it a subordinate role in the sense that they related it to procreation. The cooperation of husband and wife was certainly necessary for procreation itself. It was also necessary for the proper education of the child. These theologians then saw this mutual assistance in terms of the good of the child rather than that of the spouses themselves. Others followed closer to the Augustinian tradition and saw it as a good of the spouses themselves which could be achieved apart from offspring and even sexual relations, but, like Augustine, they did not give it any priority.

As pointed out, what is new in the Catechism is the place given to companionship or mutual assistance as the first reason for marriage. In assessing this, it should be remarked first that the Catechism is presenting reasons why men should get married, not God's plan for marriage itself. It contrasts these reasons with other reasons, e.g., heredity, beauty, which it says should not be condemned so long as they are not contrary to the sanctity of marriage, but are not sufficient in themselves. Also, although it gives mutual assistance first place, it does not require that it be present, but

---

[22]*Catechismus Concilii Tridentini* (Turin, 1891), Pars secunda, c.8, n.13.

simply says that some one of the reasons mentioned must be present. Finally, the Catechism says that the only reason God created marriage was procreation, and concludes from this that it is a terrible crime to prevent conception or cause an abortion. One can argue from this that even if he married for companionship (or relief from lust), it could not be achieved at the expense of procreation in this sense.

As in previous treatises, the Catechism deals with the love aspect of marriage under the heading of *sacramentality*. An intimate love relationship is assumed as basic to the sign value of marriage. The reference is not merely to the spiritual union involved in the original marriage commitment. It is clearly to the sexual relationship of husband and wife. In fact, the Catechism uses the expression *divinam copulationem* in reference to the union between Christ and the Church to bring out the parallel with sexual relations. In finding the sign value of marriage in the love commitment of the spouses and its expression in sexual union the Catechism was simply confirming a long-standing tradition.

It was not until the nineteenth and twentieth centuries that theologians and the Church began to use the terms *primary* and *secondary* in referring to the specific goals of marriage. They gave the primacy to procreation and considered mutual assistance and the relief of concupiscence as secondary ends. This approach eventually made its way into the Code of Canon Law published in 1917. The new terminology clarifies the relationship between the various goals of marriage in God's plan but leaves the tradition intact. What should be emphasized for our purposes is that the clarification in no way affected the traditional role love has played as the dynamic force underlying marriage. Unfortunately, in some pre-Vatican II treatises on marriage, love is identified with companionship and given only a secondary goal in marriage. Reducing love to a secondary role in marriage seemed to be dictated by concern for the problem of contraception. But it is a perversion of the tradition we have seen which makes love basic to the marriage relationship.

PIUS XI AND PIUS XII

The next document of importance in our study is the encyclical *Casti connubii* (1930) of Pius XI.[23] The encyclical discussed marriage from the viewpoint of the Augustinian goods. It is of interest because it makes an explicit connection between the good of fidelity and marital love, and tells us fidelity will flourish more readily if it springs from this love. This love, it says, pervades all the duties of married life and even holds a certain

[23]*Casti connubii*, 23.

primacy. Conjugal fidelity requires this special love which the encyclical must compare with the love of Christ for His Church.

This love must show itself in action. It must also include more than ordinary mutual help in the home; it must extend as well to the growth of the spouses in love of God and neighbor, and the pursuit of perfection. In a sense this growth can be considered a primary cause and reason of marriage if it is looked upon not so much as an institution for the procreation and education of children but in a broader sense as a total communion of life. In other words, marriage as a way of life has as its ultimate goal the goal of all life. It is through marriage that spouses will achieve their salvation and perfection. Pius XI tells married couples that this same love must rule and regulate all the other rights and duties of marriage so that in following the prescription of the Apostle charity as well as justice will prevail in their relationship.

Briefly, then, Pius XI sees charity behind the whole of marriage. It is a charity also which aims not only at the goals of marriage but also at the goal of life itself. Some see in this approach of Pius XI the beginnings of a new attitude toward the role of love in Christian marriage. We hope that we have shown that, while it is more explicit, it is not really new but in continuity with a long standing tradition.

In the first half of the twentieth century a development took place which served to bring out the importance of the love dimension, especially in relation to human procreation. This was the advent of technological reproduction in the form of artificial insemination. Procreation could now take place apart from a conjugal act. But would it be morally acceptable? The question brought to attention an aspect of human procreation that perhaps has been taken too much for granted. Prior to this time the Fathers and theologians made frequent mention of the need for a permanent and exclusive relationship between husband and wife. They undoubtedly had in mind the educational needs of the child. They also saw the importance of a love relationship between husband and wife to guarantee this kind of permanence and fidelity. It was also assumed that conjugal love is the underlying force behind sexual union between husband and wife, although theoretically it might have been absent. Whether it was actually required by the procreative nature of the act, however, was a question that never forced itself on their attention. With the advent of artificial insemination, and even more, with *in vitro* fertilization, the separation of procreation from sexual intercourse was achieved. This raised the whole question of the moral requirements of human procreation and more specifically, the part that love must play in human procreation. In an allocution on the subject Pius XII stated unequivocally that human reproduction is not just an act of bringing two germ cells together.[24] This might suffice for reproduction on the animal level but not for human reproduction. Even sexual union in itself would not suffice for this. It is the presence of a love relationship in the procreative act that makes it human, and different from procreation either on the animal level or the laboratory level. What is needed is not simply the desire or love of married couples for offspring; it is the love of the spouses for each other and the expression of this love in sexual union that is called for. Obviously, married couples can express their love for each other in many ways not necessarily related to procreation. Pius XII was expressing here the necessity of conjugal love for human procreation.

Before going on to Vatican II attention should be called to a very important observation made by Karol Wojtyla in a book which he published at about that time.[25] It had to do with *mutuum auxilium* which theologians were recently speaking of as a secondary goal of marriage. He cautioned against confusing this with conjugal love. It might lead one to believe that love was secondary to procreation in marriage. As we have already pointed out, some theologians, due to a fear of weakening the argument against contraception, had done just this.[26] The truth is that both procreation and *mutuum auxilium* (as well as relief from concupiscence) must flow from conjugal love. It is not secondary to anything in marriage. Nor is it necessary to make it so to firm up the position against contraception. As already pointed out, although love has always been basic in the Christian tradition, it has never been normative. One does not justify an act automatically by relating it to love.

VATICAN II AND *HUMANAE VITAE*

We saw that *Casti connubii* spoke of marital love apart from its role as a sacramental sign, relating it to the *bonum fidei*. It saw marital love penetrating the whole of married life, and attributed to it a certain primacy

---

[24]Allocutio, October 29, 1951: *AAS* 43 (1951) 850.

[25]*Love and Responsibility* (New York: Farrar Straus Giroux, 1981), p. 68.

[26]John C. Ford, S. J., and Gerald Kelly, S. J., *Contemporary Moral Theology*, II (Westminster, MD: Newman, 1963), p. 18, speak of conjugal love as a secondary end of marriage and the marriage act, and cite *Casti connubii* (n. 59) to this effect. As mentioned earlier, this was also done by other theologians. Their concern was that in a personalist context conjugal love might be given an independence it did not possess. The concern was real. But as we have already pointed out, even though in the tradition love was always considered basic to marriage it did not enjoy moral independence. So giving conjugal love the key role in marriage did not break its moral ties with procreation or give it an independent status.

in marriage. Vatican II takes up at this point and also sees conjugal love permeating the whole marriage, although expressing itself uniquely in the acts proper to marriage.[27]

It sees it consequently as ordered by nature to the procreation and education of children. It does this without underestimating the role it is meant to play in reference to the other ends of marriage.[28] These ends traditionally have had to do with the good of the spouses themselves. Married love serves as the source or the help they can provide for each other, and in its sexual expression, as a relief from concupiscence. It has meaning, then, even in situations where children are not forthcoming. It even calls for permanence and fidelity independently of the needs of the offspring.

The atmosphere of modern culture is quite conducive to the emphasis the council put on conjugal love. Vatican II was undoubtedly referring to this when it said that although "the profound changes in modern society" have produced difficulties they also "reveal the true character" of marriage. In a society where marriages were arranged by parents and the extended family was common, the role of love in marriage may have been less obvious. In such an environment there may have been no love relationship between spouses before marriage. Even after the marriage the need for intimacy was lessened by the presence of the extended family. The importance of a love relationship is seen more clearly in a society where marriages are the product of this relationship. It is also clearer in a society where the nuclear family prevails and married couples are more isolated. The need of love and companionship in marriage even apart from the good of offspring becomes more evident. As we have emphasized in this paper, it would be a mistake to claim that prior to the council love played only a subsidiary role in marriage. We have tried to show that love always occupied a central role in the theology of marriage. What is recent is that conjugal love is discussed not only as the basis for the sacramental dimension of marriage but as the element which permeates the whole lives of the spouses.

[27]Pastoral Constitution on the Church in the Modern World *Gaudium et spes* [*GS*], 48.

[28]*Gaudium et spes*, and later, *Humanae vitae* did not use the terms *primary* and *secondary* that had become customary in treatises on the ends of marriage. By giving it priority this terminology certainly provided support to the procreative role of marriage and the conjugal act. At the same time, however, it seemed to reduce conjugal love to a very subsidiary role. Conjugal love was viewed as a secondary product of the conjugal act rather than as its source. It also seemed to set up a tension, or even opposition between procreation and conjugal love. Instead of tension or opposition *GS* and *HV* saw marriage and conjugal love naturally ordered to procreation. Rather than undermine the role of procreation this approach reinforces it. *HV* will say later that conjugal love itself will call for respect for the procreative nature of the act.

We are tremendously indebted to *Humanae vitae* both for a recognition of the place conjugal love has in marriage and a clear description of its nature.[29] Unfortunately, this part of the encyclical has never been given the attention it deserves because of the distraction caused by the birth control issue. But it is key to an understanding of the important role love plays in marriage. Paul VI tells us that a proper understanding of this role will come from the realization that conjugal love has its origin in God, who is Love himself and the source of all love. He is undoubtedly referring here to the creation text in Genesis where God creates woman to be a companion to man and makes possible a kind of intimacy that surpasses all other human relationships. This is the meaning of conjugal love. Conjugal love, then, and marriage are not something man just happened upon or the product of some kind of evolution of unconscious natural force. The union of husband and wife is a realization of God's design in creation. It is a union, moreover, which looks not only to the good of the spouses but beyond it, since it is through this union that God's creation is carried on. It is through the love of their marital union that husband and wife continue God's creation from one generation to another.

For the baptized, the encyclical tells us, marriage and marital love take on a new dimension. They are symbols of the love which Christ has for his Church. Some medieval theologians located this symbol in sexual intercourse itself, since there the union of spouses was the closest. For most, however, the commitment and union of souls which is effected by the marital consent was constituted the basic sign; marital intercourse completed it. But marriage is not just a sign; it is a sacrament in the full sense. In other words, it is a source of grace. It achieves the closeness with Christ necessary to meet the challenge of the sign. The Council of Trent tells us that this grace perfects the love of the spouses, makes their union indissoluble and accomplishes their sanctification.[30]

The encyclical then goes into an explanation of the characteristic marks and demands of conjugal love. It advises us that it must, first of all, be fully human, involving not only instinct and sentiment, but man's highest faculties, especially his will. Conjugal love is not just something that happens to people; it involves deliberate choices. People may "fall" in love, and perhaps even at first sight, but this is not yet love which is fully human. Love is much more than a passive reaction to a sexual attraction. If it is to be fully human, it must engage the whole person, especially his or her spiritual faculties. Conjugal love will grow and develop only by free

[29]*Humanae vitae*, 7 ff.
[30]*DS* 1799.

giving of self. This giving must become habitual, even though it may at times call for great sacrifice. Although emotion and sentiment are important components of this love, it must go beyond them and rise above them.

According to the encyclical conjugal love is also total. It is a most comprehensive type of love in which husband and wife share without reserve. The reason is that the partner is loved for what he or she is, not simply for what he or she does or has to offer. Nor is it measured by response. Even if the response were limited, it would not limit the love. It is total giving, not total possessing. In fact, if it is genuine love, it is not possessive at all, but respects the autonomy of the other person. Husband and wife will become two in one flesh, but they do not lose their own individuality or personality. As Pope Paul says elsewhere: "each personality remains distinct, and far from dissolving . . . affirms and refines itself. . . ."[31] The union may be the most intimate one they can enter, but they never become entirely one (nor should they) except in their offspring. They remain two persons with their own unique personality and one of the most important gifts they give to each other is respect for this individuality. Such respect will not be divisive but will deepen and strengthen their love.

The encyclical tells us that conjugal love must also be faithful and exclusive to death. Although the terminology is a little different, this is clearly a reference to the traditional goods of fidelity and permanence. What is new is that they are pointed to as qualities of conjugal love. In the past, as already pointed out, they were spoken of as goods of marriage and might have been referred to more in terms of the good of procreation. Referring these two goods to conjugal love makes one see them more readily as important to the good of the spouses themselves. Vatican II (*GS* 48) makes this very clear when it tells us that "this intimate union, . . . and the good of the children, demand total fidelity from the spouses and require an unbreakable unity between them." This relationship needs emphasis in a society where they are often seen only in terms of the good of the children and couples may stay together only for this reason.

The final quality of conjugal love the encyclical refers to is its fecundity. This is its most distinctive quality. Other kinds of love terminate in their object. They look only to the good of the beloved. Conjugal love certainly includes this but also transcends it. It is not exhausted by the love of husband and wife for each other or the sharing of goods between them. It is destined to share love and life itself with a new human being their love will bring into existence. Apart from this the love of husband and wife could

---

[31]Address to the International Congress "Equipes de Notre Dame," n. 6 (May 4, 1970).

degenerate into a selfish kind of relationship, what the French call an *egoisme à deux*.

The encyclical says that the expression of love in the conjugal act is inseparable from the procreative meaning of the act. Love, of course, can be expressed in many ways outside the procreative act. So it is not inseparable in this sense. Even in the conjugal act it is not inseperable in the sense that procreation must follow every loving embrace. There is no way, of course, in which this could be provided for. In fact, it would be counterproductive if every act of intercourse were procreative, since even the intervals of sterility are for the good of procreation. It is entirely proper for couples to express their love in circumstances in which they know it will not be fertile because of the nature of the procreative mechanism. There is nothing wrong either if they intend this sterility, since it is already in God's plan. What the encyclical condemns is any effort to change God's plan by destroying or inhibiting the procreative function itself. This condemnation is not new. What is new in the encyclical is that this is seen not only as a violation of the power to transmit life but a violation of conjugal love as well.

The encyclical discussed contraception in terms of conjugal love precisely because of the arguments some were making that love might demand the practice of contraception. The encyclical argued that rather than call for contraception it would demand respect for the procreative process. Violating the power to transmit life would be wrong, of course, even for those who had no special love obligation. But given the total commitment of conjugal love, the compromise becomes more conspicuous. In an analogous way, euthanasia involving spouses is a more serious crime than homicide between strangers or enemies. The assumption is, of course, that the act in question is morally wrong. As mentioned earlier, love is not normative. It does not tell us what is morally right or morally wrong. But once it is decided that something is morally right or morally wrong, a special love relationship will make a difference. This is particularly true of conjugal love because of its intimate relationship with procreation.

SUMMARY

We hope that we have shown that love has always occupied a central role in Christian marriage. Right from the creation texts of Genesis marriage has been looked upon as a unique love relationship between man and woman, more intimate than that between parent and child. It was never looked upon simply as a procreative institution. As we have seen the Fathers viewed it as something aimed not only at the good of offspring but at the good of the spouses themselves. It was seen as a relief from concupiscence. It was seen also as the source of mutual assistance. If one looked only at the three goods of Augustine, one might be tempted to conclude that he and those who followed him looked upon marriage only as a procreation institution. Even the fidelity and permanence called for could be viewed as a requirement of human procreation since it demands a continued commitment to the child. Anyone who reads Augustine and the Fathers will know that they did not consider marriage this kind of relationship. Augustine said that love is (or at least should be) the source of conjugal relations and also of the mutual help spouses might give to each other. But the role he gave love is particularly evident in what he and his followers say about marriage as a sacrament. Following St. Paul they urge husbands to love their wives as Christ loves the Church and stress the sacramental and permanent aspect of this love. What they failed to do was elaborate on the relationship between love and the other two goods of marriage. This may have been because they simply assumed this relationship and it offered no problem. The conflict was between procreation and concupiscence, or procreation and various dualistic theories.

The kind of dualism that considers procreation evil never received much attention in the Christian era, but the problem of concupiscence carried over into the Middle Ages. St. Thomas Aquinas adopted an approach to this problem different from that of Augustine. He did not see the desire of pleasure as evil (or good) in itself: its goodness or badness was related to the morality of the act to which it was attached. On the other hand, he did not consider it a legitimate goal of sexual activitiy. Hugh of St. Victor was the medieval writer who spoke most explicitly of marital love in relation to procreation and the other goods of marriage. He saw marriage as a *foedus dilectionis*, a union of souls as well as bodies. This was why God principally created marriage. From this union flow the goods of marriage, not only procreation but the companionship and mutual assistance spouses provide each other. After the Fall relief from concupiscence also came from this union. Although more explicit about the role of love than the other scholastics, Hugh considered himself in the same tradition. In fact, he traced his views back to Augustine.

If one asked why even the scholastics did not give more attention to the role of love in marriage, the answer may be in the way they approached the whole concept of love. Since love was never considered normative, discussing it would not have contributed much to the solution of the moral problems they were dealing with. What was needed was an analysis and discussion of the special problems to which the unique kind of love relationship marriage was gave rise. So this is what the scholastics, as well as most of the Fathers, devoted their time to.

In the Roman Catechism love was still given consideration only under the sacramentality of marriage. It put in order the reasons why people should get married, giving first place to the mutual help couples can give each other. During the nineteenth and twentieth centuries theologians were still discussing the purposes of marriage and ordered them as primary and secondary, first place being given to procreation, second to mutual help and (or third) to healing concupiscence. The ordering did not in itself change anything from the past. Some theologians, however, began to identify mutual help or companionship with love, thus giving the latter only a secondary role in marriage. This was contrary to the tradition which saw the love relationship as key to the whole marriage.

It was not until the twentieth century that love began to be related explicitly to marital fidelity and procreation. Pius XI in *Casti connubii* saw it behind the fidelity as well as the permanence of marriage. Pius XII related it to procreation itself in discussing technological reproduction. Vatican II, then, and *Humanae vitae* related it explicitly to the problem of birth control and responsible parenthood.

CONTRIBUTORS

Rev. John R. Connery, S.J.

John Connery, S.J., is a native of Chicago, entered the Society of Jesus in 1932, and was ordained a priest in 1944. He holds a doctorate in sacred theology from the Gregorian University. He has taught moral theology at West Baden College, Bellarmine School of Theology, and Loyola University in Chicago where he was promoted to the Cody Chair of Theology in 1983. He is now Professor Emeritus.

A member of the Catholic Theological Society of America and the American Society of Christian Ethics, Father Connery has written numerous articles on moral and ethical issues. He has served as consultant and advisor to various committees of the American bishops and various institutions and church organizations in the United States.

Rev. Thomas P. Doyle, O.P.

Thomas P. Doyle, O.P., a member of the Dominican Province of St. Albert the Great, was ordained in 1970. He served as an associate pastor for five years before beginning studies in canon law. He received his doctorate in canon law from The Catholic University of America in 1978. In addition, he holds master's degrees in philosophy, theology and political science.

Father Doyle served first as an advocate and later as a judge with the Chicago Metropolitan Tribunal. Since 1981 he has been the secretary-canonist at the Apostolic Nunciature in Washington, D.C. His articles have appeared in *Studia Canonica, The Priest, Listening, U.S. Catholic* and *Marriage Studies.* He is a regular columnist for the Arlington Catholic Herald and is editor of *Marriage Studies.*

Rev. Raymond C. Finn, O.P.

Raymond C. Finn, O.P., a native of Springfield, Massachusetts, entered the Dominican Province of St. Joseph in 1962. He was ordained in 1970. He received his undergraduate education at Providence College and graduate education at the Pontifical Faculty of the Immaculate Conception in Washington, D.C. He pursued canonical studies at the Pontifical University of St. Thomas Aquinas (Angelicum) in Rome where he received the J.C.D in 1978. Father Finn has tribunal experience and is presently Vicar Provincial for the Dominican Province of St. Martin dePorres.

DR. PAUL C. GLICK

Paul C. Glick, presently adjunct professor in the Department of Sociology at Arizona State University in Tempe, received his Ph.D. in sociology from the University of Wisconsin in 1938. Since that time he has served as senior demographer for the U.S. Bureau of the Census, Assistant Chief for Demographic and Social Statistics, U.S. Bureau of the Census, and Chief, Social Statistics branch for the same agency. Since 1982 he has taught at Arizona State University.

Doctor Glick has published a number of works on marriage and families. He has served as advisor and officer in several professional organizations including the U.S. Sociological Society of which he was president. He has received a number of awards for his work.

REV. THEODORE MACKIN, S.J.

Theodore Mackin, S.J., entered the Jesuit California Province in 1940. After ordination to the priesthood he completed his doctorate in sacramental theology at the Gregorian University in Rome (1958). Father Mackin has taught sacramental theology with a concentration on marriage at Santa Clara University since 1958.

Father Mackin has published numerous articles on marriage theology in theological and canonical journals. He has also published two volumes on marriage: *What Is Marriage* (1982) and *Divorce and Remarriage* (1984). A third, *Marriage As Christian Sacrament* is in preparation.

REV. THOMAS RINCON

Thomas Rincon Perez was born in Abades, Province of Segovia in Spain. He completed his seminary studies in Segovia and in the University of Salamanca. He received his doctorate in canon law from the University of Navarre where he has also held a position on the Faculty of Canon Law. Presently Father Rincon is professor of administrative canon law and editor of the review *Ius Canonicum*. He has published a number of articles and monographs on matrimonial jurisprudence and administrative law.

REV. MSGR. ROBERT J. SMITH

Robert J. Smith, a priest of the Diocese of Erie, Pennsylvania, was ordained in 1970. After serving as an associate pastor for four years he began studies in Canon Law at The Catholic University of America, receiving the J.C.L. in 1976. Upon completion of studies he was assigned as assistant chancellor and secretary to the bishop. Since 1978 Monsignor Smith has been vice-chancellor and in 1983 was named vice-officialis.